To Elena —
you are extra o
you continued s
of your life. You
so Keep up the great work.

Best Always,
Susan
Murphy
7/3/2[4]

LifeQ

How to Make Your LIFE Your Most Important BUSINESS

**Dr. Susan A. Murphy &
Jasenka Šabanović**

© 2021 Susan A. Murphy, Ph.D., MBA and Jasenka Šabanović.

All rights reserved. No part of this publication may be reproduced, distributed, or transmitted in any form or by any means, including photocopying, recording, or other electronic or mechanical methods, without the prior written permission of the publisher, except in the case of brief quotations embodied in critical reviews and certain other noncommercial uses permitted by copyright law. For permission requests, contact DrSusanMurphy@LifeQbook.com.

FIRST EDITION

ISBN-13: 978-1-09833-765-0 (paperback)

ISBN 978-1-09833-766-7 (ebook)

Published by BCG, Inc., Rancho Mirage, CA

Printed in the United States of America

For more information: www.LifeQbook.com

TABLE OF CONTENTS

ACKNOWLEDGMENTS

LifeQ: How to Make Your Life Your Most Important Business is a labor of love by two friends and business partners who combine their knowledge, business experience, and humor with a passion for making this world better. We are from different generations, different countries and, although our relationship began many years ago as a mentor and mentee, we have found that now we often mentor each other.

We gratefully acknowledge the thousands of clients, colleagues, friends, and associates with whom we have worked throughout the years. We have learned something important from each of you. We appreciate your trust as you allow us to share your challenges and successes on your path toward fulfillment. You inspire us every day,

Several colleagues have contributed to the development of this manuscript. Ginger Applegarth brainstormed ideas that led to our *LifeQ* concept that encompasses IQ and EQ. Anne Wright, Cathy Bromley, and Lisa Fitzgerald helped with editing and structure. Kip Garrett expertly brought the *LifeQ QUIZ* on-line. Carlos Gonzalez, our IT tech-savvy Millennial, makes our website *www.LifeQBook.com* interactive and user-friendly. Rachel Druten, artist and renowned author graced our book with creative illustrations.

Spouses of authors earn outstanding credit for being cheerleaders, filled with great ideas, patient, supportive, funny, and great cooks. Jasenka's husband, Antonio, and Susan's husband, Jim, should win a gold medal for their contributions to our *LifeQ* book. We thank both of you and love you.

Our families are a vital part of our projects and encourage us to be resilient and to make a positive impact. Our families have always believed in us and continue to motivate us without prompting.

And now, we acknowledge you, the reader. Thank you in advance for being open to examining your *LifeQ*.

ABOUT THE AUTHORS

Dr. Susan Murphy and Jasenka Šabanović are co-founders of **SynerQ**, a software company that measures and improves employee engagement. **SynerQ** is the business side of **LifeQ** and provides comprehensive solutions for transforming corporate cultures. The authors have extensive backgrounds in the areas of leadership development and personal growth. Our purpose is to serve as positive catalysts in the optimum development and performance of people and their organizations.

Dr. Susan Murphy's career combines the three worlds of corporate leadership, academia, and international management consulting. She has been an executive in two Fortune 500 Corporations and served on the graduate faculty at both the University of San Francisco and Vanderbilt University. Susan has performed management consulting with 300 businesses and organizations, including NASA Jet Propulsion Lab, Stanford University Medical School, SAP, and U.S. Air Force. Her education includes an M.B.A., a master's degree in O.D., and Ph.D.

Susan is a sought-after speaker, business consultant, coach, and best-selling author who is known for her "Wit and Wisdom." **LifeQ: How To Make Your Life Your Most Important Business** is her 11th book. She co-authored **In the Company of Women** with Dr. Pat Heim. *Good Morning, America, the B.B.C., Forbes,* and *Time Magazine* have featured **In the Company of Women,** and *Harvard Business School* named it *"Book of the Month."* Susan's leadership book, **Maximizing Performance Management, Leading Your Team to Success,** is part of the curriculum at *Harvard University,* and several other organizations. In 2004, Vanderbilt University honored Susan with a *Lifetime Achievement Award.*

Jasenka Šabanović is a visionary coach whose message and work have directly impacted thousands of people all over the world. She is passionate about human development and people's success.

Jasenka is native from Bosnia, moved to United States in 1999 after flee-ing the civil war. Embracing this second chance, she decided to turn her life into a success story and discovered that her story and pain could be a path to healing. After earning degrees from the University of California, Berkeley, Jasenka decided to use her experiences to help clients overcome obstacles, compose their vision, create peace, and find fulfillment.

Jasenka has coached and facilitated in different cities and countries and in 4 different languages. Being a multi-lingual, she holds an uncanny ability to tackle the life's hardships and struggle of different diverse cultures in a way only a native could do. She holds an immense passion for helping people acquire the all-important balance in their lives and she delivers her insight through individual and business coaching.

She was cover feature in *LQ Magazine*, and voted one of the 40 under 40 most successful business owners, and Professional Coach in *Palm Springs Life Magazine*. Jasenka was featured on *Patti Gribow TV Show*, 92210 and many radio shows.

PREFACE

Businesses create strategic plans so they can be successful. Could you use that same process to create a business plan for your life?

The answer is **YES!** After all, your personal life is your most important business!

In our coaching practices, we apply the same strategic planning principles we use in business to help clients achieve success in their lives. When it comes to coaching, we mean business!

What will you learn?

Consider this book a "Do It Yourself Toolkit" for living your life based on your values and purpose. Once you discover your *LifeQ*, you will be able to enhance your life quantitatively and qualitatively! Taking the *LifeQ QUIZ* is your first step.

You will learn how businesses create strategic plans and how to use these same elements in your life. The three parts of the plan are:

1. Become aware of your current reality - confirm your purpose and values, calculate your *LifeQ* score to show you where you are and steps to take you where you want to be, and eliminate obstacles that are blocking you.

2. Develop a winning strategy - set SMART goals, make promises, and identify your Personal Board of Directors.

3. Take action and prepare for setbacks as you execute your plan - learn to act plus how to get back on track when you are off-course.

In every chapter, we share case studies to show everyday examples from clients, offer research and expert advice from our experience, provide practical exercises, and often give examples of how we apply these business principles in our lives.

Who can benefit from *LifeQ*?

LifeQ is for *you* if you want to achieve break-through, long-term results in your personal and professional life. It could be that you want to examine your career path, overhaul your financial plan, or create a retirement strategy. Maybe you want to find new love, thrive as you become an empty nester, develop better relationships, get healthier, or develop a new talent or skill. Perhaps you are just curious and want to measure how well your life is going and clarify the areas going well. Maybe you are at one of life's crossroads and need to make crucial decisions, or perhaps you are stuck and need help figuring out your next steps.

What is unique about *LifeQ?*

LifeQ is a system that measures the quality of your life based on what *you* think is essential. It is like a GPS that shows you where you are and then how to get where you want to be. It is based on *your* values, *your* purpose, and how you see *your* destiny. You can develop your own personal strategic plan, tailored to *you,* and that provides a roadmap and milestones for leading the life you choose to live.

The *LifeQ QUIZ* illustrates how well you are doing in 12 parts of your life. You will see clearly which Components are going well so you can appreciate and celebrate those areas. Plus, it will provide you specific steps you can take to improve scores in the Components with lower scores.

Is it hard to think strategically?

No, some people do it naturally. Others can learn it. By using the same 3-part process that we use in our book, we have acted strategically throughout our lives, even before we heard the words "strategic planning" in business school. Below, we describe an example from our early adulthood when we were stuck and applied the 3-part process for creating our personal plan by assessing our current reality, developing a winning strategy, and taking action. We have since learned that most people do not make changes until the pain becomes intolerable, or the pleasure is so great that it is worth the effort to change. As you will see in our stories below, we were in pain when we decided to change. Our stories may remind you of times in your past when you have already been thinking and acting strategically.

Susan's story:

It was a cold, dreary evening in Boston when it hit me that I was 25 years old and not very happy. Although I had carefully made the move from Atlanta to Boston one year before for adventure and growth, my spirits were at an all-time low. I was tired, lonely, and my job was zapping all my energy. It was time for a change and to take action. So, I did what I named my "Self-Analysis."

I assessed my current reality and then developed my plan. I wrote three lists: Assets (things going well), Liabilities (things not going well), and Action Plan.

First, I wrote down my Assets: education, health, a loving family, good job, good income, close friends, sense of humor, faith.

Secondly, I listed my Liabilities: fatigue from working shifts and not sleeping well, limited outside activities despite moving to Boston for adventure.

Thirdly, I created my Action Plan for living a happier, more joyful life: focus on having more fun, take exciting classes, work fewer off-shifts and evaluate how working 4 days per week (vs. 5) would affect my take-home pay, meet interesting men, pray every day.

Results of Planning and Taking Action: Within two months, I was working four days per week. Within 4 months, I was taking a Fannie Farmer cooking course, met some fun people outside of my job, and attended some classes at Harvard. I began dating interesting men, one of whom I married.

Jasenka's story:

When I am at a crossroads in my life journey, I use a type of SWOT analysis. Several years ago, after going through many challenging personal changes, I was unsure which path to take. Although I had found shelter in San Francisco as a Bosnian refugee, I was depressed. I had been through a war and survived. Now what? I knew there was something more I had to do – I knew I had to find my Purpose.

I wrote down my Strengths that the war had not taken from me: education, health, risk-taking, persistence, a loving family, close friends, sense of humor, spirituality.

Next, I listed my Weaknesses: pain and anger I carried from war, inability to create deep connections with people, no time for fun, plus I disliked my job.

Then, I evaluated my Opportunities and Threats (which included my limiting beliefs). What were my options? What could be obstacles? I started therapy and learned to ask for help.

My Action Plan began with finding my Purpose and then starting a career search aligned with it. Additionally, I began to practice gratitude, have fun, and meet new people.

Results of Planning and Taking Action: I found a mentor who guided me into my coaching career that reflects my Purpose of helping others find peace. I started working for a coaching company, took salsa classes, and met many interesting people. This same strategic planning process continues to guide my decision-making.

Why did we write this book? Why now?

Hundreds of our clients and other coaches have asked us for several years to create this toolbox that contains the **LifeQ QUIZ**, business theory, client stories, exercises, and planning worksheets. The **LifeQ QUIZ** has been life-changing for many. Clients have found the business principles are logical and invaluable, and their results have been extraordinary and long-lasting.

As a result, we became determined to share our coaching methods. When was the last time you became focused on an idea, and you could not stop thinking about it? It could have been developing a product idea, buying a red sports car, or traveling to Hawaii. For us, it has been our goal to create the *LifeQ QUIZ* and write this book that we knew could help others live more abundant, joyful lives with measurable results. We have succeeded in our goal of providing a reader with measurable tools for improving your life. We have wanted to do it for years!

How do you begin your journey?
We recommend that you begin your journey by first reading through the *LifeQ* book to introduce yourself to the concepts, exercises, and flow. Then you can understand the context and process for building your plan and creating the abundant life that you want. Once you know the fundamentals of your personal plan, then you can design it.

Your life journey started at your birth and will continue until your last breath. You have already traveled many miles on your journey and had many successes and probably some setbacks. This *LifeQ* book involves a dynamic process that you can enter at any point in any chapter, but each chapter is an essential building block. Each part is fundamental and impacts others.

No matter where you are on your path, this book will allow you to measure your *LifeQ* and will teach you to think strategically just as businesses do.

We invite you to take this journey with us. Work at your own pace and enjoy the journey.

As you read this book, we would love to hear from you. Our website is *www.LifeQBook.com* where you will find the *LifeQ QUIZ*, plus bonus articles, exercises, workbook, and resources. If you are undecided about whether this is the right time for you to take the dive into *LifeQ*, ask yourself, *"If not now, WHEN???"*

#### CHAPTER 1

THE BIRTHDAY PARTY

Imagine your family and friends are throwing you a party for a milestone birthday. They have hired a videographer to interview the special people in your life who have come to help you celebrate. Some smile as they answer the questions. Others appear quite serious. You are curious about what they are saying. When the videographer spots you across the room and approaches you for an interview about your life, the questions are thought-provoking. *"What are your accomplishments?"* *"What are your regrets?"* *"What advice would you like to pass along?"* *"What will your next chapter be?"*

You are the Producer, Director, and Actor of your life. It is empowering to realize you add chapters every day as you create your life story. Are you working toward the life you want? What will be your legacy to your children, your community, and humanity? How will people remember you?

How will you feel about your accomplishments, and how fulfilled will you feel by the journey? What is your destiny?

This book is about creating the life you want and creating the story of YOU. We are all here for a purpose, and the most crucial task you have is to clarify it. The second challenge is to fulfill it. We wrote this book to help you celebrate what is going well for you and guide you to renovate and transform the parts of your life that are not. You *can* live the life that you want every day. It does not matter how long you have been doing whatever you have been doing, and it does not matter how old you are. It is never too late to start living the life that you feel called to live and to align yourself with your real purpose and passion.

LIFE IS 5% WHAT HAPPENS TO YOU & 95% WHAT YOU DO WITH IT

We believe that life is 5% what happens to you and 95% what you do with it. Living a conscious life of mindfulness enables you to be truly alive, present, and connected with what you are doing and with others around you. It brings your body and mind into harmony and makes your actions more deliberate. From now on, you can proactively live your values and purpose, visualize opportunities, change destructive underlying beliefs, and create magic along your journey. It does not matter what your past has been. Your future is spotless.

LifeQ vs. IQ

In this book, we will introduce you to your Life Quotient (*LifeQ*). You will assess the level of fulfillment in your life by *your* standards and then be able to consciously choose the strategies and your next steps to create the life story that *you* want – not someone else's standards or strategies.

Remember when you were young, and you took intelligence tests to determine your Intelligence Quotient (IQ)? And remember how scary it was to think that *one* test could decide whether or not you were considered *intelligent*? A negative result could crush your dreams of pursuing a particular career or applying to a specific university. But what if you didn't allow that lower-than-expected score to determine what you were capable of doing? What if, instead, you just continued to pursue what made you feel excited, joyful, and fulfilled? Rather than allowing your IQ score to determine your future, what if you could take the reins and do so yourself?

Of course, we now know that tests like those IQ tests only assess a particular type of intelligence, and we also know that there are a multitude of contributors we should look at when evaluating intelligence. Even though no one may have told you that you are next Albert Einstein or Marie Curie, successful people learn to highlight their great personalities or their abilities to communicate well with others. They may use their humor to defuse potentially volatile situations or tap into their ability to listen and be sensitive when others feel discouraged. What is important is that successful people do not give up on themselves, and they continue to strengthen their talents and abilities.

Obviously, merely scoring well on an IQ test does not guarantee anything about how fulfilled people will be with their intellectual lives. Just as IQ test results do not predestine you, consider the concept of *LifeQ* as a measure of contentment with your life as a whole. Even though you may not be currently satisfied with many elements of your life, that does not mean that you are fated to continue living that life. By becoming more aware of the various aspects that contribute to your satisfaction and dissatisfaction, you begin to acquire the self-consciousness needed to carve out and work toward the life story that you want to be living. You can create a higher, stronger *LifeQ* if you choose to do so.

A DO-IT-YOURSELF TOOLKIT

Consider this book a "Do It Yourself Toolkit" for living your life based on your values and purpose. We will show you how to take steps toward gaining the life that you want and removing those things in your life that you do not. Once you discover your *LifeQ*, you will be able strategically to plan to enhance your life, both quantitatively and qualitatively! The **LifeQ** Tool provides concrete actions that you can take to increase the scores in each of your 12 **LifeQ** Components. Chapter by chapter, you will explore a step-by-step manual filled with practical research, thought-provoking exercises, and examples from actual clients. Throughout the book, we will weave illustrations from our personal lives of how we apply the principles of **LifeQ**. We will share with you our values, purpose, use of Law of Attraction, a d strategic planning process.

You will gain insight into YOU as well as enhance your skills to focus on the areas that are truly important to you. These tools are building blocks that can transform your life. We organized this toolkit so that you can increase your **LifeQ** by creating a strong foundation built on self-awareness and carefully designing your plan.

THREE SECTIONS TO YOUR LifeQ PLAN

The book is divided into three parts: **Part 1: Become Aware of Your Current Reality, Part 2: Develop Your Winning Strategy,** and **Part 3: Take Action and Turn Your Setbacks Into Comebacks.**

As you gain awareness and begin to transform your life, we will serve as your personal coaches. You were born with great potential, and it is your personal responsibility to develop it. However, it is always helpful to have experienced guidance along the way. To realize your full ability and create your best future, you must not only focus on what you want but how you are going to get there and the tools needed to accomplish your arrival. As the Cheshire Cat said in *Alice In Wonderland, "If you don't know where you're going, any road will take you there."* You have some underlying beliefs about the world, money, success, power, love, and commitment. Could these beliefs be blocking you from creating the life story that you want? We will support you to clarify your values and purpose, to become more aware of your patterns of behavior, underlying beliefs, your self-esteem level, the impact of significant events in your history, and then help you use the Law of Attraction in your life. We will help you choose your Personal Board of Directors.

TRAVEL AT YOUR OWN PACE

Travel at your own pace as you work your way through the chapters. There is no rush. As you develop your roadmap, it is better to take your time.

The more thought you contribute to each session, the more likely you will gain a more vital and more purposeful understanding of the work you are doing in your life. This toolkit contains proven techniques and processes for self-knowledge, goal setting, self-management, and transformation. Many people have found it useful to read through the book once to get a feel for the strategic planning process. Once they understand the fundamentals, then they start doing the actual work of strategically designing the abundant, fulfilling life that fulfills their destiny.

Just as many businesses are open and operating when we begin work with them, so it is with you and your life. You have been operating as you for a long time. You have already had many successes and possibly some failures. At any time during this process, you can apply tools as you see fit. Each chapter is freestanding. You don't need to wait until you get to that section to try them out.

IT IS TIME TO FOCUS ON YOURSELF AND TAKE CARE OF YOU

At the beginning of every airplane flight, the flight attendant says, "In case of turbulence, put on your oxygen mask before assisting others." Now is the time to put oxygen on yourself and focus on YOU. It is OK to focus on yourself, so you can enrich not only your own life but positively impact those around you, too. Often, people operate as a service station open 24 hours per day, filling up everyone else's fuel tank, while their own is empty. It is illogical to think that always putting other people's needs before your own helps anyone over the long haul. You cannot pour from an empty cup. So, just as your cell phone needs recharging when the battery is low, you need energy and recharging to function at optimal levels. Now is the time to recharge your battery, take care of you, and get ready for this next adventure.

You have probably heard that "a body in motion tends to stay in motion, while a body at rest stays at rest" … so get off the proverbial couch and begin your transformation! Wake up and enjoy this journey into your best life ever!

What you will need:

- Workbook for *LifeQ* or your notebook

- Your favorite pen

- 30 minutes per day that is committed to your *LifeQ* Toolkit

WHAT'S NEXT?

The next chapter, CREATING YOUR PLAN, introduces you to the concept of creating a strategic plan for your life just as most executives create a strategic plan for their businesses. Also presented in Chapter 2 are five frequent regrets that many people have so you can guard yourself against those regrets in your Personal Strategic Plan.

LifeQ PRACTICE #1.1 Questions To Ponder As You Begin Your Transformation

DIRECTIONS: Answer YES / NO

Do you have a clear idea of your most fundamental principles, values, interests, and gifts?

YES: _____ NO: _____

Do you have a sense of purpose in your life?

YES: _____ **NO:** _____

Do you almost always have a positive attitude about life and wake up each day excited about life?

YES: _____ **NO:** _____

If your life ended tomorrow, would you be satisfied with who you were, how you spent your time, your relationships, your service to others, and what you accomplished?

YES: _____ **NO:** _____

Will you leave a legacy that impacts others in your circle in a positive way?

YES: _____ **NO:** _____

Will your life story be a legend passed on by future generations?

YES: _____ **NO:** _____

SCORING: There are six questions. The more questions you can answer "YES," the more you are living your life with Purpose as you begin the journey with us. Each YES represents a lot of work and self-reflection. Our goal is that when you have completed the work in this *LifeQ* journey, you will score YES on all six questions.

LifeQ PRACTICE # 1.2 THIS WEEK'S ACTION PLAN

- What have you learned about yourself after reading this chapter?

- What actions will you take this next week to start to design the life that you want to live?

#### CHAPTER 2

HOW TO BUILD A PERSONAL STRATEGIC PLAN

Have you ever noticed how much easier it is to clean and organize someone else's closet, or how much quicker it is to recognize and carry out the repairs at someone else's house? This same concept seeps into the way people live their lives. Many people develop meaningful working strategies for their companies but feel their personal lives are not as fruitful as they would like.

Does Carmen's story resonate with you?

> ### *Carmen's story:*
>
> *Carmen knows it is time for a change. She is 35 years old and has discovered that most of the time, she feels like a hamster in a cage running mindlessly on its wheel with no purpose or destination. Carmen lives in a mid-sized city where she has been a psychologist for seven years. For four years, Carmen has lived with her long-time boyfriend in a relationship that is going nowhere. As a psychologist, she can recognize her behavior patterns: staying with men who do not want to commit, feeling too worn out to exercise or have hobbies, and working long hours helping others sort out their values and goals, while always putting her own secondary to others. She knows something must change, although she is not quite sure how to start.*

All successful enterprises use strategic planning to develop a roadmap for success. Leaders must clarify in what direction they want their organizations to go and then create the strategy to get them there. We have worked for many years side-by-side with clients, helping and guiding them as they developed a roadmap to achieve desired fiscal and organizational successes. Our passion has been to provide business leaders with the best tools and processes for clarifying their organization's purpose, values, and goals, taking full advantage of their strengths, and overcoming the obstacles that inevitably arise. In this book, we help you do the same for your essential journey through life. Our clients continue to inspire us by their tangible success as they transform their lives, creating abundance and purpose. Their success drives us to share what we have learned with you.

COMPONENTS OF STRATEGIC PLANS

The three vital elements of a business plan are: 1.) become aware of your current reality, 2.) develop a winning strategy, and 3.) take action and turn your setbacks into comebacks.

PART 1: BECOME AWARE OF YOUR CURRENT REALITY

Awareness is one of the most challenging yet essential elements in helping you achieve a more focused and meaningful life. As Socrates said, "*The unexamined life is not worth living.*" Think back to our earlier question about how much easier it is to organize or repair someone else's home. Doesn't it feel safer to help a friend toss out old clothes or lay new tiles in his entryway? Of course, any second thoughts or mistakes are someone else's problem, not yours. That apprehension you feel most likely stems from a lack of clarity about your wants and needs. Becoming aware of your current reality gives you the confidence you need to know that the decisions you make are working to create a stronger, more satisfied you.

Before designing your pathway to success, it is crucial to take stock of where you are now. Often, we know we want to change our situation, but are not clear about what needs our attention or where to begin the journey. So, how do you apply the elements of a strategic business plan to your personal strategic plan? Understanding what is important to you and where you envision yourself are crucial parts of your journey. After assessing your **LifeQ** in Chapters 3, 4, and 5, we will ask you to think about how aware you are of the following when you make decisions in your life:

- Your values

- Your purpose

- Your belief system, patterns, and self-esteem

- Your strengths, weaknesses, opportunities, and threats (SWOT)

Clarify Your Values

Your values are your most important and enduring beliefs or ideals about what is good or desirable and what is not. Values exert a significant influence on your behavior, drive priorities, and provide a framework for making decisions. Values define what you stand for and include family, love, compassion, kindness, loyalty, integrity, power, money, integrity, contribution and recognition.

In Chapter 6, we will help you discover if you are living your values and, if not, why not. For example, many people say that their top value is family, but once assessed, they realize that they do not invest time or resources in this value.

Define Your Vision and Your Purpose

Just as successful businesses often create a formal mission statement, so do successful people. Your *mission statement* defines the fundamental purpose of your life, succinctly describing why you exist. Your *vision* is a picture of who you want to be in the future in the long-term view. What is your vision for your life personally and professionally, and will you arrive there? The clearer you are about your purpose and your vision, the easier it is to make decisions when you encounter forks in the road during your life journey. In Chapter 7, we will help you define your purpose.

Perform Your SWOT Analysis

Assessing Strengths, Weaknesses, Opportunities, and Threats is an integral part of a successful strategic planning process in business.

- *Strengths* are skills, talents, qualities, and personality characteristics that will enable you to be successful in living the life you want.

- *Weaknesses* are areas where you do not excel.

- *Opportunities* are a set of circumstances that make it possible to do something, for example, a chance for you to be promoted or find a new job.

- *Threats* are possible obstacles, challenges, or hindrances.

In strategic planning for businesses, many organizations use a process called *Appreciative Inquiry* that identifies what is going well and then builds on these areas of distinctive competence. In other words, they play to their strengths and talents. Appreciative Inquiry can be an uplifting and positive approach for you too. Weaknesses are also essential to understand. Once you identify them, you can determine whether it is important to strengthen these areas or not. There may be some knowledge gaps where you need to develop your skills to enhance your ability to be successful. It could be that some areas where you do not excel now will not serve as obstacles. In that case, it is often more productive to focus on your strengths and talents. Opportunities are another critical part of the SWOT analysis. Once you have determined your purpose, values, and strengths, focusing on your opportunities can be uplifting and energizing. The fourth part of the SWOT analysis is examining the threats that may serve as obstacles to living your fulfilling and purpose-driven life. In personal strategic planning, the most critical threat is usually in your conscious and subconscious mind, the underlying beliefs and patterns that serve as possible obstacles, challenges, and hindrances to living the life you want.

Throughout this do-it-yourself toolkit, you will find these elements of your SWOT analysis interspersed among the research, case studies, and exercises.

Take Advantage of the Law of Attraction

Chapter 8 explains how to use the Law of Attraction and what prevents you from using the Law of Attraction successfully. By understanding and using the Law of Attraction, you can successfully attract what you want in your life. You must decide what you want, resolve any unresolved negative beliefs you have developed about your ability to obtain what you say you want, and take strategic steps to make your desires your reality.

Implement Strategies for Embracing Change

By the time you reach Chapter 9, you will be ready to put what you have learned into action and start thinking about welcoming the change you want to see in your life. We will review the four stages of change *resistance, confusion, exploration,* and *commitment* and the personal behaviors and feelings that occur at each stage. We will discuss how to stay committed to your goals on a day-to-day basis, a task that is fundamental to creating the life story that you want. Preparing for your initial emotional resistance to change is an essential part of transforming your life.

Uncover Your Beliefs

Your belief system is the set of principles by which you live your daily life. Your beliefs govern your thoughts, words, and actions. *Core beliefs* are those things you just know and trust to be true. They serve as an internal "guide to life," telling you how to behave and react to the world. In Chapter 10, you will start to uncover the genesis of your beliefs, and you may begin to alter them. You will discover that some things you have been telling yourself for many years are based on a skewed perspective of something that happened to you when you were a child. The good news is that when you release an unfounded core belief, a core truth automatically comes to replace it.

Uncover Your Patterns

Just as significant as understanding your belief system is acknowledging your patterns. Chapters 10 and 11, will also help you recognize the patterns (or scripts) that control all your unconscious actions. Every time there is a situation in which you take action without conscious thought, you are using a pattern. Right now, you are using patterns to read this page. The voice that you hear in your mind is your script, and this script shapes both conscious and unconscious actions.

Boost Your Self-Esteem

Related to understanding your belief systems and uncovering your patterns or scripts is another vital element for success that is your self-esteem. In Chapter 12, you will explore your level of self-esteem: how well you value and respect yourself, your accomplishments, relationships, abilities, and sense of responsibility, and how others perceive you. You will discover if the *impostor phenomenon* is interfering with your optimal **LifeQ**, and if so, ways to deal with it.

PART 2: DEVELOP YOUR WINNING STRATEGY- CREATE YOUR PLAN

Awareness alone leaves you in an inactive state. The process of clarifying your beliefs, values, and purpose is essential. However, once you work through those ideas, you want to act. Be cautious about acting too quickly; successful organizations take some much-needed time first to develop a plan that will be in line with their mission. You also can use this technique in making decisions that are important to you, whether it is deciding to take up a new hobby or change careers.

Along the way, we will help you set specific goals that align with your values. We will then work together to design that personal plan and create the action steps you need to get there. We will show you how to define short- and long-term goals and create a powerful Personal Board of Directors.

Define Short-Term and Long-Term Goals

To facilitate your goal setting, we have included worksheets and examples for creating action plans like ones we use with our business clients. In Chapter 13, we will illustrate how to set SMART (Specific, Measurable,

Attainable, Relevant, and Time-bound) goals. In the SMART goals chapter, you will learn how changing the word *goal* to the word *promise* can make a big difference in success.

When you set SMART goals and promises, it is easy to tell when you have successfully reached them. If a goal is too broad (for example, "I want to make a lot of money" or "I want to lose weight" or "I want to be more self-disciplined at work"), it is hard to tell when you reach it. Your goals and promises can be made SMART by declaring:

- "I see myself making at least $100,000 per year beginning next year."

- "I see myself at my ideal weight by December 31."

- "I am home for the family dinner four evenings per week."

- "I am in a healthy, loving relationship by my next birthday."

A vital part of a SMART goal is the "T" for time bound. A dream without a deadline is merely a wish. With these action plans in place, you will have a roadmap to living the life that you want to live.

Create a Powerful Personal Board of Directors

The people in your inner circle influence how you spend your time, resources, thoughts, and emotions. To transform your life and to create the story that you want, you must choose trustworthy, supportive, and talented people to travel life's journey with you. We will discuss how to do this in Chapter 14. We will introduce you to the Johari Window, a model for designing effective relationships with your board members as well as with every significant person in your life. The four quadrants of the Johari Window reflect how well you know yourself, how well others know you, and what is hidden from you about yourself.

PART 3: TAKE ACTION AND TURN YOUR SETBACKS INTO COMEBACKS

Part 3 of your *LifeQ* Plan is to TAKE ACTION! Nothing happens if you do not take action. Dreams without action are illusions. A goal without a deadline is merely a wish. Therefore, many readers of Law of Attraction books fail to achieve their dreams. Nothing happens if you do not put in the work needed. Opportunities come and go. When they arrive, you have got to answer the call with action. Without understanding this, it is impossible to create a fulfilling and joyful life that you want.

This section will help you pull it all together and ensure you are moving forward. In business, there is a syndrome known as *analysis paralysis* where taking action is delayed, procrastination occurs, and the leaders want to conduct an additional analysis. In Chapter 15, we will show you how to take those initial actions and then how to harness resilience. We will also show you how to turn your setbacks into comebacks. You will learn how to take those first steps and what to do when you hit inevitable obstacles and experience setbacks.

COMMITMENT TO YOUR PLAN - LIVING YOUR LIFE ON PURPOSE

Strategic planning is a dynamic process that continues until you take your last breath. It is often challenging to stay on track toward goals when so many factors in your busy world compete for your time, energy, and focus. Relatives, friends, your boss, social media, weather, the economy, equipment failures, and illnesses are just a few. You will need discipline, tenacity, personal awareness, and clarity of Purpose in your roles as the producer, director, and actor in your life story.

CREATING YOUR PERSONAL STRATEGIC PLAN

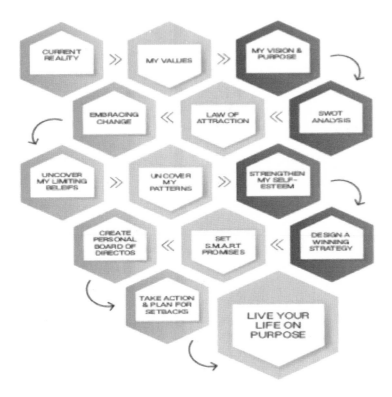

FIVE REGRETS DYING PEOPLE HAVE - CONSIDER IN YOUR STRATEGIC PLAN

A Chinese proverb that describes the importance of learning from the experience of others: *To know the road ahead, ask those coming back.* As you develop and create your goals in this first draft of your strategic plan, it may be helpful to consider another angle. An Australian hospice nurse, Bronnie Ware, wrote an international best-selling book, *The Top Five Regrets of the Dying*, about hospice patients' regrets during the final weeks of their lives.[1] Note that there is no mention of physical beauty, status, or revenge among them.

1. *"I wish I'd had the courage to live a life true to myself, not the life others expected of me."* The most common regret of people was that many of their dreams have gone unfulfilled.

2. *"I wish I hadn't worked so hard."* Many people regret spending so much of their lives, making a living versus making a life.

3. *"I wish I'd had the courage to express my feelings."* Many of the hospice patients had not talked about their feelings. As a result, many even developed illnesses relating to bitterness and resentment carried.

4. *"I wish I had stayed in touch with my friends."* Many had become caught up in their own lives and had drifted away from precious friendships.

5. *"I wish that I had let myself be happier."* Many had not realized that happiness is a choice. They had stayed stuck in old patterns, and their fear of change had prevented them from being content.

With these five lessons from hospice patients in mind, contemplate which ones you can incorporate into your personal strategic plan.

WHAT'S NEXT?

The next chapter, **WHEEL OF LifeQ** *and* **MINI LifeQ QUIZ,** *introduces you to 12 Components of your life. On every journey, it's critical to know your starting point. Chapter 3 will acquaint you with the holistic view of your life and help you calculate your starting point for your journey. The hub of your* **MINI LifeQ QUIZ** *and* **WHEEL OF LifeQ** *contains your Values and Purpose.*

LifeQ PRACTICE #2.1 BEGIN TO THINK ABOUT YOUR EULOGY

Begin to think about your eulogy.

- What would you like to have written about you at your death?

- What is your contribution?

- What road did you create for others?

- What is your legacy?

- How will your headstone be inscribed?

- Create a bulleted list of what you wish people would say about you. This list is an essential step for developing your mission statement that is your foundation and purpose.

LifeQ PRACTICE #2.2

Begin your SWOT (Strengths, Weaknesses, Opportunities, Threats) analysis by considering questions about your strengths, talents, accomplishments, and assets. Define each category broadly.

- What are your strengths?

- What are your talents? What have you done with them, and what would you like to do with them?

- What have you accomplished so far in your life? List your accomplishments, big and small.

- What kinds of tangible assets (financial, property, jewelry, etc.) do you own? Do you feel you have sufficient tangible assets to facilitate the life you want to live?

- What do you enjoy most?

- What energizes you?

LifeQ PRACTICE #2.3

Now consider the areas in which you feel you do not excel and the skills, knowledge, and talents that would be useful for you to improve.

- What are some areas that you would like to improve to make your life more fulfilling and abundant? For example, you may be disorganized. Your home and workplace may be cluttered, which drains your energy and distracts you. Another example might be that you are impatient and become discouraged easily.

- What skills would be useful to acquire? Where do you have gaps in knowledge or skills that you will need to address?

- What talents would come in handy?

- What drains your personal energy?

- Which areas of your life are not enjoyable to you? What is uncomfortable or unpleasant about them?

- What opportunities are available to you right now?

- What threats could serve as obstacles to deter you from living your fulfilling and purpose-driven life? In personal strategic planning, the most critical threat is usually in your conscious and subconscious mind. Your underlying beliefs and patterns can serve as challenges and hindrances to living the life that you want.

LifeQ PRACTICE # 2.4 THIS WEEK'S ACTION PLAN

- What have you learned about yourself after reading this chapter?

- What actions will you take this next week to start to design the life that you want to live?

PART 1

BECOME AWARE OF YOUR CURRENT REALITY

#### CHAPTER 3

WHEEL OF LIFEQ AND MINI LIFEQ QUIZ

I n Chapter 2, you began the process of personal strategic planning. You learned you could create a strategic plan for personal success in the same way companies create strategic plans for business success. The goals of your Personal Strategic Plan, however, are far more profound than those of any business plan because *your life is at stake!* Your definition of success and the ability to create steps to achieve success will affect your level of fulfillment as a whole person. If you are more content *whole*-istically, you will be more successful in all areas, including your business.

Abby's story below shows how by examining her life holistically, she strategically set new goals and proactively steered her life in a new direction.

Abby's story:

Abby has always been healthy and athletic. For as long as she can remember, daily workouts and a healthy diet have been a way of life. Four years ago, Abby won a full scholarship for soccer at a four- year college. While at college, she was captain of the soccer team and led the team to several championship titles.

With her extraordinary leadership talent and her great people skills, Abby has developed strong relationships with both men and women. Abby earned her college degree in business administration and always thought that she would figure out her future once she had moved on from college. Now, as a new grad, Abby realizes it is time to get serious about her career and start earning some money. Abby is one of the lucky young people who can move back home with her parents and take a little time to strategize about her career. Even though Abby and her boyfriend are pretty serious, both want to wait for their careers to take off before considering a lifetime commitment.

Abby contacted us to help her with her career planning. We explored with Abby her values and interests as well as the types of careers she would enjoy and be successful. Abby also researched the types of workplaces she would want. The next step was to perform her SWOT analysis. Abby evaluated her Strengths, Weaknesses, Opportunities, and Threats. Many of her skills are transferable from her soccer career leadership and relationship-building as well as communication and conflict management. Her Weakness is primarily her lack of business experience. Opportunities for Abby include that she lives in a big city with a booming economy and a variety of industries. One of Abby's Threats is that she has no income at this time, so she may start to feel pressure to take a job before her ideal one comes along. Abby set a goal to begin her career within four months after her graduation.

Next, we encouraged Abby to arrange informational interviews with people established in fields that interest her. During those interviews, Abby learned what skills she needed to be successful in those companies. She realized that at some point in her career, she might need to obtain a master's degree or additional certification. Additionally, we provided Abby networking tips so that she can use her exceptional relationship-building skills to aid in her career search.

Now, Abby is feeling encouraged and hopeful about her future and is ready to implement her strategic plan to discover the ideal position to begin her career path.

HOW DO YOU DISCOVER YOUR *"LifeQ"*?

When we meet with our clients, their first assignment is to conduct a self-assessment of their current achievement level in the 12 Components of the **WHEEL OF LifeQ** (Life Quotient). Using our two **LifeQ** quizzes: **MINI LifeQ QUIZ** or Overview and a **LifeQ QUIZ** or Detailed Assessment, we invite you to measure the level of fulfillment in your life by *your* standards. Once you see your life today, you will be able to consciously choose the strategies and next steps to create the life story that you want. You will not be acting based on someone else's standards and judgments. Your process will be the ones you choose to change your life.

THIS *MINI LifeQ QUIZ* EXERCISE HAS THREE MAIN GOALS

These goals are:

Awareness: To make you aware of the importance of *all* **12 LifeQ Components** and show where you believe you are in each.

Inspiration: To inspire you to commit to increasing the score in each life area regularly.

Action: To develop actions you can take immediately to increase your **LifeQ** score.

DIFFERENCES IN YOUR IQ, EQ, AND *LifeQ*

Ever since the term *Intelligence Quotient (IQ)* was coined more than 100 years ago by German psychologist William Stern, the idea of measuring an individual's "Intelligence Quotient" has been controversial. *Intelligence* is the "ability to learn or understand things or to deal with new or difficult situations."[1]

Daniel Goleman, Ph.D., re-examined the definition of intelligence and believes intelligence includes an emotional element that he named "Emotional Intelligence Quotient." This has "the capacity to be aware of, control, and express one's emotions, and to handle interpersonal relationships judiciously and empathetically." [2] It is possible to have a high IQ and low EQ and vice versa. You have probably met bright people who have prompted you to think, "He might be smart, but he hasn't got a clue about dealing with other people." Conversely, you have met others who connect brilliantly with others and yet score poorly academically.

Your *LifeQ* includes both your IQ and EQ among the 12 Components. We call these **MindQ** and **EmotionQ** in the *LifeQ QUIZ*. Your basic intelligence and knowledge, as well as your ability to read other people's emotions, act accordingly, and manage your own, are an integral part of each of the 12 Components. It can be challenging to increase your IQ and challenging to increase your EQ. However, by looking at your life holistically and paying attention, you can enhance your *LifeQ* and your IQ and EQ as well.

YOUR *LifeQ* HAS 12 COMPONENTS

We believe life is 5% what happens to you and 95% what you do with it. All too often, we hear people saying, "I'm feeling unfulfilled and dissatisfied with my life. There must be something wrong with me. Maybe I am just not one of the lucky few who has been given a stimulating, abundant life." *Given*? No! You are not *given* a life to lead any more than you are *given* a job, significant other, or a promotion. You must *work* for the life that you want.

If you want to get to know yourself, you need to spend the time figuring yourself out. Once you determine where you are in your personal GPS, you can strategize and prioritize how to navigate toward the life you want to live.

If you look at the center of the **MINI WHEEL OF LifeQ**, you will see Values and Purpose. That is because Values and Purpose are the cornerstones of your life, and therefore of your *LifeQ*.

Chapters 6 and 7 provide detailed information about defining your Values and your Purpose. Your *Values* are what you stand for and what you believe in. Deciding what is important to you is critical to living a life of purpose and having a high *LifeQ* because your deeply held values fuel the energy behind your life purpose. Your *Purpose* gives your life meaning. Having a specific purpose (mission) provides you with guidance and keeps you from getting sidetracked on your life journey.

Your *LifeQ* Score is composed of 12 Components. **(See FIGURE 3.1)** Each Component has a quotient ("Q") that measures how well you are doing in that aspect of your life. The sum of all the quotients reflects your *MINI LifeQ QUIZ* score.

COMPONENTS OF *LifeQ*

- *MindQ*: Intellectual health

- *SoulQ*: Spirituality/personal growth and contribution

- *EmotionQ*: Emotional health and awareness

- *BodyQ*: Physical health

- *FunQ*: Recreation, fun, and relaxation

- *EnvironmentQ*: Satisfaction with your physical surroundings

- *MoneyQ*: Satisfaction with your income, assets, and life savings plan

- *CareerQ*: Satisfaction with your career

- *LoveQ*: Relationship with significant other

- *CommunityQ*: Satisfaction with your contribution to the world, community, volunteer efforts

- *FriendsQ*: Relationship with people whom you consider friends

- *FamilyQ*: Relationship with members of your family

MORE IS LESS

If you have been struggling to balance two life areas, you may be surprised to know that masterfully juggling 12 life areas can be more fulfilling and more comfortable. This sounds counterintuitive, and yet it is true. How can that be?

If you thought that life balance is only about your work and your family life, you might have been ignoring your physical, spiritual, mental, emotional, and relaxation needs. Often, people try to convince themselves that once they have their career or family life under control, they can then make time for health, spirituality, personal growth, and so on. People frequently feel this way until they experience a significant event in their life that triggers a need for them to start to examine other aspects of their life. This wake-up call could be a health crisis, job loss, death of a close friend, or simply feeling that their life is empty of meaning.

WHY YOU NEED BALANCE TODAY

You may believe that too many other things need to be done before achieving balance. However, every day you avoid addressing the imbalance, it will grow. Reasons to start balancing now include understanding that every Component of your *LifeQ* is essential, your Components reinforce each other, and a low score in one Component may be caused by other Components.

Balancing All Your Qs

Every Component of Your *LifeQ* Is Important

Imagine neglecting your health for a few years while you focus on your career. You will not usually suffer the consequences of that decision during those years. However, we all know, neglecting your health tends to show up with long-term effects. Perhaps you are pre-diabetic but do not know it because of continually postponing your doctor's appointment. You could be damaging your internal organs, your eyesight, and your circulation.

Your *LifeQ* Components Reinforce Each Other

All your *LifeQ* **Components** are connected. You can enhance your family life with good health, recreation, and fun. You can boost your career through good social connections and emotional development. Each *LifeQ* **Component** influences others. By neglecting some of the *LifeQ* areas, you could be inadvertently sabotaging the success in another place that you want.

A Low Score in One Component May Be Caused by Your Score in Other Components

Have you ever tried to improve one area of your life and been unable to do so no matter how hard you worked at it? For example, your low score in *LoveQ* may be caused by a low score in *EmotionQ* or *BodyQ*. Perhaps you have an undiagnosed health issue that contributes to fatigue and depression. If you are feeling lousy, you are probably not projecting your best self. A low *BodyQ* score could affect your *CareerQ.* You may not have enough stamina to be productive and creative at work. It could affect your ability to have a successful love life.

Enhancing your *LifeQ* is up to you

You must *work* for the life that you want. Invest time figuring out yourself and determining where you are in your personal GPS. Once you calculate where you are, you can strategize and prioritize how to influence your destiny and live the life you want to live.

[FIGURE 3.1]

WHEEL OF LifeQ

DIRECTIONS FOR SCORING *MINI LifeQ QUIZ*

CUSTOMIZE FOR YOUR LIFE

As noted at the beginning of this chapter, an essential step in living an abundant life is to figure out where you are NOW. Only then can you begin to create your personal strategic plan. In business, we call this assessing your current reality. Once you have accurately assessed your current reality, you can plot the path and milestones to your destination.

You will find the *MINI LifeQ QUIZ, LifeQ PRACTICE #3.1, Page 42,* at the end of this chapter. There are *12 Components*, and you will rate each of the **Components from 0 – 100 with 100 the highest score possible.** *To make addition easy, rate each component as a multiple of 10 (for example 10, 20, 30, 40, 50, etc.)* Next add the **12 Components** together on the worksheet to find your *MINI LifeQ score.* The highest *MINI LifeQ* score possible is 1,200. Because of the complexities of life, no one gets a perfect score!

If a Component does NOT apply to you, give that Component a score of 100 which is the top score for a Component. That way, results are not negatively skewed by a Component that is not relevant to you. For example, you may not be interested in having a significant other or you may be retired and not interested in a career. Your **MINI LifeQ QUIZ** is customized to your life now and the way you WANT to live your life in the future.

"YOU ARE HERE."

Look at the *MINI WHEEL OF LifeQ* in **Figure 3.2 below.** The Wheel's 12 sections represent *12 Components* of your life. The center of the wheel is 0 and outer edge is 100. For each of the 12 Components, draw a horizontal line corresponding to the number you score on your **MINI Life QUIZ (for example 10, 20, 50, 80...).** The higher you score a component, the closer to the outer edge you would draw your line. This wheel is a visual representation of your **MINI WHEEL OF LifeQ.** It illustrates which areas you feel good about and which ones you do not. If you are like most people, your wheel is crooked and out of balance.

FIGURE 3.2 Example *MINI WHEEL OF LifeQ.* Center of the Wheel is 0 and Outer Wheel is 100.

MINI WHEEL OF LifeQ

[FIGURE 3.2]

FIND BOTH: MINI LifeQ QUIZ (LifeQ PRACTICE #3.1) and **MINI WHEEL OF LifeQ (LifeQ PRACTICE #3.2)** at the end of this chapter. Draw your **MINI WHEEL OF LifeQ** based on your **MINI LifeQ QUIZ.**

WHAT'S NEXT?

The next chapter, INTRODUCTION TO YOUR "LifeQ" quantifies how you see your progress in the 12 Q Components of your life. You will calculate your LifeQ Score. LifeQ, your Life Quotient, is the foundation for your Personal Strategic Plan, and this chapter reinforces that this book is all about YOU, your Life, your Values, and your Purpose. The LifeQ QUIZ will provide you with specific ideas about which areas are going well and will help you determine what you want more of and less of to create your fabulous life story.

CHAPTER 3 *LifeQ* -TIPS AND CHAPTER RECAP

The purpose of the *MINI LifeQ QUIZ* is three-fold:

- **Awareness:** To make you aware of the importance of *all* **12 LifeQ Components** and show where you believe you are in each.

- **Inspiration:** To inspire you to commit to increasing the score in each **LifeQ Component** regularly.

- **Action:** To develop actions you can take immediately to increase your **LifeQ** score.

LifeQ PRACTICE # 3.1 (*MINI LifeQ QUIZ*)

Rate each Component from 0-100 with 100 the highest score. *To make addition easy, rate each component as a multiple of 10 (for example 10, 20, 30, 40, 50, etc.)* **Next add the 12 Components together to find your MINI LifeQ score. The highest MINI LifeQ score possible is 1,200.**

If any of these Components do NOT apply, give that Component 100 points (i.e. CareerQ or LoveQ).

MINI LifeQ QUIZ 12 *LifeQ* Components	Score
BodyQ: How is your physical health? Are you generally fit and well?	
MindQ: How is your mental health? Are you mentally fit with good memory and the ability to make sound decisions and learn new things?	
EmotionQ: How is your emotional health? Are you emotionally balanced with the ability to laugh, cry, grieve, love, and forgive?	
SoulQ: How strong is your sense of meaning and purpose in your activities and relationships? Have you been growing spiritually?	
FunQ: Do you take time to relax and enjoy life? How often do you have fun?	
EnvironmentQ: Do you like the areas where you live and work? Is your home comfortable and safe?	
FamilyQ: Do you have valuable relationships with your family? How close are you to them?	
FriendsQ: Do you have valuable relationships with your friends? How close are you to them?	
LoveQ: Do you have/want a partner and soulmate? Do you share values and intimacy?	
CommunityQ: Do you demonstrate that you care about contributing to society by making a difference in your community?	
MoneyQ: How well are you planning for financial freedom? Do you earn and save enough?	
CareerQ: If working, how satisfied are you with your career? Your job? Does it reflect your values?	
TOTAL *MINI LifeQ* Score (max 1200)	

LifeQ PRACTICE # 3.2

GRAPH YOUR *MINI WHEEL OF LifeQ* from PRACTICE #3.1. Draw your scores on the wheel below (inner circle is 0, outer circle is 100). Refer to FIGURE 3.2, p. 41 for example of *MINI WHEEL OF LifeQ*.

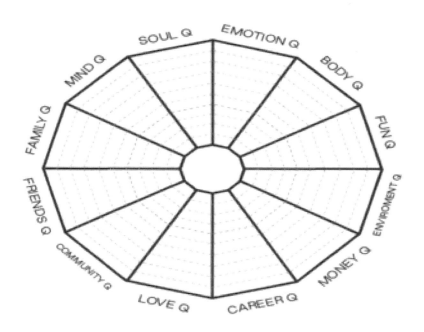

How bumpy is your ride if this were a real wheel?

LifeQ PRACTICE #3.3

REVIEW YOUR RESULTS. HOW DO YOU FEEL ABOUT THEM?

- Are you surprised at the results? Why?

- Which Component is the most surprising for you? Why?

- What areas are going the way you would like them to go?

- What areas are not going particularly well or are not very satisfying?

- For the areas with lower numbers, how do you feel about them?

- Is it OK with you that you are less satisfied in some areas of your life than in others?

- Choose one area in which you would like to see change.

- What actions can you take to start moving the number up the scale?

- What action could you take now to increase your score by this time next week?

LifeQ PRACTICE #3.4 THIS WEEK'S ACTION PLAN

- What have you learned about yourself after reading this chapter?

- What actions will you take this next week to start to design the life that you want to live?

CHAPTER 4

LIFEQ QUIZ

YOUR *LifeQ SCORE*

Now that you have completed the ***MINI LifeQ QUIZ*** in Chapter 3, it is time to dig deeper and discover your current ***LifeQ***. You may be saying to yourself, "Wait a minute! I just completed the ***MINI LifeQ QUIZ*** in the last chapter. Isn't that enough?" As we have found from many years of working with clients, the difference is in the details!

In the ***MINI LifeQ QUIZ***, we asked you to give a number for each of the 12 Components. The numbers may feel right to you, but the reality is that they come from a lifetime of influences about which you may not even be aware (like your values, purpose, patterns, underlying beliefs and self-esteem). These influences affect how you think about your achievements. We will discuss these factors during the next chapters so you can better understand why you think like you do.

The single number that you gave for each Component in the ***MINI LifeQ QUIZ*** is based on your gut feelings, not a quantitative assessment. It reflects the way you think about yourself on a snapshot, a day-to-day basis, and it usually drives your behavior and your thoughts. The numbers you chose in the ***MINI LifeQ QUIZ*** reflect the way you think about each Component *right now,* and how you answered is very dependent on your mood, recent events, and long-held patterns and beliefs. For example, a happy mood will likely produce higher scores than a depressed mood. A recent job promotion will probably cause you to overlook aspects of your career that are unsatisfying. As another example, if your parents always told you that you are not good with money, you may believe that about yourself regardless of any financial success you have achieved.

It is easy to think that things are better (or worse!) than they are. Human minds have all kinds of tricks to keep from seeing reality. Did you know that, on average, a person has 17,000 thoughts a day? Of those 17,000 thoughts, approximately 90% (more than 15,000) are repeated. [1] The **MINI LifeQ QUIZ** helps to expose your repeated thoughts and the stories you tell yourself.

LifeQ QUIZ DIGS DEEPER, IS QUANTITATIVE, PROVIDES SOLUTIONS

When we first meet with clients, they complete the **MINI LifeQ QUIZ**. The QUIZ shows us what they think is working and what is not. Next, they take the **LifeQ QUIZ**, which allows them to dig deeper and develop an awareness of current reality. It is when we dig deep and ask specific questions that a more accurate reality reveals itself. That awareness must be precise for constructive change to occur.

Another benefit of answering the 10 specific questions in each **Q** is that they can provide solutions as well as identify problems. By comparing the results of the two quizzes, clients can see the difference between what they have been telling themselves about their lives and what their actual reality is. Additionally, *the **LifeQ QUIZ** provides specific action steps to take to improve their current reality.

Through Brian's story, you will see how a low score in one area can be caused by the influence of other areas. Brian strategically clarified his values, discovered what made him feel fulfilled, assessed the different Components, and then took action. By using strategic thinking and planning as Brian did, you can raise your overall **LifeQ** score and live the life you desire. We will refer to Brian's story throughout this chapter.

Brian's story:

Brian grew up in Colorado, where he spent weekends and summers camping and hiking. He always felt most himself and alive in nature. Brian was an intelligent and hard-working student who had always been interested in finance. When he got into Wharton School of Business, he headed east without a look back. He worked hard and was offered a coveted job in a prestigious New York bank upon completion of his MBA. He was thrilled. For the first few years, Brian was happy doing the work he loved as well as enjoying the excitement of being young, single, and living in New York City. His income reflected his hard work.

At the beginning of his third year with the bank, Brian received the promotion that he had been working hard to get, and with it, he earned a massive increase in an already generous salary. Yet, it was around this time Brian found himself frustrated. He developed a quick temper and was not as happy as he thought he would be with his success. His career focus and 12-hour workdays had prevented any serious love interest from having a chance. It was on a trip back to Colorado over Christmas that Brian realized that his life was not as fulfilled as he wanted. He knew he was missing his connection to nature and fun times with family and friends. Brian figured that a love relationship would naturally follow once he had more balance and more happiness in his life.

On the plane ride back to New York, Brian committed himself to evaluate his life and come up with concrete ways to reconnect with nature and develop relationships, despite his business schedule and many pressing commitments. He realized that overwork and fatigue were skewing both his outlook on life and his actual life balance. A friend suggested to Brian that we could help him, and he began to work with *us, starting with the completion of the snapshot* **MINI LifeQ QUIZ** *and the detailed* **LifeQ QUIZ.**

Brian's was excelling in the **MoneyQ** *and* **CareerQ** *Components. His salary kept rising, and his job promotions were frequent and on track with his career plan. However, his overall* **WHEEL OF LifeQ** *was unbalanced. His* **Q** *Components were low due to lack of fun, relaxation, peacefulness, and exercise. Brian had become short-tempered and missed his Colorado natural environment. He was lonely despite New York City having almost 9 million people.*

Brian began with small steps. He started by running three mornings a week in Central Park.

Brian also joined with some colleagues and rented a house in Vermont for a winter ski vacation. Additionally, he spread the word that he was interested in dating. These small changes reinvigorated Brian. He promised himself that at least once a month, he would research and find a place outside of the city to go hiking or skiing, depending on the season. Although there was an occasional month, he could not get away, he found that he was working better the weeks right before or after each of those trips. He also noticed that he felt clearer of mind and better able to make business decisions after a run through the greenery of the park.

Brian then focused on making long-term plans with his new priorities in mind. He continued to advance at work and to strengthen his financial position so that he would have flexibility if a job change presented itself. A few years later, Brian was offered another promotion at the bank. Instead of accepting it, he decided to move back to Colorado and start his financial advisory firm. He had been able to balance his need for a specific type of physical environment while developing himself as a financial professional. Brian also reconnected with his college sweetheart who had returned to Colorado because she also missed the Colorado lifestyle. With his professional credentials and assets at a certain level, Brian was now able to have the professional life he desired while living in an environment that fulfilled him the most. He also committed to redoing his LifeQ QUIZ every six months to make sure he is on track to meet his goals.

Later in this chapter, after you have completed the *LifeQ QUIZ*, you will be able to compare the two results: what you tell yourself about your life (*MINI LifeQ QUIZ*) and what is going on (*LifeQ QUIZ*). You may be amazed to see the differences. Most of our clients are. With this information, you will be able to start the process of uncovering *why* your life is the way it is now and how you can change that reality to achieve and live the life you deserve! You may find that you have a more pessimistic view of your life and see your "glass as half empty" no matter how well things are going. With a negative outlook, you may be limiting the abundance that is available to you because you are envisioning the worst possible outcome in situations. Or it could be that you have more of a Pollyanna view of your life, and that may prevent you from seeing obstacles that surprise you. By having an accurate picture of current reality, you could be strategically planning to surmount those obstacles.

LifeQ QUIZ IS QUITE EASY

The *LifeQ QUIZ* sounds complicated, but it is relatively easy. Your *LifeQ QUIZ* score is the sum of 12 *LifeQ QUIZ* Components. How do you find out your personal **LifeQ QUIZ** score? Each of the 12 Components has 10 questions. The bottom-line? In only 120 questions, you will be able to see your current *LifeQ* score. We guarantee you will be surprised and enlightened by the results. Expect a few "Aha!" moments. Your *LifeQ QUIZ* is self-rated and self-scored. It is based on how YOU want to live YOUR life. If you believe it is low compared to where you would like it to be, the questions themselves will give you a starting point for making positive changes.

The more progress you make in increasing your Q scores, the higher your *LifeQ* score will climb.

We encourage you to complete all the questions now. You may have great intentions of completing a few Components now and then finish the rest "someday." We have found, however, that our clients' "someday" may never come, because "someday" is not a day in a week. It is too easy to procrastinate, especially when you see some progress is occurring. If you are pressed for time, you can answer those questions at this time if you set a firm deadline for when you will complete the *LifeQ QUIZ*. As you will see, though, the different Components may strongly influence others. You will get more out of the *LifeQ QUIZ* if you complete it in its entirety at one time.

The charts that follow contain all 120 *LifeQ QUIZ* questions. Start by answering the questions in the Components most vital to you. You may want to focus on problem areas of your life, but we encourage you to take the time now to complete all the Components. That is because all the Components are related, and they influence each other. ***Remember that if any Component does NOT apply to your situation, give that Component a score of 100.*** As mentioned in Chapter 3, you may not be interested in having a significant other, or you may be retired and not interested in a career. Your *LifeQ QUIZ* is customizable to the way you live your life now and the way you WANT to live your life in the future. **FIGURE 4.1** serves as a reminder of the **12 *LifeQ* Components.**

FIGURE 4.1 *LifeQ QUIZ* COMPONENTS

EmotionQ: Emotional health & awareness

SoulQ: Spirituality, personal growth & contribution

BodyQ: Physical health

MindQ: Intellectual health

FunQ: Recreation, fun, and relaxation

EnvironmentQ: Satisfaction with your physical surroundings

MoneyQ: Satisfaction with your income, assets, and life savings plan

CareerQ; Satisfaction with your career

FamilyQ: Relationship with members of your family

FriendsQ: Relationship with people whom you consider friends

LoveQ: Relationship with significant other

CommunityQ: Satisfaction with your contribution to the world, community, volunteer efforts

CHAPTER 4 *LifeQ*-TIPS AND CHAPTER RECAP

- How you assess your success is dependent on your mood, recent events, and long-held patterns and beliefs. Therefore, a quantitative assessment like the **LifeQ QUIZ** can be a more consistent way to measure improvements in your level of abundance and fulfillment.

- On average, a person has 17,000 thoughts per day, and 15,000 of those thoughts are repeated – approximately 90% are repeated. Your mind can play tricks on your view of reality.

- When strategically designing your next steps to develop your *LifeQ* Plan, think of times in your past when you made successful changes. Most likely, you made changes slowly, building confidence one step at a time. There are different approaches you can take, depending on what you have found works the best for you.

- Start where YOU want to start. You are just beginning the process of change, and you want to stay motivated to make those positive changes in your life.

- Start in an area that will give you the most satisfaction, even if it may not be the most comfortable place to start. You know from experience that your extra effort will make other changes seem much more manageable.

- Start in an area that will give you the fastest results and will motivate you to continue to the other areas.

WHAT'S NEXT?

*In Chapter 5, we will illustrate examples of how to use the Components in your **LifeQ** Plan by using the **LifeQ** questions to help guide you to solutions. Using information from the **LifeQ** QUIZ, you will be able to translate your scores into your plan to design and embrace the destiny that you want. At the end of Chapter 5, you will find your unique **LifeQ** worksheets to help you set goals in each area and then list specific actions you plan to take to reach those goals.*

LifeQ QUIZ

12 Components

120 Questions

DIRECTIONS: The next 12 pages contain the *LifeQ* **QUIZ.** There is one Component per page. Each of these 12 Components has 10 statements that relate to that Component.

Read each statement carefully and rate how much that statement describes you on a scale of 1 to 10 (10 is highest). Each component has a maximum of 100.

IMPORTANT: If any Component does NOT apply to your current situation, give that Component a SCORE OF 100 and do not worry about rating that Component. For example, you may not be interested in CareerQ or LoveQ at this point in your life although you may change your mind in the future.

DIRECTIONS: *Read each statement carefully and rate how much that statement describes you on a scale of 1 to 10 (10 is highest). Each Component has a maximum score of 100.*

BodyQ – QUESTIONS	TOTAL
I am conscious of my body and fitness level and exercise regularly.	
I honor my body with activities that it deserves (massages, stretching, nature walks).	
I rest and have enough quality sleep.	
I have a good relationship with food without addictions, starvation, or overeating.	
I base my diet on fruits and vegetables, high protein foods and grains, and drink lots of water. I limit my intake of processed foods, sugar, and animal products.	
I am free from disease and injury.	
I approach my health proactively through regular physical and dental exams, addressing pain promptly, practicing good personal hygiene.	
I am free from substance abuse (drugs, cigarettes, alcohol).	
My energy levels are consistently high throughout the day.	
I moisturize my skin daily and use sunscreen that is free from harmful chemicals.	
TOTAL SCORE – *BodyQ*	

DIRECTIONS: Read each statement carefully and rate how much that statement describes you on a scale of 1 to 10 (10 is highest). Each Component has a maximum score of 100.

MindQ – QUESTIONS	TOTAL
I am mentally healthy and fit with a good memory and ability to make sound decisions.	
I have high integrity with what I think, say, and do.	
I practice mindfulness every day by being "present" when eating, in conversations, walking, and driving.	
I stretch the analytical, logical, critical thinking part of my brain every day.	
I stretch the creative, artistic, musical part of my brain every day.	
Every day I think about what is important to me and intentionally imagine those things in my life.	
I am an expert in at least one area of knowledge and continue to learn in that area.	
I am aware of my negative self-talk and can manage it healthily.	
I deal with stress and change in a healthy manner (no addictions, conflict, self-sabotage).	
I welcome feedback from others. I often ask myself and others, "How can I improve? What do I need to change?"	
TOTAL SCORE – *MindQ*	

DIRECTIONS: *Read each statement carefully and rate how much that statement describes you on a scale of 1 to 10 (10 is highest). Each Component has a maximum score of 100.*

SoulQ - QUESTIONS	TOTAL
I have a sense of meaning and purpose in my activities and my relationships.	
I know my values and passions and honor them daily.	
I accept myself and take 100% responsibility for my life (no victim nor blame behaviors).	
I take time every day to be peaceful, quiet, pray, or meditate.	
I am involved with activities that contribute to others who can benefit from my help through community services, church outreach, or other volunteer efforts.	
My calendar and checkbook reflect that I spend significant time and resources (money, knowledge, energy) on my purpose in life and my values.	
I practice daily gratitude for my life and show generosity toward others.	
I have self-confidence. I know what I deserve, and I am receiving it daily.	
I regularly engage in activities where I grow and expand my level of mindfulness and awareness (i.e., reading, writing, listening, studying).	
I forgive others and forgive myself for past transgressions.	
TOTAL SCORE - *SoulQ*	

DIRECTIONS: Read each statement carefully and rate how much that statement describes you on a scale of 1 to 10 (10 is highest). Each Component has a maximum score of 100.

EmotionQ - QUESTIONS	TOTAL
I am emotionally balanced with the ability to laugh, cry, grieve, love, and forgive.	
I have a great sense of humor, including the ability to laugh at myself.	
I express my emotions and feelings in a positive manner.	
I let others know what I want and need, and can say "NO."	
I take responsibility for my feelings and reactions in a relationship. I can name my feelings and know how to manage them.	
I can understand or feel what another person is experiencing from his/her perspective.	
I believe worrying is a futile, non-productive activity. I can control my worrying and live in the present without worrying about the future or regretting the past.	
I know how I deserve to be treated. I ask/expect others to honor me. I allow myself to pursue my goals and dreams.	
I can trust myself and others.	
I set aside time regularly to address my needs, fears, and goals (journaling, coaching, therapy).	
TOTAL SCORE - *EmotionQ*	

DIRECTIONS: *Read each statement carefully and rate how much that statement describes you on a scale of 1 to 10 (10 is highest). Each Component has a maximum score of 100.*

FunQ - QUESTIONS	TOTAL
I have defined what fun and recreation are for me (hobbies, passions, or avocation).	
I create time to do the things I enjoy.	
I smile and laugh a lot.	
I do not take life too seriously. I can relax and enjoy my life.	
I take breaks to nourish my mind, soul, and body (travel, sports, music, movies, books, or cooking).	
I have a good mix of fun and work in my life.	
I participate as often as I want in clubs, sports, classes, and groups that add enjoyment to my life.	
I try new things with a spirit of adventure, curiosity, and fun.	
I take a vacation at least once a year where I shut off work-place communications and demands.	
I am guilt-free when I participate in fun activities, so I can be present and participate fully.	
TOTAL SCORE - *FunQ*	

DIRECTIONS: Read each statement carefully and rate how much that statement describes you on a scale of 1 to 10 (10 is highest). Each Component has a maximum score of 100.

EnvironmentQ - QUESTIONS	TOTAL
I enjoy my home, its décor, and furnishings.	
I am surrounded by things I enjoy and that have meaning to me.	
My home serves as a safe haven for me where I feel nourished, supported, and re-energized.	
The level of order in my surroundings is appropriate to my needs (amount of clutter in my home, garage, car, closets, on my desk).	
I enjoy my neighborhood, and I feel safe.	
I feel comfortable, safe, and have good self-esteem when in my car, bike, or other modes of transportation.	
I feel proud of my city and country and choose to live there.	
My wardrobe reflects who I am and my values. I enjoy wearing my clothes.	
I enjoy my office or workspace, its décor, and furnishings, and I can be creative and productive there.	
I keep my appliances, technology, equipment, car or bike in excellent working condition.	
TOTAL SCORE - *EnvironmentQ*	

DIRECTIONS: Read each statement carefully and rate how much that statement describes you on a scale of 1 to 10 (10 is highest). Each Component has a maximum score of 100.

MoneyQ - QUESTIONS	TOTAL
The state of my finances is excellent.	
I have a financial plan that will keep my financial picture healthy throughout my life.	
I have a financial budget that I use to guide my income, expenditures, and savings.	
I have at least six months of expenses in a designated "rainy day" fund.	
I have a will, an advance directive, and durable power of attorney. I have plans for my dependents and pets if I am unable to take care of them.	
My tax payments are current and up-to-date.	
I have appropriate insurance coverage for healthcare, disability, auto, belongings, and home.	
I have enough money to do things I want to do and to accomplish things that are important to me. My financial future feels robust and sustainable.	
I am free from worry and anxiety about money. I live with a feeling of abundance and "having enough."	
I manage my financial affairs and my records well.	
TOTAL SCORE - *MoneyQ*	

DIRECTIONS: Read each statement carefully and rate how much that statement describes you on a scale of 1 to 10 (10 is highest). Each Component has a maximum score of 100.

CareerQ - QUESTIONS	TOTAL
I am aware of my talents, skills, and professional achievements.	
I have good relationships at work with my clients, colleagues, and my management.	
I receive positive recognition with my job. My job increases my self-esteem.	
I have job flexibility to deal with family, personal emergencies, and appointments. I feel I have some control over my workload.	
I have an optimal commute/travel schedule/video conferencing with my job.	
My job makes me feel energized and engaged and aligns with my personal value system.	
I am aware of the areas in which I do not excel nor enjoy.	
I have my professional goals and dreams documented in my career plan.	
My career path will provide the financial remuneration and benefits that I need and want.	
I see the opportunity for advancement, growth, and development in my current position.	
TOTAL SCORE - *CareerQ*	

DIRECTIONS: Read each statement carefully and rate how much that statement describes you on a scale of 1 to 10 (10 is highest). Each Component has a maximum score of 100.

LoveQ - QUESTIONS	TOTAL
I am able to be in a committed relationship that is joyful, loving, stable, and intimate. I am free from past resentments or blame.	
I love and respect myself, and I believe I deserve love and respect from a partner.	
I have evaluated which characteristics, values, and behaviors I want in a partner, and I am exhibiting the same.	
I am in a committed relationship with a partner who has the characteristics, values, and behaviors I want.	
I can be authentic, honest, and trustworthy with my partner.	
I enjoy spending time with my partner, and we have fun and romance together.	
My partner treats me respectfully with kind words and actions daily.	
My partner brings out the best version of me. My partner believes in me and is encouraging and supportive.	
I bring out the best version of my partner every day. I believe in my partner and am encouraging and supportive.	
I am satisfied with the level of physical and sexual connection that I have with my partner.	
TOTAL SCORE - LoveQ	

DIRECTIONS: Read each statement carefully and rate how much that statement describes you on a scale of 1 to 10 (10 is highest). Each Component has a maximum score of 100.

CommunityQ- QUESTIONS	TOTAL
I care about contributing to society and have found a way through my career, job, relationships, or activities to do so.	
I donate time, energy, or resources to charities that are important to me and aligned with my values.	
I vote in every election for representatives and legislation that impact my neighborhood, my city, and my country.	
I know at least two of my neighbors and have exchanged contact information with them. I watch out for my neighbors.	
I do random acts of kindness several times per week. I pay it forward daily (buy coffee, let someone pass, share information, compliment).	
I serve as a mentor and role model for others.	
I care about the environment, and I follow three R's: Reduce, Reuse, Recycle in my daily life.	
I am active in organizations that help my community (schools, hospitals, jails, seniors, mentoring, children, safety, animals, food banks).	
I support local businesses and the local economy (I buy food, art, clothes, attend events) in my community.	
I behave as a good citizen who obeys laws, cares about others (safe driving and biking, respectful of public spaces).	
TOTAL SCORE - *CommunityQ*	

DIRECTIONS: *Read each statement carefully and rate how much that statement describes you on a scale of 1 to 10 (10 is highest). Each Component has a maximum score of 100.*

FriendsQ - QUESTIONS	TOTAL
I have created the experience of family in my life, whether or not it is with my biological relatives.	
I have close positive friends who cheer me on and bring out the best version of myself. My friendships nourish and sustain me.	
I am a good friend, and I make myself available to my relationships. I am dependable, caring, and a good listener.	
I behave in a trustworthy manner with all my friends. I am loyal, tell the truth, keep my promises, and keep discreet information confidential.	
I limit my time with relationships that are negative, sarcastic, or do not encourage me to achieve my goals.	
I enjoy and make the most of my time with my friends.	
At least one person in my life will provide me with honest and trustworthy feedback.	
I am committed to keeping positive, supportive people in my inner circle (no judgment, no envy).	
I am stretching myself to meet the kinds of people who support me to grow as a person.	
I let others know what I need and want. My relationships are reciprocal. My friends and I devote the same amount of energy and time to our relationship.	
TOTAL SCORE - *FriendsQ*	

DIRECTIONS: Read each statement carefully and rate how much that statement describes you on a scale of 1 to 10 (10 is highest). Each Component has a maximum score of 100.

FamilyQ - QUESTIONS	TOTAL
I am free from past resentments or blame about my childhood experiences and family.	
I feel a deep connection to at least one family member who provides honest, trustworthy feedback. If needed, he or she would respond immediately.	
I have evaluated the characteristics and behaviors of family members with whom I want to be connected and close.	
I limit my time with family members who are negative, sarcastic, or do not encourage me to achieve my goals.	
I am satisfied with the level of closeness I have with each member of my family.	
I am satisfied with the role I play and the level of contribution I have in my family.	
I am satisfied with the amount of contact I have with my family.	
I let my family members be themselves and accept them for who they are.	
I schedule family time (in-person, phone, or virtually) each week and do not let other activities get in the way of it.	
I behave in a trustworthy manner concerning my family.	
TOTAL SCORE - *FamilyQ*	

LifeQ PRACTICE # 4.2 YOUR *LifeQ* SCORE

DIRECTIONS: Enter your scores for each Component on the chart above and columns below:

LifeQ:	Score	*LifeQ:*	Score
BodyQ		**CareerQ**	
MindQ		**MoneyQ**	
EmotionQ		**LoveQ**	
SoulQ		**CommunityQ**	
FunQ		**FriendsQ**	
EnvironmentQ		**FamilyQ**	
SUBTOTAL		**SUBTOTAL**	
TOTAL LifeQ SCORE			

LifeQ PRACTICE # 4.3 *WHEEL OF LifeQ vs. MINI LifeQ*

Please return to Chapter 3, *LifeQ* **PRACTICE # 3.2, p. 44** and fill in your new LifeQ score on the wheel with a different color pen or broken line as in the example below:

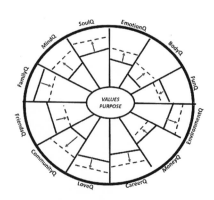

COMPARING *MINI LifeQ* QUIZ AND THE *LifeQ* QUIZ

Now it is time for one more step, and it is a critical one. In the **MINI LifeQ QUIZ,** the numbers you wrote down reflect the widespread beliefs you have about each of the Components. These are the ideas you carry around in your head and are the basis of overall attitudes about yourself. Let's face it, most people engage in negative self-talk even when they have all the evidence in the world that they should be praising themselves. ("I'm not good with money." "I'm too fat/boring/don't know what I'm doing with my life." "I don't know why I don't have close relationships.")

In contrast, to complete the *LifeQ* QUIZ, you answered 10 specific questions for each of the Components. It was not just your "off the top of the head" assessment; it forced you to confront the reality of how well your life is working in the details.

When you complete *LifeQ* **PRACTICE # 4.4 "COMPARING THE Qs CHART"** below, you will have a chance to instantly compare the ideas you carry around in your head (the **MINI LifeQ QUIZ**) with reality ((the *LifeQ QUIZ*).

Most people have substantial differences in some areas. You cannot make changes until you see the reality of your situation. In the spaces provided under "Observations," write down any ideas you have about why the numbers are so different. It is essential to treat yourself with humor and respect. Now is your chance to assess the current reality of your life. You will find your accurate location on your personal Global Positioning System (GPS), celebrate the parts of your life going well, and determine what changes you want to make, so you live your life on purpose and honor your values.

LifeQ* PRACTICE # 4.4   **COMPARING THE Qs CHART**

Use the numbers from Chapter 3, *LifeQ* **PRACTICE 3.1** (the **MINI LifeQ QUIZ),** and Chapter 4, *LifeQ* **PRACTICE 4.2** (Your *LifeQ QUIZ* totals) to complete the "Comparing the Qs" chart.

MINI LifeQ QUIZ vs. LifeQ QUIZ

LifeQ	MINI LifeQ QUIZ Score	LifeQ QUIZ Score
BodyQ		
MindQ		
EmotionQ		
SoulQ		
FunQ		
EnvironmentQ		
CommunityQ		
FriendsQ		
FamilyQ		
LoveQ		
MoneyQ		
CareerQ		
TOTAL SCORES		

- How do you feel about the differences in these scores? Are you surprised? Why?

- Describe your observations about differences in scores:

WHAT NOW?

You have done it! Congratulations on completing the **LifeQ QUIZ!** Now, you have discovered which **Qs** are going well and which could be improved. You now know where you are in the primary areas of your life story.

The 120 statements that you just answered are useful tools in themselves and show you precisely what you can do to make progress toward a life of abundance, balance, and joy.

Once our clients have completed their **LifeQ** score, it is often overwhelming. They may see a snapshot of their lives clearly, sometimes for the very first time. Remember, Brian, our nature-loving finance expert? Brian originally answered the *MoneyQ* and *LoveQ* Components in his *LifeQ QUIZ* and was shocked to find his *MoneyQ* score was 88 and his *LoveQ* was only 25. He finally had visual proof of what he had felt and somehow known for so long. Quantifying it with numbers made it much easier to understand. He felt more motivated than ever to balance his life and increase his *LifeQ* score. So, where do you start?

- Think of times in the past when you have made successful changes. Most of us succeed long term by making changes slowly, with one success engendering confidence to take the next step. Here are several different strategies to help you take the first step. Pick the one(s) that best fit your personality and work method.

- Start where YOU want to start. You are just beginning the process of change, and you want to stay motivated to make those positive changes in your life.

- Start in an area that will give you the most satisfaction, even if it may not be the most comfortable place to start. Your extra effort will make other changes seem so much easier.

- Start in an area that will give you the fastest results. That will motivate you to go on to the other areas. In business, this is "picking the low hanging fruit."

LifeQ PRACTICE # 4.5 CHOOSE ONE COMPONENT YOU WANT TO IMPROVE

Component:

- What is one step you will take during the next week to increase that score?

- Describe what your plans are, including the start-date.

LifeQ PRACTICE # 4.6 THIS WEEK'S ACTION PLAN

- What have you learned about yourself after reading this chapter?

- What actions will you take this next week to start to design the life that you want to live?

#### CHAPTER 5

PUTTING LIFEQ INTO YOUR PERSONAL STRATEGIC PLAN

Now, you can begin putting your self-reflection into your strategic plan. We will illustrate how to use the *LifeQ QUIZ* as a tool for change. First, we will give examples of how to use the Components in your plan. Next, we will provide some case studies to show you how others have found success so that you can envision how to design your plan and achieve the balance and fulfillment you want. We will show you how the **WHEEL OF LifeQ** helped a new grad, a 20-something, an empty nester, a lonely accountant, and a married banker approaching retirement. At the end of the chapter, you will find your unique *LifeQ* worksheets. These will help you set goals in each area and then list specific actions to take to reach those goals. Remember to use the *LifeQ QUIZ* questions to help guide you to solutions.

LifeQ COMPONENTS

Now that you have scored your *LifeQ QUIZ*, you have specific steps you can take to create a more fulfilling and abundant life. As you explore your **WHEEL OF LifeQ,** you may decide to start focusing on some of the Components that you can impact right away. From experience you may know that to be successful, you want to start small and not take on too many changes at once.

BodyQ, FunQ, and *SoulQ.*

If you choose to focus on your health first, you could start with your *BodyQ, FunQ,* and *SoulQ.* Health is "a state of complete physical, mental and social well-being and not merely the absence of disease or infirmity."[1] You may decide to make changes during the next month in two of the *BodyQ* areas: in #3 "I rest and have sufficient amount of quality sleep," and in #10, "I moisturize my skin daily and use sunscreen that is free from harmful chemicals." Also, you may decide to focus on the part of #5 and drink more water. To honor those areas in your *BodyQ* and improve your score, you promise yourself that during the next month, you will:

- Be in bed, ready for sleep by 10:30 p.m. at least five nights per week.

- Make taking care of your skin a priority. Every morning you will apply lotion with sunscreen on your face, neck, arms, and legs.

- Drink eight more ounces of water every day than you do now.

In the *FunQ* area, you might decide that during the next month, you are going to smile more frequently and laugh at least three times per day. Start by smiling at yourself when you first look in the mirror each morning. You will be amazed at your immediate attitude improvement.

If you decide to increase your *SoulQ*, you could focus on the following statements of the *LifeQ QUIZ*: "#9. I take time every day to be peaceful, quiet, pray, meditate," and "#10. I forgive others and forgive myself for past transgressions." To increase these scores, you might commit to setting aside 20 minutes every morning to be peaceful, quiet, pray, or meditate. You decide to schedule time on your calendar. You also realize that you have difficulty forgiving others, so you commit to reading more about forgiveness. Make a list of those people you would like to forgive. You may want to put your name on that list. Forgiving yourself is often the most challenging kind of forgiveness. So, start by being gentle with yourself as you begin to focus on forgiving yourself and others. Studies show that forgiveness improves both your physical and emotional health, and the primary beneficiary of forgiving others is you.

LoveQ

As you plan your next few months, you may decide to focus on the relationship part of your life. *Once again, if you are NOT interested in being in a romantic love relationship, give yourself a score of 100 for LoveQ.*

That way, results are not negatively skewed by a Component that is not relevant to you. If you decide to increase your low **LoveQ** score, you may choose to focus on the following statement from the **LifeQ QUIZ**: "#3. I have evaluated which characteristics, values, and behaviors I want in a partner and believe that I am exhibiting the same." You promise that during the next month, you will compile a comprehensive list of the characteristics, values, and behaviors you want in a partner. Do not make the mistake of falling back on past negative habits and relationships. Learn from your mistakes! Patterns *can* change; the first step is recognizing them. As you are compiling this list, examine your own life to ensure you are exhibiting the same characteristics, values, and behaviors that you are pursuing in another. If you identify malicious behavior that is sabotaging your chance for a positive love relationship, commit to change.

CommunityQ

Next, you may decide to set some goals in **CommunityQ**. The questions you focus on are: "#4 I know at least two of my neighbors and have exchanged contact information with them. I watch out for my neighbors," and "#5 I do random acts of kindness for others several times per week. I pay it forward daily (buy coffee, let someone pass, share information, sincerely give a compliment)." You may realize that you already know one of your neighbors and have his or her contact information. There is a new neighbor next door with whom you have only exchanged pleasantries. During the next two months, you promise to invite him over for coffee and to exchange contact information. You decide to put a yellow sticky note on your bathroom mirror and set a reminder on your phone to prompt yourself to do one or more random acts of kindness every day. You will perform these random acts at home, at work, at the store, which also could impact several of your **Q**s. The great news is that behaving positively towards others increases your endorphins so that you feel better about yourself. Talk about a win-win!

MoneyQ

As you review your scores, you note that your *MoneyQ* score is 50. You could decide to focus on the following statements that you gave low scores: "#2. I have a financial plan that will keep my financial picture healthy throughout my life" and "#5. I have a will, an advance directive, and durable power of attorney. I have made plans for my dependents and pets should I become unable to take care of them." You decide to ask your friends and colleagues for some references for a good fee-only financial planner who could help create a personal financial plan that focuses on the areas of most importance for your current and future financial goals. The National Association of Personal Financial Advisors (www.napfa.org) is an organization that can help. Members earn fees, not commissions, so there are no conflicts of interest. Some NAPFA members specialize in investing, retirement, and education planning, while others can help you create a budget and get out of debt. You recognize that you need to develop a will, an advance directive, and durable power of attorney. You set a goal to obtain these signed legal documents within the next four months.

CareerQ

If you decide that your focus should be your *CareerQ,* you may choose two areas that are low for you. For example, you can select "#1 I am aware of my talents, skills and professional achievements" and "#5 I have an optimal commute/travel schedule/video conferencing with my job." To gain confidence and reinforce your knowledge of your talents, skills, and professional achievements, update your resume and study it. This way, you can evaluate if you are in a position that matches your gifts and talents and keeps you growing professionally. If you travel for work or have a very long commute, you probably already realize that your schedule is negatively affecting several areas of your *LifeQ*. The impact of traveling so much of the time has perhaps affected several Components that directly impact you physically, mentally, and emotionally. You cannot see your family and friends as often, kids are usually in bed when you get home, and it is hard to exercise late at night in your hotel room.

CASE STUDIES FROM SUCCESSFUL CLIENTS

The following are five examples of how others have used the insights they gained from *LifeQ* to make positive changes in their lives.

CASE 1 Natalie is about to become an empty nester. Now that her youngest son is preparing to go away to college in another state, Natalie realizes her life will change significantly. For the past 25 years, she has taken her role as a wife and mother very seriously and has spent time, money, energy, and focus raising her three children and helping her husband John in his business. What a super job she has done! Her daughter is in medical school, one son is in his last year of college, and now her youngest son is leaving home to start college. In addition, the business has become so successful that John can hire the help he needs. Suddenly, there will be two people in that big house: John and herself. Natalie knows her life is about to change and wants to be proactive so that she has a busy, fulfilling schedule in place when "empty-nest syndrome" hits. Natalie knows from experience that without one, she is likely to become depressed. Natalie completes the **LifeQ QUIZ** *and asks John to do the same so that they can approach this new phase of their life in sync.*

Natalie decides to establish new goals in the areas of **LoveQ**, **BodyQ**, *and* **CommunityQ**. *She asks John to get involved with the goal setting, which will immediately increase Natalie's* **LoveQ** *score. They decide to get new bikes and set a goal to ride together three times per week, which will help* **LoveQ**, **BodyQ**, **FunQ** *and* **EmotionQ**. *Natalie decides to average eight hours of sleep per night, which seemed impossible with three growing kids. Now, she commits to being in bed by 10 p.m. at least four nights per week. She also plans to have both medical and dental check-ups since she had been delaying these visits because of her packed schedule. Natalie commits to* *examining options in the community for a charity where she wants to devote some newfound time and energy.*

CASE 2 Alicia is a successful attorney who needs more balance. *Alicia's dreams of being a successful attorney are coming true. On her 10th anniversary with the law firm, Alicia reflects on her career experience. Not only has she won several impressive legal cases, but she has also paid back her student loans, bought her first home, and is financially on track with her 401(K). On her* **WHEEL OF LifeQ** *diagram, Alicia scores herself high in the areas of* **CareerQ** *(90) and* **MoneyQ** *(80). However, she gives herself low scores in the areas of* **FunQ** *(10),* **LoveQ** *(10),* **FriendsQ** *(30), and* **FamilyQ** *(40). Alicia hesitantly increases her* **BodyQ** *score to 50 because she signed up yesterday for Zumba classes at a health club near her office, although the classes do not start until next month. Alicia knows that her life has been "lopsided" for several years. She has been okay with focusing on her career and finances, but now it is time to take back her life in the other areas. As she studies her* **WHEEL OF LifeQ**, *it becomes clear that she should make some life changes, and it is time to set some new SMART goals. Some goals can overlap areas. For example, Alicia could invite some friends to join her at the Zumba class and get together afterward for dinner. These plans could positively impact her Components for* **BodyQ**, **FriendsQ**, *and* **FunQ**. *Also, Alicia may meet a new love while out with her friends, or perhaps her friends may know of some available men or may encourage her to sign up for online dating.*

A picture is worth 1,000 words, and as Alicia looks at the picture of her **WHEEL OF LifeQ**, *she commits herself that by her 11th work anniversary, her* **WHEEL OF LifeQ** *will be more balanced, and her* **LifeQ** *will be higher.*

CASE 3 At age 28, Jordan is tired of the bar scene where he and his buddies hang out every Friday night. It has turned from fun to a monotonous ritual where they seem to tell the same stories repeatedly, drink too much, and then start the weekend with a hangover. Jordan has not been in a committed relationship for five years when his then-girlfriend abruptly told him she wanted to date other guys. He is not sure how to break free from his routine, meet new women, or develop some new interests. Jordan came to us for coaching. Jordan's **WHEEL OF LifeQ** *shows what he sensed already. His high scores are in* **CareerQ (90)** *and* **MoneyQ (80)** *because Jordan's profession as an architect fulfills his passion for creating new building designs. His* **LoveQ (10),** **EmotionQ (40),** *and* **FunQ (40)** *are the areas where Jordan wants to focus first. Jordan's initial exercise is to think about his ideal partner.*

What attributes and values does she have? What kinds of hobbies or interests? What does she do for a living, and what type of education does she have? What beliefs does she have? Another assignment is to tune into his emotions. Jordan never explored his breakup five years ago and the impact on his ability to trust. He has never clarified what he wants and needs in relationships. Over time and through hard work and introspection, Jordan is developing more self-confidence, strengthening his ability to trust women, and improving his ability to understand his emotions. We encouraged Jordan to continue to exhibit a passion for his architectural career because many women are attracted to men who are passionate about their work. We also implored Jordan to explore his interests and hobbies, and Jordan became re-ignited with his love for photography and cinematography. After Jordan assessed the type of woman he wants as a partner, we presented situations and social media sites where Jordan could find women for him to meet. Jordan is looking forward to his next chapter.

*CASE 4 Kevin has been an accountant for 15 years. His dad was an accountant for 45 years. Kevin became an accountant because he was groomed from childhood to take over his father's successful accounting firm. Kevin has been a workaholic since college trying to please his father, although accounting has never been easy for Kevin. He has always felt different and being gay did not help. Kevin's true love is jazz music, which he plays loudly during his commute and after work hours. Kevin is shy and lonely, and music is the only thing that makes him feel alive. Kevin decides it is time to expand his horizons. At 36 years old, he suddenly realizes he does not want to live this way for the next 30 years. Kevin takes the **LifeQ QUIZ** and discovers he is high in **MoneyQ**, and that is about it. Kevin examines his values, which include loyalty, family, and relationships (even though he is shy).*

*Kevin decides to set goals in **LoveQ** and **FunQ**. He commits to set more goals in the future, but his "comfort zone" is being deliberate and precise, and he wants to achieve first things first. Kevin buys a set of drums and signs up for 10 jazz music lessons on Wednesday evenings. He plans to join a jazz ensemble within two years. In looking at questions from **LoveQ**, Kevin decided to envision a partner, something he had never taken much time to do because he was afraid it would be a useless exercise and just get his hopes up. Kevin made a list of characteristics, values, and behaviors he wants in a partner. He knows with his shyness that meeting people may be difficult, so he includes in his plan that he will read books and articles about overcoming shyness. He starts immediately with small steps. He commits to joining the local Jazz Society because he will share a common interest with other members and easily be able to talk with them about music. (He knows that no one wants to talk about accounting!) Kevin also wants to "get ready" to have a partner, so he decides to get his hair professionally styled and ask if his local department* store has a personal shopper to help him upgrade his wardrobe and change his image. Although Kevin is a little nervous about making these changes, he is excited and open to this next chapter in his life.

CASE 5 Darlene will be retiring next year after 40 years at the bank. *She started as a teller after college. Through a combination of working full time while earning graduate degrees and certificates, Darlene's banking career has consumed many hours of every day throughout the years. She is now a senior vice president. Even when not at work, Darlene has been mentally on the job during mergers, downsizing, politics, new regulations, deregulation, and so forth. She freely admits that her career success and work focus were significant factors in her divorce 10 years ago from her high-school sweetheart. Her ex-husband had resented Darlene's success and attention to her career while he was content with the same, blue-collared job during their 30-year marriage. Because Darlene has watched many friends and colleagues retire, she realizes this is going to be a significant change in her life. She has been active as a volunteer, and physically Darlene is in good shape. She loves being in nature and enjoys leading hikes for a local outdoor group.*

What will be her next act after such a busy, structured life? Darlene takes the **LifeQ QUIZ** *and finds that her* **WHEEL OF LifeQ** *is already quite full, although she realizes that next year, she will have 50+ hours per week that will be unscheduled. Darlene wants to expand her* **FunQ, CommunityQ,** *and* **SoulQ.** *She has a small group of hiking friends who have always talked about climbing Mount Kilimanjaro in Kenya "someday." Darlene decides that "someday" has arrived, and she convinces two of her hiking buddies to join her on her "trip of a lifetime." Darlene realizes this will require physical training for several months before going to get in tip-top shape for the climb, and she arranges a regular hiking and conditioning* *schedule for her and her friends, which will increase her* **FunQ**. *For her* **CommunityQ**, *she plans to check out the city program to help struggling school kids with reading. Darlene went to mediocre public schools growing up, and she wants to help other children succeed.*

Regarding strengthening her **SoulQ**, *Darlene is excited about having some quiet time to reflect and meditate. She commits to writing five minutes a day in her journal and signs up for a mindfulness meditation class at the local hospital. Darlene knows she will miss the structure and stimulation of working full time, but with all these plans in place, she is now looking forward to this next chapter of her life. Darlene realizes that gratitude and attitude are essential lifelong values, so she plans to nurture those values in herself and others for her entire life.*

WHAT'S NEXT?

The first of the three parts of the personal strategic planning process is BECOME AWARE OF CURRENT REALITY. The next chapter will help you CLARIFY AND PRIORITIZE YOUR VALUES that will guide your Personal Strategic Plan. You will learn the benefits of saying "No" to honor your values and increase your **LifeQ**. *Having specific values can make decision-making more straightforward and will add focus and purpose to your Personal Strategic Plan as well as your daily actions.*

CHAPTER 5: *LifeQ* -TIPS AND CHAPTER RECAP

- Every life area of the **WHEEL OF LifeQ** is essential. Life areas reinforce each other.

- There is no need to put your happiness on hold.

- By using the questions on the **LifeQ QUIZ**, you can learn specific steps to take to increase your **LifeQ** Score.

- Your success in your life depends on how you perceive your progress in fulfilling your purpose, living your values, and focusing on your priorities.

- Life is 5% what happens to you and 95% what you do with it.

LifeQ PRACTICE # 5.1 - SET GOALS FOR EACH *LifeQ* COMPONENT

Now it is time to start working on your **LifeQ** plan. The first step is to look at the results of your **LifeQ QUIZ** and decide which goals you want to set in each of the **12 Components** so that you can achieve a life of balance, abundance, and joy. Do not worry about reaching all of your goals now; you will gradually be able to find success in all your goals over time.

What can you do today to increase your *LifeQ*?

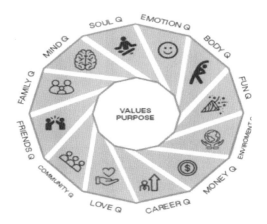

Let's set your *LifeQ* goals and start taking action! Think of all the activities you can do in one Component to advance in that area.

For example, ask yourself this question: *"What can I do to advance my life in the Component of CareerQ?"*

Possible answers include: *"I could enhance my skills, take a class, talk to my boss about opportunities, and research which jobs match my expertise/ experience/ interests, or start my own business."*

List all the options open to you in that area. Be as specific as possible.

Move to another area and ask yourself what you can do to improve your LifeQ score in that area.

Consider activities that stretch across several life areas. This process is where you can feel the power of the *WHEEL OF LifeQ*. You can satisfy several needs through a single action. For example, rather than exercise in the gym, ride bikes with your friends. You may even meet someone who could help you with your *CareerQ* during your bike ride. Perhaps you may find a new love along the way to enhance your *LoveQ*. Be creative in coming up with ways you can advance several life areas at the same time.

Select the activities you want to start with for the *LifeQ* areas: Choose the things that you can apply today or during the next week or month from the above lists. Take your time. These are significant decisions. Choose carefully. Over time, make sure that you cover them all. Start with what is most important to you. No matter how minor the activity or action is, if you are increasing your *LifeQ* score in that area, you are making progress and improving your quality of life.

BodyQ	Score

• **Goal 1:**
   ✓   Action Steps:
 	
• **Goal 2:**
   ✓ Action Steps:	

MindQ	**Score**

• **Goal 1:**
   ✓   Action Steps:
 	
• **Goal 2:**
   ✓ Action Steps:	

SoulQ	**Score**

• **Goal 1:**
   ✓   Action Steps:
 	
• **Goal 2:**
   ✓ Action Steps:	

EmotionQ	**Score**

• **Goal 1:**
   ✓   Action Steps:
 	
• **Goal 2:**
   ✓ Action Steps:	

FunQ	Score

• **Goal 1:**
   ✓   Action Steps:
 	
• **Goal 2:**
   ✓ Action Steps:	

EnvironmentQ	Score

• **Goal 1:**
   ✓   Action Steps:
 	
• **Goal 2:**
   ✓ Action Steps:	

MoneyQ	Score

• **Goal 1:**
   ✓   Action Steps:
 	
• **Goal 2:**
   ✓ Action Steps:	

CareerQ	Score

• **Goal 1:**
   ✓   Action Steps:
 	
• **Goal 2:**
   ✓ Action Steps:	

LoveQ	Score

• **Goal 1:**
  ✓ Action Steps:
 	
• **Goal 2:**
  ✓ Action Steps:	

CommunityQ	Score

• **Goal 1:**
  ✓ Action Steps:
 	
• **Goal 2:**
  ✓ Action Steps:	

FriendQ	Score

• **Goal 1:**
  ✓ Action Steps:
 	
• **Goal 2:**
  ✓ Action Steps:	

FamilyQ	Score

• **Goal 1:**
  ✓ Action Steps:
 	
• **Goal 2:**
  ✓ Action Steps:	

LifeQ PRACTICE #5.2 THIS WEEK'S ACTION PLAN

- What have you learned about yourself after reading this chapter?
- What actions will you take this next week to start to design the life that you want to live

THE VALUE OF VALUES

*V*alues are what you stand for and what you believe. Deciding what is important to you is critical to living a life of purpose and having a high **LifeQ**. Your deeply held values can fuel the energy behind your life purpose or calling. Simply put, *values* are the standards and principles that are important to you. "If you don't stand for something, you'll fall for anything" are lyrics from a country-western song. [1]

Read the two case stories below. How does Oscar's claim that family is his most important value compare with Ellie's claim?

Oscar's story:

Oscar is a 50-year old executive with a high-pressured job. He travels internationally every week, smokes two packs of cigarettes a day, is 40 pounds overweight, and lists his love for his family as his most important value. Oscar says he understands that he is a high risk for a stroke or heart attack and wants to change his life. He cuts out butter, smokes a half pack per day, and answers ads for a new job. After three months, Oscar says the timing is not right for changing jobs or changing his lifestyle. It is just too hard right now. He resumes his previous smoking and eating habits. He promises that he will try again next year. Is Oscar's love for his family really his most important value?

Ellie's story:

*Ellie is a 37-year old medical assistant who has been married for 17 years and is the mother of two daughters. Three months ago, Ellie packed her suitcase and moved into an apartment. Before moving, she began meeting her single girlfriends after work for happy hour and was feeling relieved of the pressures of being a full-time mother, wife, and employee. She got involved in charity work and enjoyed the spotlight and public recognition. When she moved out, she was full of resentment that she had gotten married so young. Living alone in her apartment, Ellie was confused, guilt-ridden, and not at all happy when she sought coaching from us. We asked Ellie to assess her **WHEEL OF LifeQ**. Next, we helped her reaffirm her values and determine her life purpose. After much soul-searching, Ellie realized that her family is the most essential part of her life, and the best path for living her life's purpose is to partner with her husband to raise her children in their family home. Ellie moved home, entered marriage and family counseling with her husband and daughters, and now focuses on creating a life where everyone in her family identifies, discusses, and explores their needs.*

WHAT ARE YOUR VALUES?

What do you consider the most important and valuable in your life? It may not be what first comes to mind. To continue on the path of self-awareness, you must do some research. Clarifying your values is fundamental to living the life that you want.

How aligned are your values with your behavior? If you examine how you spend your resources (that is, time, energy, focus, money, and efforts) and compare them to what you say is valuable, you might see a disconnect. An exercise to quantify your use of resources can be to review your bank statements and calendar. The way you manage your time and your money indicates the things that you view as necessary, the things you value.

WHAT YOUR BANK STATEMENTS TELL YOU (See *LifeQ* **PRACTICE # 6.1** at the end of this chapter). Review your bank statements for the past year. These statements will show where you have invested your *money*. Look closely at the investments above and beyond the necessities of food, mortgage/rent, and clothing. Do you pay for health club membership? Did you buy new tires for your car? Did you buy a new car? Did you give money to any causes that are meaningful to you? As you look over the statements, do you see excessive expenses in any area(s)? How many ATM withdrawals did you have, and do you remember where you spent that cash?

WHAT YOUR CALENDAR TELLS YOU (See *LifeQ* **PRACTICE # 6.2** at the end of this chapter.) Your calendar will show where you have invested your *time*. How many hours did you put in at work? Did you take a vacation? Volunteer in your community? Did you spend time with your family and friends? Did you spend time taking care of your physical body? How about your professional development? Have you gone on a retreat to feed your soul? This review is an excellent way to show what has been important to you. Have your actions matched what you say that you value?

CLEAR VALUES AID DECISION-MAKING

By clarifying what is important to you, you can make decisions more efficiently on how to spend your limited resources of time and money. For example, if you determine that health is a value, it becomes easier for you to select healthy food, make time for exercise, get enough sleep, and get regular medical and dental checkups. You may be less tempted by sweets, a cigarette, or a drink. As another example, if you hold integrity as a value, you admit your mistakes and endure the consequences rather than lying or blaming someone else. Two powerful models of individuals who clearly understood their values and made decisions accordingly in their own lives were Benjamin Franklin and Alfred Nobel. The decisions they made affected not only their own lives and times but continue to influence us today.

BENJAMIN FRANKLIN'S VIRTUES FOR VALUES

In 1726 when he was 20, Benjamin Franklin decided to cultivate his character by selecting 13 "virtues" to practice, and he continued to practice them in some form for the rest of his life. *Webster's Dictionary* includes "values" as a synonym for "virtues." In Franklin's autobiography, *Memoir,* he wrote about "The Art of Virtue" and lists his 13 virtues. [2]

1. *Temperance* Eat not to dullness, drink not to elevation.

2. *Silence* Speak not, but what may benefit others or yourself; avoid trifling conversation.

3. *Order* Let all your things have their places; let each part of your business have its time.

4. *Resolution* Resolve to perform what you ought; perform without fail what you resolve.

5. *Frugality* Make no expense but to do good to others or yourself; i.e., waste nothing.

6. *Industry* Lose no time; be always employed in something useful; cut off all unnecessary actions.

7. *Sincerity* Use no hurtful deceit; think innocently and justly, and, if you speak, speak accordingly.

8. *Justice* Wrong none by doing injuries, or omitting the benefits that are your duty. ·

9. *Moderation* Avoid extremes; forbear resenting injuries so much as you think they deserve.

10. **Cleanliness** Tolerate no uncleanliness in body, cloths, or habitation.

11. **Tranquility** Be not disturbed at trifles, or at accidents common or unavoidable.

12. **Charity** Rarely use venery, but for health or offspring, never to dullness, weakness, or the injury of your own or another's peace or reputation.

13. **Humility** Imitate Jesus and Socrates.

Franklin did not try to work on these virtues all at once. Instead, he would work on one and only one each week, "leaving all others to their ordinary chance." By his own admission, Franklin fell short many times of living these virtues. Nevertheless, he believed the attempt to live by them made him a better man and contributed significantly to his success and happiness. He devoted more pages in the *Memoir* to this plan than to any other single point. "I hope, therefore," he wrote, "that some of my descendants may follow the example and reap the benefit."

Franklin was a prodigious inventor. Among his many inventions are the lightning rod, Franklin stove, bifocal glasses, and the flexible urinary catheter. In his zest to live by his "virtues," he made the decision not to obtain patents on his many inventions.

To us, this decision seems to relate to his 13th virtue: *Humility. Imitate Jesus and Socrates.* In his autobiography, Franklin wrote, "... as we enjoy great advantages from the inventions of others, we should be glad of an opportunity to serve others by any invention of ours; and this we should do freely and generously."

ALFRED NOBEL AND THE NOBEL PEACE PRIZE

Alfred Nobel, a 19th-century scientist, and inventor of dynamite became one of the wealthiest men in Europe. He held 355 patents. Alfred Nobel somehow read the eulogy that the press had prepared to be published upon his death. For well-known people like Nobel, the press prepares their eulogy ahead of time so it will be ready immediately for publication upon their death. When Nobel read the description of his life, he was shocked and disappointed because he wanted to be known more for helping humanity than for his inventions like dynamite. To rectify this, he founded the Nobel Peace Prize, which has been given for more than 100 years and has caused Nobel's memory to stay alive and strengthened each year. He is remembered not only as of the inventor of dynamite but as a great benefactor to mankind. The Nobel Peace Prize was created because Alfred Nobel wanted to be known for his value of helping humanity.

While Nobel was still alive, he was able to enhance his list of benevolent deeds. Most of us dread the thought of dying but having values and a vision of how we want to be remembered can inspire greatness in us.

ARE YOU LIVING TRUE TO YOUR VALUES?

When people are not living their *true* values, they are not at peace with themselves. It is crucial to determine the roots of *your* values. You may have unconsciously adopted your values from others. During the formative years, the environment in which you live can influence and develop your values. For example, you may be acting in ways that fulfill your parents' values, not your own. Perhaps your parents were workaholics, and you adapted that behavior for yourself. You may say that you value more work-life balance but find that you are working 24/7. Until you can clarify your own set of values, you may be frustrated and exhausted. It is imperative for living a purposeful and healthy life to frequently examine your values, decide what is truly important to you, and then strategically make life choices based on those values. *The story of two wolves provides a great example of how we make choices.*

A wise Cherokee Indian Chief was speaking to his grandson about the meaning of life. "A fight is going on inside of me," he said to the boy. "It is a terrible fight, and it is between two wolves. One is evil. He is anger, envy, sorrow, regret, greed, arrogance, self-pity, guilt, resentment, inferiority, lies, false pride, superiority, and ego. The other is good. He is joy, peace, love, hope, serenity, humility, kindness, benevolence, empathy, generosity, truth, compassion, and faith. And the same fight is going on inside you and inside every other person, too."

The grandson thought about it for a minute and then asked his grandfather, "Which wolf will win?"

The old Indian Chief simply replied, "The one you feed." (Author unknown)

Everyone must make decisions in life on how to react to situations and how to behave when having a difficult time. Although you cannot control many of the events that occur in life, you can control the way you act and your responses. When you have clarified your values and committed to leading your life by them, they become evident in what you think, say, and do.

Your life is a product of the thoughts, emotions, and feelings that you let impact you, whether for the better, or the worse. The beauty of this story about the two wolves is that it applies to everyone. Anything from misplacing your car keys to a tragic event in life can be factored into this story of two wolves. If you let positive values and emotions manifest instead of negative ones, a situation will become much easier to handle. You can prevent the evil wolf from taking control of your life story. Clarify your values and let them manifest. Choose to feed the good wolf.

HONORING YOUR VALUES EVERY DAY

The following anecdote is well known universally and repeated often. It clearly illustrates the importance of honoring your values every day.

A professor stood before his class and held up a large and empty glass jar. He then filled it with rocks and asked his students if the jar was full.

They all said, "Yes."

Next, the professor picked up a bag of pebbles and poured them into the jar, shaking the jar lightly as he did so. The pebbles settled between the rocks. He asked the students again if the jar was full.

Again, they said, "Yes."

Then the professor picked up a bag of sand and slowly poured it into the jar. The sand found its place between the rocks and pebbles. He asked the students a third time if the jar was full.

They said, "Definitely."

The professor then said, "This jar represents your life. The rocks are the most important things, like your health, your loved ones, and your dreams. The pebbles are the other things that also matter to you, like saving for a beautiful home, going on an incredible vacation, buying a luxury car, and donating money to a great cause. The sand is everything else—the small stuff. If you put the sand into the jar first, there is no room for the pebbles or the rocks. The same goes for your life. If you spend all your time and energy on the small stuff, you will never have room for the things that are important to you."

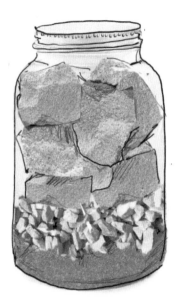

If you fill your jar with sand and pebbles first, there is no room for rocks.

What are the "rocks" in your life? How about the "pebbles?" Do you ever find yourself not having time for your "rocks" because you are putting the "sand" in your schedule first?

ANNOUNCING YOUR VALUES CLARIFIES AND REINFORCES THEM

By announcing your top values to the world, you can clarify and reinforce them in your mind. Our highest values guide our words and actions. Jasenka's values include consciousness, spirituality, personal growth, authenticity, knowledge, peace, love, joy, fun, persistence, courage, and making a difference. Susan's values include kindness, authenticity, contributor, family, leadership, hope, self-supporting, optimistic, trustworthy, wisdom, spirituality, joy, and health.

LEARN TO SAY "NO" TO HONOR YOUR VALUES

Learning how and when to say "No" are essential to living a life that honors your values. One of life's most empowering skills is the simple, unheralded ability to say "No." It is also one of the most difficult, whether it is to your boss, spouse, friends, overtime, recreation, and social engagements. It is also one of the most valuable. Learning to say "No" becomes a way to honor your values and increase your *LifeQ* score. You must spend your time, money, energy, and other limited resources wisely to live your most productive, purpose-centered, fulfilling life. Spend them on activities that support your values, your purpose, and your **12 Qs.**

When you say "Yes" to one thing, you're saying "No" to something else. Time is a limited commodity, and each person has 24 hours per day. Once you invest that time, it is irretrievable. Frequently when you are helping others accomplish their "to-do lists," you are not investing your limited resources in your priorities.

Why is it hard to say, "No?" Saying "No" can elicit intense negative emotions. You may feel guilty, embarrassed, and ashamed. You may fear it makes you look selfish, lazy, or appear to be a bad team member. To avoid those feelings, you often say "Yes," even when you know it is the wrong answer! By doing so, you may become resentful and angry. What are the benefits of saying, "No?" When used deliberately, "No" can empower you to be more in control of your life. You can invest your time, energy, and money to focus on your priorities and *LifeQ* areas. To help you learn to say "No:"

- *Clarify your life's purpose, priorities, and values so you can make important decisions about how to spend your time, energy, and money.* Block out time on your calendar for your priorities to "pay yourself first" by investing in your values and priorities. (Chapter 7 describes how to define your purpose.)

- *Understand that you probably believe others judge you more harshly than they do.* Most people move on to ask someone else once you have declined their request.

- *Quickly and politely decline right away if you are sure you are not going to accept the assignment.* That way, you do not delay anyone else's plans. If possible, suggest an alternative who might be able to take your place.

- *Have criteria for when you say "Yes," and when you say "No."* This makes decision-making easier! Ask yourself: "Do I want to do this? What do I gain from attending this event or doing this task? What has this person done for me lately? How close of a friend is this person? What else will I do with my time or money if I don't do this?"

- *Ask yourself if you have a fear of missing out (FOMO)?* Does your FOMO get in the way of your purpose and priorities? Facebook, Instagram, and other social media sites can make you feel like you need to overextend and say "Yes"!

- *Practice makes perfect when it comes to saying, "No."* Say "No" as often as you can to get more comfortable saying the word. Sometimes, repeating the word is the only way to get a message through to persistent people. Eventually, they will get the message.

- *Say, "I don't," not "I can't."* This simple shift that suggests that your refusal comes from your firmly held beliefs. "I have a policy that I don't lend money to friends." When your boss wants you to take on new assignments and you believe you are spread too thin to take on more work, consider saying to your boss, "I'm not sure I can add this considering my current projects. I would appreciate your thoughts on how to prioritize."

Bottom Line: "No" is a complete sentence. Try it!

WHAT'S NEXT?

*Now that you have clarified your fundamental values in life, the next step is to decide on your PURPOSE and create a VISION. These are essential in determining your path and will impact each of your **LifeQ** Components. It is incumbent upon you to live a purpose-driven life each day to live your most fulfilling and abundant life.*

CHAPTER 6: *LifeQ* -TIPS & CHAPTER RECAP

- Values are what you stand for and your belief system.

- Taking time to clarify and prioritize values is critical to living a purposeful life.

- Decision-making is easier when values are clear.

- Your deeply held values can fuel the energy behind your life purpose or calling.

- How you spend time and money, your two primary resources, indicate what is important to you.

- Limit your focus on one or two values per week. Focusing on too many simultaneously will blur your focus and cause you to be less effective.

- Learning how and when to say "No" are essential to living a life that honors your values and strengthens your *LifeQ*.

- Simple ways to say "NO."

    □ "At the moment, I can't commit to this. My plate is already full."

    □ "I'm in the middle of something, so this is not a good time for me. Can we reconnect at another time?" Then recommend a time to reconnect.

- "I would love to, however…"

- "Let me have some time to think about it. I promise to get back to you with my answer."

- "This is not what I need at the moment, but if the situation changes, I will keep you in mind."

- "I don't think I am the best person to do this. Maybe you can ask…?

- "No!"

- "Sorry, I wish I could!"

LifeQ PRACTICE # 6.1 REVIEW YOUR BANK STATEMENTS

Review your bank statements for the past year. These statements will show where you have invested your *money*.

As you look over the bank statements, notice:

Have you been paying for a health club membership that you are not using? Did you buy a new car?

Did you give money to causes important to you?

Do you see excessive expenses in any area(s)?

How many ATM withdrawals did you have, and do you remember where you spent that cash?

LifeQ PRACTICE # 6.2 REVIEW YOUR CALENDAR

Your calendar will show where you have invested your *time*. This review is an excellent way to show what has been important to you.

How many hours did you put in at work? Did you take a vacation?

Did you volunteer in your community?

Did you spend time with your family and friends?

Did you spend time taking care of your physical body?

Have you worked on your professional development?

Have you gone on a retreat to feed your soul?

This review is an excellent way to show what has been important to you.

Have your actions matched what you say that you value?

LifeQ PRACTICE # 6.3 CONSIDER THE IMPACT OF SAYING "NO".

WHEN I SAY 'NO' TO	I AM SAYING 'YES' TO
No!	Yes!
Going to the gym 3x week and eating healthy	*Extra weight, low energy, possible disease, low self-esteem*

LifeQ PRACTICE # 6.4 PRIORITIZING YOUR VALUES

Review the list of values and definitions at the end of this chapter (Or if you feel compelled, define your values). Prioritizing your values is essential for a healthy fulfilling life.

TOP 10 VALUES

- Narrow your list to 10 values and write them below

- Define what that value means to you.

1.	
2.	
3.	
4.	
5.	
6.	
7.	
8.	
9.	
10.	

TOP 5 VALUES

Narrow your list of values to 5 based on importance to you.

1.	
2.	
3.	
4.	
5.	

TOP 3 VALUES

Narrow your list to 3 based on importance.

1.
2.
3.

TOP # 1 VALUE

1.

LifeQ PRACTICE # 6.5 CORE VALUES WHEEL

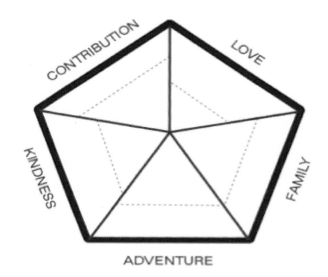

- *Write each of your top values in one section of the Core Values diagram below.*

- *For each value, rate how well you are currently living that core value by drawing a straight line between 1-10 in each section*

- *If you are fully living that value to its maximum, it will be a 10.*

- *If you are only living that value some of the time, it might be a 5.*

- *If your life is out of alignment for that value, it will likely be less than 5.*

LifeQ **PRACTICE #6.6**

CORE VALUES WHEEL

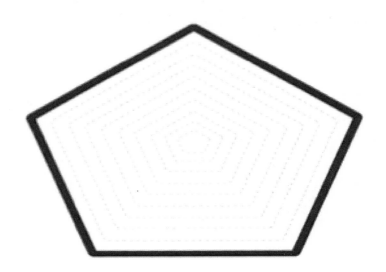

Core Values Insights

- *What did you feel when directed to give up a core value?*

- *Have you ever felt this feeling before, at home, or work?*

- *What values do you sell out on first?*

- *What is stopping you from honoring your values?*

- *How do you want to handle this situation in the future when it arises?*

Now, look at the top three values on your list.

- *What do they mean exactly? What are you expecting from your-self–even during challenging times?*

- *How would your life be different if those values were prominent and practiced?*

- *What would your organization/relationship/friendship be like if everyone lived up to those values?*

- *What is the price you pay for not honoring your values?*

- *What is stopping you?*

LifeQ **PRACTICE #6.7**

VALUES AND OBSTACLES WORKSHEET

Describe what the value means for you	Honoring Score	How is the value honored by you?	Obstacle to honoring value
Family – supporting, strengthening & respecting my family unit & relationships	5	Spending significant quantity of time & quality of time with my family	My work schedule

LifeQ PRACTICE #6.8

VALUES ACTION LOG

Does the way you live your life reflect your most important values? If so, good for you! If not, how would your life be different? What would you do differently if those values were prominent and practiced in your life? Decide what actions you will take to practice those values and record them in the Values Action Log.

Value	Action to be taken to Increase Score	By When?
Example: *Family*	*Learn to say "No" to outside events that are not meaningful to me so that I can spend more time with people most important to me.* *Be in the present (control distractions, for example, cell phone) when with my family.*	*Start today*

LifeQ PRACTICE #6.9 CHAPTER REFLECTIONS & ACTION PLAN

- What have you learned about yourself after reading this chapter?

- What actions will you take this next week to start to design the life that you want to live?

LifeQ PRACTICE – Samples of values and definitions

Abundance a massive quantity of something, plenty, prosperity	Acceptance be accepted as you are for who you are	Accessibility live and work in a place that provides access to what is needed for quality life	Achievement sense of accomplishmen t, attainment, an internal standard of excellence	Accountability takes responsibility for both actions and outcomes
Advancement moving forward toward clearly defined goals or flexibility altered goals	Adventure new heights, new challenges, adrenalin rush, taking risks, thrills, excitement	Altruism selfless concern for the well-being of others	Authenticity the quality of being true, genuineness	Authority legitimate right to make decisions based on the position of power
Balance balancing time and effort between money, family, friends, health, faith.	Beauty make life more beautiful or have time to appreciate beautiful things	Belonging to feel part of a group or association of others	Camaraderie importance of personal relationships and warm working relationships	Celebrity being famous, known, recognizable
Challenge invent or revitalize thoughts, ideas, processes or approaches	Charity voluntary sharing, giving money, materials, supports, kindness to needy	Comfort free from anxiety, feeling relaxed and pain	Commitment being bound emotionally or intellectually to a course of action, dedication	Compassion caring about others, watch out for pity which is the near enemy of compassion
Competitiveness working against others where there are clear win/lose outcomes	Competence possessing the skill, knowledge, and ability to perform effectively	Consciousness the state of being awake and aware of one's surroundings, awareness by the mind of itself and the world	Consensus general agreement or accord, harmony with others	Consistency precision with little tolerance for errors or unpredictability
Contribution service, giving to or supporting a charity or cause, have your work make a difference	Control to exercise restraint or limitation on others or situations	Cooperation collaboration, working with others for common goals	Courage willingness to take calculated risks, operating outside of one's comfort zone	Creativity being imaginative, innovative, inventive, original, out-of-the-box, unique
Decisiveness assess and eliminate all alternatives	Discipline calm, controlled, conscious behavior; a systematic approach to behavior	Directness to speak honestly and without avoiding important or unpleasant points	Diversity seeking and valuing contact with others different from you	Education the act or process of imparting or acquiring general knowledge
Effectiveness the ability to produce a desired effect or outcome	Efficiency creating results in a timely manner with minimal waste, expense or unnecessary effort	Empowerment gaining power, authority or ability to accomplish	Environment commitment and dedication to the earth and the physical world in which we live	Excellence standard of being outstandingly good and having exceptional merit

Expertise	Fairness	Faith	Family	Fitness
to value and be valued for your knowledge, wisdom, experience, abilities	treating people and being treated equally, equitable, moral rightness	belief in a higher power that guides you	being with family both quality and quantity of time, a strong commitment	being physically fit, regular physical activity, optimal well-being
Forgiveness letting go of feelings of resentment, pardoning actions or situations	**Freedom** able to move about without bounds or restraints, liberty	**Growth** investing in lifelong learning, personal development, self-education	**Happiness** good fortune, pleasure, contentment, joy	**Harmony** agreement, accord, harmonious relations
Healing helping others become healthy or maintain their health	**Health** physical and psychological well-being, vigor, strength	**Honesty** being truthful, sincere	**Honor** honestly, fairness, or integrity in one's beliefs and actions	**Hope** maintaining an optimistic or enthusiastic outlook
Humility the quality or condition of being humble, having a modest opinion of self	**Independence** free from the influence, guidance or control of others	**Influence** being a compelling force on actions, behavior, opinions, etc. of others	**Innovative** creating new and different objects, ideas, experiences	**Integrity** beliefs and actions are congruent, being true to who you are, doing what you say
Intimacy close, familiar and often affectionate or loving personal relationship	**Kindness** caring, excellent and charitable behavior, concern for others, pleasant disposition	**Knowledge** subject matter expert, education via experience or study	**Leadership** ability to influence and direct others, guidance	**Legacy** directing resources to causes you care about to make a long-lasting difference in the world
Love intense feelings of compassion and affection for others	**Loyalty** devoted or faithful to a person, an ideal, a custom, a cause or a duty	**Make a Difference** to have an effect; to matter; to change the outlook or situation	**Mastery** proficiency excellence in a given field or area	**Materialism** acquiring material possessions as a sign of success
Mindfulness mental state achieved by focusing one's awareness on the present moment, while acknowledging, accepting one's feelings, thoughts, & bodily sensations	**Obedience** the act or practice of obeying, dutiful or submissive compliance	**Openness** accessible, as to appeals, ideas or offers	**Organized** importance of order, structure, neatness, systems, tidiness	**Passion** intense emotional excitement, boundless enthusiasm
Peace mental calm and serenity, without anxiety, making sure you and others get along without conflicts	**Perfection** the highest attainable standard	**Perseverance** the resilient never giving up regardless of challenges or problems	**Persistence** firm or obstinate continuance in the course of action despite difficulty or opposition	**Personal growth** development as an individual
Physical challenge performs activities, sports that require labor, test your physical limits	**Pleasure** enjoyment, delight, gratification	**Power** authority, control, command, clout	**Precision** accuracy, exactness, meticulousness, correctness	**Professionalism** setting and maintaining boundaries to be effective, produce strong results

Public Exposure	Recognition	Respect	Responsibility	Results
dealing with the public, day-to-day contact, in the public spotlight	giving and receiving acknowledgment for achievements	want admiration and acknowledgment from others	being accountable for results, conscientious, reliable, trustworthy	to be concerned with outcomes of efforts or focus
Security protection or precautions are taken against escape, loss, custody	Self-control control or restraint of oneself or one's actions, feelings, etc.	Self-identity having self-respect, pride, dignity, confidence	Service give support, information, and advice to others	Significance holding a position of importance, high standing or prestige
Simplicity lack of complexity / complication	Spirituality beliefs, the meaning of life/existence, faith existentialism	Stability predicable routines, schedules, providing security, constancy, regularity	Status position, prestige or ranking of an individual in relation to another or others	Structure formality, processes, systems
Superiority the quality or condition of being superior to something or someone	Teamwork cooperative, a collective effort by a group or team	Thoroughness attention to detail and accuracy, being complete and without omission	Tolerance a fair, objective and permissive attitude towards others	Toughness strong and durable, not easily broken or overcome
Tranquility calmness, peacefulness, quiet, serenity	Trust a firm reliance on the integrity, ability or character of a person or thing	Truth a verified or indisputable fact, proposition, principle or the like	Unity absence of diversity, unvaried or uniform character	Urgency fast-paced, swift, action-oriented
Variety diversity of cultures / lifestyles / experiences	Victory a success or triumph over a challenge or enemy in battle or war	Virtue morally excellence, goodness, righteousness	Winning achieve victory or success by defeating an opponent, gaining something of value by skill or luck.	Wealth have, or maintain a high economic standard of living. high net worth.
Wisdom having deep understanding, insight, knowledge, ability to make sound judgments.	Zen a state of calm attentiveness in which one's actions are guided by intuition rather than by conscious effort	Youthfulness having or showing the freshness, energy innocence and hope of someone young		

CHAPTER 7

FINDING YOUR PURPOSE

Your purpose gives your life meaning. Having a clear purpose provides you with guidance through life's challenges and enables you to make decisions more easily because you will choose the option that is aligned with your purpose. Without a purpose in life, it is easy to get sidetracked on your journey, wandering and drifting without accomplishing very much.

The story of Sean's transformation will demonstrate that when you strategically focus on your purpose and make life changes that reinforce your purpose, you can bring abundance and fulfillment into your life.

Sean's story:

Sean was impatient and aggressive with clients, partners, and his family. He worked 15-hour days, couldn't sleep, took anxiety pills, and had lost his close relationship with his wife and children. Sean was empty, depressed, and felt exhausted and defeated. Every day started the same way alarm clock ringing, grumbling, four cups of coffee, disheartened wife, employee problems, customer complaints, and turmoil and destruction at every turn. Sean was miserable, hated his life, and didn't know what to do. He thought, "something bad is going to happen unless something changes." He knew he was not living the life he wanted to live.

Sean sought coaching and has searched deeply for answers to rescue him from his disastrous trajectory. Fortunately for Sean, he met Jasenka at a party, and she immediately recognized his pain. She broached some tough questions that evening: "How much success and money is enough? What would you do after your wife and children leave? What is your purpose on earth? What is the quality of life you want?"

Sean was ready to begin to transform his world. The pain had gotten so severe that he knew it was time to make some drastic changes. The first step was to recognize and honor his values. Number one was the family he had been neglecting. Sean began the journey of designing his personal strategic plan to discover and create the man he would want to be in 1 year, 5, 10, and 35.

After much soul-searching, Sean realized his purpose is to be a leader and make a positive difference in the lives of his family members and his employees. He identified his talents of seeing the big picture, business development, finance, and created a clear vision for his company. Sean also started to understand his behavior patterns and the ways his ego-system was controlling his life. Sean discovered he needed to control his ego, not other people in his life.

When Sean examined his **LifeQ** score, he was low in many of the 12 Components. He decided to create goals in the areas of **LoveQ**, **FamilyQ**, and **BodyQ**. He realized that increasing his **LifeQ** scores in those areas would spill over to increase other dimensions like **CareerQ**, **SoulQ**, and **FunQ**. Sean's strategic plan included dates with his wife, weekends and nights without a phone, running with his son, and playing guitar with his daughter.

Today, Sean has a thriving family, great business, and sleeps well at night without anxiety drugs. Sean's life has been transformed. Sean is fulfilling his vision, purpose, and values, his life is abundant, and his **LifeQ** is high.

A CLEAR PURPOSE AND VISION ARE FUNDAMENTAL TO STRATEGIC PLAN

In all successful organizations, the Vision, Mission Statement, and Values are fundamental elements to their strategic plans. It is impossible to develop an optimum strategy when the core elements have not been clarified and endorsed. The same is valid for creating a meaningful personal strategic plan for your life. Without the fundamentals, the structure is not grounded. There are no anchors to secure it to solid ground. Thomas Merton said, "It's incredibly easy to get caught up in an activity trap, in the business of life, to work harder and harder at climbing the ladder of success only to discover it's leaning against the wrong wall."

FINDING YOUR PURPOSE

In Chapter 4, you became aware of your *LifeQ* score and the 12 Components of the *WHEEL OF LifeQ*. In Chapter 6, you defined your most important values. Now you are ready for the next strategic step: to figure out your purpose.

Most people dread the thought of dying and find it challenging to think about it. However, having a vision of how you want to live your life, as well as the legacy of how you want others to remember you, can inspire greatness. Remember the story of Alfred Nobel from Chapter 6? Over 100 years ago, Nobel created the Nobel Peace Prize as his legacy. When you have a compelling life purpose, it is possible to do great things that have a long-lasting impact on your family and society.

WHAT IS YOUR PURPOSE IN LIFE?

It is up to you to figure out who you are, clarify what is important to you, and decide what you will do with your life. In other words, you must define your purpose. In business, the purpose is often called its *Mission Statement* and describes its purpose or reason for existing. Your Mission Statement describes *your* unique purpose in life; *your* personal mission is not that of your mother, father, teacher, or spouse. If you do not feel passionate about a particular purpose, then it is not *your* purpose.

It includes what you want to accomplish, plus the contributions and impact you want to make. When developing your personal mission statement, focus on those unique qualities and talents you have now and those you wish to build. You may have several in your life, some personal, some professional. You may discover they have a common thread.

Later in this chapter, you will have the opportunity to begin creating your purpose or mission statement. It may not be quick or easy. For the moment, keep these questions in mind. They will guide your thinking. Answering them will take much thought and soul-searching.

- *What is your professional purpose? For example, if you are a teacher, it may be to help students who are having an incredibly difficult time succeeding.*

- *What is your personal purpose? For example, it may be merely being an honest, loyal friend.*

- *How do you want to be remembered? For example, as a good friend, a person who helped others become stronger.*

- *How can you utilize your talents and qualities while fulfilling your purpose? For example, if you love gardening, volunteer to look after a community rose garden for others to relax in and enjoy.*

- *Is there a common thread?*

Once you discover your purpose, it will most likely stay the same throughout your life. Even though you play various roles like parent, spouse, professional, friend, neighbor, or colleague, your mission will remain constant. For example, if your purpose is "to inspire and empower people to achieve their dreams" or "to leave the world a better place than I found it," you can accomplish your purpose no matter what role you are playing throughout your life.

When your purpose is clear, everyday choices and decisions will either align with your mission and goals or move you farther away from them. The clearer your purpose, the easier it is to see which choices to make. Having a specific purpose does not mean it is always easy to make the right choice. However, it facilitates your knowing what the right choice is the one aligned with your purpose and values. Let us look at The Star Thrower Story.

THE STAR THROWER STORY

Once, on ancient Earth, a human boy was walking along a beach. There had just been a storm, and starfish were scattered along the sands. The boy knew the fish would die, so he began to fling the fish to the sea. But every time he threw a starfish, another would wash ashore. An old man happened along and saw what the child was doing. He called out, "Boy, what are you doing?"

"Saving the starfish!" replied the boy.

"But your attempts are useless, child! Every time you save one, another one returns, often the same one! You can't save them all, so why bother trying? Why does it matter, anyway?" called the old man.

The boy thought about this for a while with a starfish in his hand. He answered, "Well, it matters to this one." And then he flung the starfish into the welcoming sea."

Loren Eiseley, The Star Thrower [1]

Every person can help create positive change. Rather than becoming overwhelmed by thinking that it is impossible to change the whole world, start to realize that you can change a small part of it for someone. To each starfish, the boy in the story made a world of difference.

Every person can make a difference. It is up to you and everyone else to discover their purpose in living. It may seem like a small impact when you think of the billions of people in the world. However, once your purpose manifests itself to you, you must follow your destiny and do your part to improve the world. Imagine the positive impact on the planet if everyone lived his or her life on purpose and fulfilled his or her true destiny—the choices you make everyday matter.

VISION VS. MISSION

The terms *vision* and *mission* are often used interchangeably. These terms describe goals for your life and answer the questions: Who are you? What is your purpose for being here? In what do you believe? How do you want to be remembered? Where are you headed? Although both the vision and mission describe goals for your life, there is a difference between them.

- *Vision* **is a picture of what you want to look like in the future.** It engages your heart, your spirit, and captures your imagination. It should challenge and inspire you to achieve your purpose.

- *Mission* **describes your purpose.** It may explain why you are here, why you believe you exist, what you want to contribute to society, and for what you want to be remembered. It is clear, brief, sharply focused, and actionable, and provides direction for making the right decisions.

EXAMPLES OF VISION AND MISSION STATEMENTS

We developed our Vision and Mission several years ago and have used them to guide all aspects of our lives. Because of our commitment to our Vision and Mission, it is easier to make significant life decisions.

Susan's Vision and Mission:

Susan's Vision: "To be the Partner of Choice & Trusted Advisor of People & Organizations seeking peak performance."

Susan's Mission: "To serve joyfully as a Catalyst in the Optimum Development & Performance of People & their Organizations. I am driven to help people reach their goals and fulfill their potential, and to create harmonious, positive, loving, and peaceful relationships." Susan keeps her Vision, Mission, and Values displayed in her office and on yellow sticky notes on her bathroom mirror so she can see them first thing every morning.

Jasenka's Vision and Mission:

Jasenka's Vision "To synchronize people, dreams and the world. To live a life on my terms and to never settle for anything less than what I can be, do, give, or create because the secret of living is giving. To make a positive difference despite being imperfect by making it my goal to learn and grow every day. With my ability to connect, listen, and desire to serve humankind, I want my persistence and courage to help make a difference on this planet. To inspire others to dream big, take action, and dare to live life fully."

Jasenka's Mission "To remember where I have been and where I will go through maintaining positive relationships with family and friends. To find peacefulness within myself by looking inward while using my heart to guide my dreams and desires, and my mind to pursue knowledge, creating balance among all my obligations. To enjoy every moment along this journey, finding laughter, love, and happiness with each day that passes, to go through life with a smile on my face and a twinkle in my eye."

Susan's story: How her vision saved her corporate job

Several years ago, Susan was a vice president at a large Fortune 500 Corporation. She had already developed her Vision and Mission that included serving as a catalyst in the optimal development and performance of others by being a corporate consultant and executive coach. The corporation frequently experienced layoffs in the workforce. For several years, Susan had seen many of her colleagues lose their jobs, and she had always escaped the reduction-in-force, the dreaded "RIF."

One year when it was time for her performance review and time to review her goals for the next year, Susan's Director said, "This is the toughest thing I've had to do... but your position has been eliminated. The cutbacks have hit our department hard, and I've got to cut your position." Susan was shocked, and suddenly her thoughts and intuition kicked in. Her vision and mission did not include a lay-off! Suddenly, Susan heard her own voice saying, "That decision just doesn't make sense. I'm the only one in the department who has hospital experience, and this is a healthcare company! Why would they lay-off the one person who understands what our employees need, and our clients expect? Here are the goals and action plan I developed for next year to meet the needs of our clients." She just kept talking, for she's not sure how long. When she stopped, she looked at her stunned boss, whose face appeared frozen, with his mouth open.

Susan's boss finally said, "Well, let me re-assess this. At this moment, you are not laid off. I'll get back to you on this."

As it turned out, not only did she stay employed at the organization for several more years, Susan got a raise! So, between her Vision, Mission, Intuition, and probably her Guardian Angel, Susan was successful in staying in her corporate position where she could continue fulfilling her Vision and Mission.

YOUR MISSION CAN HELP GUIDE YOUR ACTIONS

Your mission will evolve and clarify over time as you have different experiences, expand your education, and meet new people. However, because your mission statement reflects your values, the fundamentals of your purpose will probably remain the same. You will recognize it when you find it. You may have an "Aha!" or "Of course!" moment. Once you clarify your purpose, it can guide your actions.

Bev developed her Mission Statement, and her behavior became deliberate and consistent, as shown in the story below:

Bev's Mission Statement

"To serve others and influence them to live healthy, productive lives which make positive contributions to society, focusing initially on my children and then others in my community."

*After Bev created her Mission Statement and reviewed her most essential values, her focus returned to her **WHEEL OF LifeQ**. She realized that to live her mission and incorporate her values, she needed to create goals in all areas of her **WHEEL OF LifeQ**.*

- ***BodyQ, MindQ, SoulQ, EmotionsQ** Goal: to successfully serve and influence others. To accomplish this, her body, mind, emotions, and spirit needed to be as healthy as possible. She needed to grow and develop also. She committed to continuous growth within herself.*

- ***FunQ** Goal: Serve as a role model for leading a balanced, joyful life. To create balance, she needed to schedule a time to enjoy hobbies like painting and playing bridge.*

- **EnvironmentQ** *Goal: to have her children feel safe and be healthy. Her home had to provide a loving, clean, organized environment for her children.*

- **FamilyQ and FriendsQ** *Goal: Keep positive, supportive, trustworthy people in her inner circle, and reciprocate those attributes to them. Her family and friends required unwavering focus, loyalty, and support.*

- **LoveQ** *Goal: Have support from her husband in living her mission. Her relationship with her husband had to be close and healthy, so she needed to schedule 1:1 time with him to build upon the strong foundation they already had.*

- **CommunityQ** *Goal: Make positive contributions to her community. She needed to learn about its needs and collaborate with others to coordinate the available resources.*

- **MoneyQ** *Goal: Feed and raise healthy children. Bev needed resources to feed and raise healthy children, so she needed to create a weekly budget that included carefully monitoring expenses plus a savings plan for a rainy day fund.*

- **CareerQ** *Goal: Have more resources so they could take vacations and getaway weekends for her family to spend time together. Bev returned to work part-time to provide more resources for her family.*

The Power of Purpose

Once you determine your purpose, you may find ways for activities in your everyday life to have more meaning. Instead of thinking of bath time for your kids as an exhausting, unwelcomed chore, it can be an act of love to keep them healthy and safe. You may transform the tiresome chore of cooking dinner for your family into a meaningful activity that fulfills your purpose of being a joyful parent and partner who nurtures your family's wellness.

When you reframe your job and align it with your purpose, it can be more fulfilling and abundant. Some examples can be seen throughout history. When President John F. Kennedy visited NASA in 1962, he noticed a janitor mopping the floor. JFK asked him what his job was at NASA. The janitor replied, "I'm helping put a man on the moon." He saw himself as helping to make history.

After the great London fire of 1666, the renowned architect, Christopher Wren, was recruited to rebuild St Paul's Cathedral. One day in 1671, Christopher Wren observed three bricklayers on a scaffold. One was crouched, one was half-standing and the third was standing tall, working very hard and fast. Christopher Wren asked the bricklayers, "What are you doing?" The first bricklayer replied, "I'm a bricklayer. I'm working hard laying bricks to feed my family." The second bricklayer, responded, "I'm a builder. I'm building a wall." But the third bricklayer, the most productive of the three, answered with a twinkle in his eye, "I'm a cathedral builder. I'm building a great cathedral to The Almighty." The third bricklayer was deeply connected to the mission and was engaged and productive.

No matter how large or small your role, you can move through your life with intention and passion and connect your various roles to the larger purpose of your life. When Susan was a hospital executive, she made a point to tell employees how their jobs contributed to the health and care for the patients. Dishwashers are often the lowest paid employees and yet dishwashers were told that their job was to prevent bacteria and other germs from being spread to patients through dirty dishes. The dishwashers felt they had an important role to help patients stay safe and directly contributed to the hospital's mission of quality patient care.

If you do not now experience passion in your work or your life, now may be a great time to consider your purpose and connect your daily activities with it so you can feel that what you do every day is worthwhile.

Having a clear purpose gives meaning to your life and provides you with guidance through life's challenges. Your important decisions will be easier to make as you can choose the option aligned with your purpose. As you well know, life can become complicated, and having a defined purpose is one of the most powerful tools that will help keep you on track during your life journey.

WHAT'S NEXT?

The next chapter will explain the Law of Attraction. The Law of Attraction is a powerful tool for bringing what you want into your life. You will learn the steps to take to get what you desire and why the Law of Attraction sometimes fails to work. Note that "Action" is the second half of the word "Attraction." You will also learn to apply Abundance Thinking and reject Scarcity Thinking in your conscious and subconscious minds.

CHAPTER 7: *LifeQ* -TIPS AND CHAPTER RECAP

- In all successful organizations, the Vision, Mission Statement, and Values are fundamental elements of the Strategic Plan.

- Your purpose gives your life meaning. Having a clear mission provides you with guidance through life's challenges and enables you to make decisions more easily because you will choose the option that is aligned with your purpose.

- It is crucial to figure out the purpose of *your* life – not someone else's. If you do not feel passionate about a specific mission, then it is not *your* mission.

- Your vision (your picture of the future you) and your mission (your purpose in life) are your life goals. There is a difference between them. Think through them and articulate them carefully.

LifeQ PRACTICE # 7.1

What is your vision of the life you want to live?

Go back and reread the examples of others' visions above. Then picture yourself, your living situation, your professional life, your friends, as you would like them to be. You could start by writing, "I see myself…"

LifeQ PRACTICE # 7.2 BEGIN TO CREATE YOUR PERSONAL MISSION

Begin to create your personal mission or purpose statement.

Earlier in the chapter, you began thinking about your purpose and pertinent questions. Now, consider them in more detail and answer them on the lines below. Remember, this is a process. Give yourself plenty of time. This process is too necessary to rush.

- *List your past accomplishments and successes. (You started this already in Chapter 2!)*

- *What unique talents, abilities, and qualities do you have?*

- *What strengths of yours have other people commented on, and how have these strengths and comments affected your accomplishments?*

- *What are some ways that you enjoy expressing your talents, abilities, qualities?*

- *If you had unlimited time and resources and you could not fail, what would you choose to do?*

- *What kinds of dreams and aspirations did you have as a child? What did you say when people asked you, "What do you want to be when you grow up?"*

- *What excites you and ignites your passion?*

- *How do you want to be remembered? What do you want others to feel or say when you are not present?*

- *What do you want as your legacy?*

- *What do you want to accomplish during your lifetime? What can you contribute?*

- *What will you regret not doing, seeing, or achieving?*

- *Imagine you could invite to dinner three people who have influenced you the most past or present. Write their names in the boxes below. Then record the one quality or attribute you admire most in these people:*

  ➢   *Name:*   *Attribute:*

  ➢   *Name:*   *Attribute:*

  ➢   *Name:*   *Attribute:*

Get Inspired by Others:

Here are a few mission statements from some folks you might recognize:

- *"To be a teacher. And to be known for inspiring my students to be more than they thought they could be." Oprah Winfrey*

- *"To have fun in my journey through life and learn from my mistakes." Sir Richard Branson*

- *"To constantly be striving to be the best version of myself in my job, with my health and fitness, with my relationships with family and friends, and with my emotional well-being." Katie Arnold*

LifeQ PRACTICE # 7.3 BEGIN TO WRITE YOUR MISSION STATEMENT

Now, keeping in mind your answers, write the first draft of your life mission statement. Think about what it would take for you to feel truly fulfilled, to be excited about getting up in the morning because you loved what you are doing.

- You could begin, "My mission is to…

LifeQ PRACTICE # 7.4 THIS WEEK'S ACTION PLAN

- What have you learned about yourself after reading this chapter?

- What actions will you take this next week to start to design the life that you want to live?

#### CHAPTER 8

LAW OF ATTR"ACTION"

The *Law of Attraction* is the belief that "like attracts like." According to the Law of Attraction, if you think positive thoughts, you will have positive results, with the converse being true as well. If you think negative thoughts, you will have negative results. You attract whatever you think about, good or bad. An everyday example of the Law of Attraction is when you start thinking of someone you care about, and suddenly she calls you. Or you realize that you have not received a speeding ticket in years and bam, the next day you get one.

Below is a true story that further illustrates the Law of Attraction in action.

Elton John story:

While driving to Las Vegas with her husband, Susan said, "I missed seeing Elvis and the Beatles in person, and I want to see Elton John in person sometime." Elton John was not scheduled to play in Las Vegas for several months.

Within 30 minutes, Susan was surprised when they passed a billboard saying that Elton John would be playing in Las Vegas the following night. They quickly called for ticket information and found the show was sold out. Because of Susan's disappointment, her husband went to the Caesar Casino ticket counter the following day to see if there were cancellations. Susan continued to visualize being at the show while her husband charmed the ticket seller, telling her of Susan's dream.

> "Go be a hero to your wife," the ticket seller told him—long story short.... Within 24 hours of Susan's stating her intention, she had a VIP seat in the Orchestra Section of Elton John's sold-out Las Vegas show. She not only high-fived Sir Elton but also danced on stage with his lead guitarist. The Law of Attraction had fulfilled a dream within 24 hours of Susan's sincere, enthusiastic, and clear intention.

Abundance Thinking

The best way to experience abundance is to agree that within the universe, there is enough for everyone. It's time for you to start thinking and feeling that there is abundance and *not lack*.

Consider your finances as an example. Abundance thinking requires that you *visualize* that you are wealthy already and are grateful for all your riches. To enter in an abundance vibration, it is crucial that what you think and say about money is aligned with what you feel and do every day. If you are continually repeating and complaining about lack of money, you are sending the energy that the universe responds to in action. If you believe you live in scarcity, you will attract scarcity.

An Attitude of Gratitude

The most critical step and easiest part of the Law of Attraction is gratitude. Gratitude is an energy that becomes magnified when it returns to you. What you put into the world is what you get out of it. If you think negative thoughts about your life, you will have a difficult life. Conversely, if you give more love, you will receive more love. If you are generous with your money, you will receive more money.

If you live a life filled with gratitude, you will always have things for which to be grateful. To live a more abundant life, you must become aware of the energy and focus you are putting on things in your life.

Examples of ways to enhance your attitude of gratitude include:

- Create a gratitude journal and capture joyful events and reasons to be grateful.

- Actively celebrate your prosperity and abundance.

- Practice being fully present at least once every day when you stop your stressful thoughts and appreciate the present moment.

- Show your gratitude and thank others for their kindness and character traits that you appreciate in them.

- Develop a ritual for bedtime reflection where you call to mind events of the passing day for which you are thankful.

- Intentionally develop a sense of awe and increase your feelings of joy.

Mantras for Positive Self-Talk

Your energy follows your thoughts, and you are continually creating and reinforcing the brain's neural pathways to accept the desires that you want.

To attract a Life of Abundance, develop mantras:

- *I have everything I need.*

- *I have all the love I desire.*

- *I live a fulfilling life.*

- *I am healthy and full of vitality.*

- *Whenever you give or receive money, say, "There is more where that came from."*

WHY DOES THE LAW OF ATTRACTION SEEM TO FAIL SO OFTEN?

Most people will not achieve positive outcomes, despite thinking positively and visualizing success. The reason is that they have subconscious beliefs, values, and habits that block their success.

Both parts of your mind affect the Law of Attraction - your conscious mind and your subconscious mind. Your conscious mind can create the images of what you want to attract to you and can consciously, logically, set goals and promises to attain them. Your subconscious, however, is the critical component that makes or breaks the Law of Attraction's effectiveness for you. Your subconscious mind controls your habits, expectations, emotions, and actions and determines your success. The conscious and subconscious mind must get into harmony. Several factors can prevent you from attracting what you want.

1. *You may dwell on the painful events and people from your past.* When you revisit thoughts about unfortunate, destructive events and people in your history, these thoughts limit and disempower you. They activate the Law of Attraction in attracting the same negative experiences to your present life. Learn from mistakes and situations, and then let go and move on. (See Chapter 12 for the importance of Forgiveness.)

2. *Your limiting beliefs and fears.* There are obstacles to the Law of Attraction that you must identify and replace by a new set of empowering beliefs. If you have limiting beliefs, you will have a limited existence. You give power to whatever you focus on, so do not focus on your fears. Override them and focus on positive outcomes. (See Chapters 10 and 11 for the importance of changing the underlying beliefs you have that drive your behaviors that are not goal oriented.)

3. *"Hoover" people.* Named for the popular and best vacuum cleaner, "Hoover people" suck the positivity out of you and your dreams

of success. Stay away from them when you are tapping into the Law of Attraction.

4. *You may feel desperate.* People generally know what they want, and they want it *now.* People often think that if they simply document what they want, they will receive it. That is not how the Law of Attraction works. The Law of Attraction brings desperate people more desperation. Instead, you must focus on the present and on generating the feeling that you would have once your desires have manifested. An abundant feeling attracts more abundance!

You Manifest What You Believe

What you believe internally manifests what is occurring externally. For example, if your subconscious believes that you are unlovable, you will not be in a healthy, loving relationship no matter how many times you say that is what you want. If your subconscious believes that you will never have enough money, you never will. If your subconscious believes that you will never be happy, you will never be happy.

Real change occurs via the subconscious level. It is critical to discover and understand your current belief system and where those beliefs originated. You will sabotage your future if you are subconsciously playing and replaying old tapes from your past experiences.

For example, let's say you believe you want a permanent, healthy relationship. You have told your friends and family, written it down on your New Year's Resolutions List, and even defined all the characteristics you want in a mate. When eligible candidates start to talk about creating a future with you, you start behaving in ways that drive away intimacy. With one candidate, you emotionally shut down and became physically untouchable. With another candidate, you became moody, erratic, and rude.

When this experience happens with clients, we help them examine their subconscious beliefs to discover the source of these beliefs. For example, many children of divorced parents have difficulty believing in permanent, loving relationships. They may think they are unlovable, and that is why the parents split. In other words, they hold on to the belief that they caused the divorce. Behaving in ways to sabotage relationships is often based on this belief.

Another example could be your subconscious beliefs about money. Many children see their parents arguing about money. When you are young, you do not know much about the meaning of money, but you may develop the belief that money is a bad thing because it makes people argue, and apparently, there can never be enough money. You may unconsciously sabotage your ability to make and save abundant money. You have learned money is scarce, and there will never be enough.

What are some self-limiting beliefs you hold in your subconscious mind?

When did they develop? Some beliefs may develop over time. Throughout your life, your religion may have encouraged you to feel guilty. An alcoholic parent may have shattered your self-esteem. There are innumerable self-limiting beliefs. As we will discuss in Chapters 10 and 11, some of those beliefs developed from significant events like bullying from a classmate that left you fearful of others, an accident that left you handicapped, or a family secret that you discovered about your parents.

If you keep sabotaging your dreams, it is time to figure out why. It is time to uncover your negative beliefs. You must take a closer look at precisely how these beliefs may be wreaking havoc in your life and blocking the Law of Attraction.

CHANGING SCARCITY/NEED-BASED THINKING TO ABUNDANCE THINKING

You *can* change the neural pathways in your subconscious. It is hard work, but the good news is you can do it! Changing a state of "need and want" to a state of "abundance" takes persistence, tenacity, focus, and time.

Need-Based Thinking

When you follow a *need-based* pattern of thinking, it is impossible to attract opportunities to create what you think you want. For example, if you are continually thinking, "I have got to earn more money, or I need at least $12,000 per month," you will stay in a state of scarcity and need. According to the Law of Attraction, when you follow this need-based pattern of thinking, you will not be able to attract opportunities for attracting money.

Stop Negative Thinking

Stop thinking negative thoughts of scarcity and need. They attract negativity into your reality.

- *I'll never have enough money.*

- *I'll never find love. My perfect soul mate doesn't exist.*

- *I'm fat and can't lose weight.*

- *I'll always have a job I hate.*

When you realize you are thinking negative thoughts, STOP IT! Immediately respond with a positive affirmation. Your negative thoughts become habits, so it is up to you to retrain your self-talk from negative to positive. You CAN change your subconscious belief system!

THE "ACTION" PORTION OF LAW OF ATTR"ACTION"

You have stated clearly and precisely your desired outcome, and you have aligned your subconscious beliefs with your desire. Now, it is time for the action portion. You need to take physical steps to move toward your outcome. Remember that "Action" is the second half of the word "Attraction."

When Susan wanted to see Elton John in person, it was not enough for her to make a wish. When they learned that Elton was in Las Vegas, Susan and her husband took action. They called for tickets, went to the ticket office, were persistent with the salesclerk, and showed up for the performance.

If you want to meet your soul mate, it is vital to state the intention, align your subconscious with your conscious desire, and then take steps to move toward your outcome. If you sit in your apartment merely dreaming of your soul mate's arrival, no one will come.

If you want to increase your sales and have aligned your subconscious with this desire, you still must take physical action to move toward those goals. Sitting idly at your desk will not achieve your desired outcome. Do your research, learn about your product, take sales training, and keep visualizing what you want.

If you want to increase the abundance in your life, behave like a person of abundance. If you want more love, give more love. If you want more compassion, be more compassionate—even the smallest actions matter. For example, you can increase the level of abundance in your life by resolving to tip more generously. By adding a few extra dollars to the server's tip, you demonstrate abundance in the universe.

STAGES OF THE LAW OF ATTRACTION

There are five stages of the Law of Attraction: 1. Decide what you want. 2. Decide that you are worthy of it. 3. Decide that you can have what you want. 4. Recognize the abundance in the world. 5. Believe that what you want will happen.

Decide what you want

Many times, people do not know what they want. It is essential to be clear about what you want. Your ambiguous goals send blurry requests and vibrations to the universe day-to-day, minute-to-minute. It is tough to attract what you want when you are continually beaming unclear descriptions. Clarify, visualize, and expect the best.

Decide that you are worthy of it

You may not believe you deserve to receive what you want to attract. This belief can be self-limiting, as we discuss in Chapter 10. Your subconscious may be sending the message to your conscious mind that you are not good enough or special enough to receive it. Your subconscious mind is more persuasive than your conscious mind and can overrule it. You must believe that you deserve the best.

Decide that you can have what you want

Another self-limiting belief to the Law of Attraction is that you do not believe that it is possible to get what you want. Even if you sincerely want to receive it, deep down, you may genuinely not believe you can do so. It is essential to take a massive leap of faith and convince yourself that you are capable of getting what you want.

Recognize the abundance in the world

Acknowledge that the world has an abundance. Again, it is part of synchronizing your conscious and subconscious mind to prevent self-limiting beliefs. The world is full of compatible partners, wealth, kind people, love, and even peace.

Believe what you want is going to happen.

Now it is time to believe that what you want is going to happen. At this stage, the temptation is that you may get sidetracked by your questions of who, when, and how. Stop worrying about HOW. The answers to these will come. Focus on what you want, recognize that it is out there in abundance, believe that you can have it and that it will come to you.

You could get stuck in each stage at times

Which stage of the Law of Attraction is the most difficult for you? You probably get stuck at times with each step. Train your mind to focus on what you want and tame your conscious and subconscious mind to work together to stop self-limiting beliefs from thwarting your progress toward living an abundant life.

WHAT'S NEXT?

It is essential to start thinking about welcoming the change you want to see in your life. The next chapter introduces you to the stages of change that you will encounter once you commit to your promises. The four stages of change are Resistance, Confusion, Exploration, and Commitment. Even positive changes in your life will trigger Resistance in you. We discuss how to stay committed to your goals on a day-to-day basis, a task that is fundamental to creating the life story that you want.

CHAPTER 8: *LifeQ*-TIPS AND CHAPTER RECAP

- **Use the Law of Attraction to gain what you are seeking.**

  - The Law of Attraction is always operating. Like the law of gravity, it never fails.

  - Knowing about this Law allows you to have more power in your life, and feel less like a victim.

  - Be clear and specific about what you want. State it in positive terms.

  - Write it down in the present tense as if it has already occurred. *"I'm so grateful now that my cholesterol is below 190."*

  - Uncover your subconscious beliefs and ensure they align with your desired outcome. Decide that you are worthy of achieving what you want *and* can have it.

  - Recognize the abundance in the world.

  - Spend time everyday visualizing that you have attained your outcome.

  - Develop action steps that will ensure the Law of Attr"ACTION" will be activated.

◦ Take the actions and do the work needed to achieve what you want.

- **Consider developing a Vision Board** or find magazine pictures to help you see and feel what you want. Look at these pictures every day.

- **If your current reality is not good, focus on what you wish to experience instead of the present situation.** When you focus on your current reality, you will attract the same life experiences you already have. Focus on what you want. Imagine what it would be like if it happened.

LifeQ PRACTICE # 8.1 DEVELOP A MANTRA OF FOUR STATEMENTS

Develop a **MANTRA OF FOUR STATEMENTS** that will support creating a Life of Abundance for you. Repeat several times daily.

LifeQ PRACTICE # 8.2 NEXT WEEK'S ACTION PLAN

- What have you learned about yourself after reading this chapter?

- What actions will you take this next week to start to design the life that you want to live?

CHAPTER 9

EMBRACE CHANGE

"*The only person who welcomes change is someone with a wet diaper,*" Mark Twain said long before the 21st century. This idea applies today more than ever. Change can be daunting for many people, even when they have dreams that require a change to achieve them. When you have dreams, the universe often sends messages and opportunities your way. You can choose to go through the doors leading to the possibilities, or you can stay where you feel "comfortable." Marco had a choice to make about whether to embrace change or resist.

Marco's story:

Marco had worked in the family auto repair business since he was 16 years old. He did not particularly enjoy the thought of working there his entire life, but this was the only business he knew. Marco was comfortable in his job and was making good money. He had dreams of moving to London and starting a life there, but he was afraid to leave his family and his secure job. He was scared of the unknown.

After Marco had worked 15 years in the family business, a new partner joined the firm. This new partner implemented many new policies and practices in the areas of technology, sales, accounting, and mandatory meetings. Previously when Marco had recommended new ways, his father had refused to listen to him. Now, this new partner began to implement many of the same practices that Marco had suggested. Marco became angry and decided this might be the time to reconsider going to London. He had been resisting change for many years. Marco started exploring all his options, examining opportunities that seemed possible. After careful review, he realized that this was a perfect opportunity to take a year off, visit London, and see what awaited him there. After a year, he could either stay there or return to the family business. Marco's dream of having a life in London finally came true.

Humans are open to change in response to either of two extremes: for pleasure or pain. Marco's pain was so severe that he was finally ready to consider making a change.

YOUR CHANGE TEMPERAMENT

How can you thrive during change? How do you shift your mindset to reach your goals and promises so you can live the life that you want to live? Let us start by looking at your change temperament. Change energizes some people and paralyzes others. When making changes in your life, it is often challenging. *How do **you** respond to change? What is **your** change temperament?* Take a moment and think about how you have reacted to some of the changes you have experienced. How easy was it for you to adjust to your new home? Was it an adventure for you to search for a new drugstore, supermarket, clothing store, or was the experience exhausting and stressful?

What happens to your mindset when you upgrade to a new cell phone or a new computer? Do you become excited by the opportunity to see what has changed since your last purchase, or do you dread having to learn the new software enhancements? It is crucial to understand how you respond to change. For example, if you know that you struggle with change, you can incorporate additional strategies into your action planning. One place to start is to strengthen your sense of humor so you can laugh at yourself and your difficulty with change.

BENEFITS OF LAUGHTER

You have probably heard many times that laughter is the best medicine. The importance of humor and laughter is even in the Bible. "A cheerful heart is good medicine, but a crushed spirit dries up the bones." [1] When you laugh, your body releases two key chemicals. Your pituitary gland releases endorphins into the bloodstream and helps relieve pain and trigger feelings of pleasure. Studies show that people can endure 15% more pain by laughing a few minutes beforehand. Additionally, when laughing, your brain releases dopamine, a neurotransmitter that creates a sense of euphoria.

Laughter is the best medicine!

Many studies show that laughter therapy has a significant impact on improving anxiety in patients with Parkinson's disease [3], improving hopefulness, confidence, and depression in women with menopause [4], and reducing worry and depression in students. [5] The overall health benefits of laughter include improved immunity, stress relief, improved cardiovascular health, reduced anxiety, and a sense of safety. [6]

So, laugh at yourself. As we like to joke, "Some days you are the bug, other days you are the windshield. Some days you are the statue, other days you are the pigeon." Make yourself a promise to smile throughout the day. Even faking a smile can make you feel less stressed and more joyful.

Let us look at the different ways that Danielle and Tom respond to change.

Danielle and Tom's stories:

Danielle is a Baby Boomer and, for many years, became easily frustrated with new computer upgrades. It seemed that as soon as she learned all the ins-and-outs of the latest equipment, it was time to upgrade. Although now Danielle realizes this and can laugh at herself, for years she seemed to freeze when the software that she was used to was changed. Recently, she purchased the latest smartphone and has already forgiven herself for asking constant questions about the applications. She has switched her frame of mind so that she is looking forward to seeing the enhancements in the new device.

Tom thrives on change and has a positive change temperament. As a member of the Millennial Generation, he enjoys computer upgrades and new equipment. He recently visited France and decided he wanted to live there just like that. Tom feels exhilarated by all the changes that living in France and having a different lifestyle has brought him. Tom has been able to make changes in several areas of his WHEEL OF LifeQ, and his LifeQ has increased. Since he has moved to France, Tom is physically healthier than ever, has made new friends, enhanced his spirituality, advanced his career, and found love. Not only is Tom's temperament change-friendly, his openness to change is an excellent example of a phenomenon we discussed in Chapter 3. We discussed how changing in one life area in

> *the **WHEEL OF LifeQ** (in this case, Tom's physical environment) often leads to positive changes in other areas.*

Use the tool "ASSESS YOUR OUTLOOK" *LifeQ* **PRACTICE # 9.1** at the end of this chapter to see where you fall on the adaptability to change scale.

CREATE YOUR PLAN FOR YOUR CHANGE

Before you begin working toward your goals, consciously make them a part of your Personal Strategic Plan. Your life is your most important business, so it is essential to plan just like companies do. Determine what the end goal looks like, what obstacles you will encounter, actions you will take to alleviate the barriers, and an action plan, including steps and due dates for each step. Find goal-planning materials in Chapter 13.

SELF-MANAGEMENT

Self-management is key to thriving on change and reaching your goals and promises. It is also the most challenging chore during times of change. It is easy to become distracted, run into obstacles, and get off course. There are "time-robbers" like emails, text messages, Facebook, Instagram, and surfing the Net. There are the Naysayers and those "Hoover people" who vacuum your positive energy and tell you that you will never make the changes you want. It is easy to self-sabotage by negative self-talk. Remember that 77% of self-talk is negative. [7] This is when self-management is critical.

Part of your plans to achieve your goals must include ways to manage distractions and unsupportive people. You also must learn to change your self-talk to powerful affirmations as we discussed in Chapter 8.

PREPARING YOURSELF FOR CHANGE

How can you prepare yourself for change? Every change involves specific dynamics. There is always some loss and letting go of the old. You must make intentional choices to grow. There is no growth without change, no change without loss, and no loss without pain. You will need to let go of some old things and then take hold of some new ones.

When a trapeze artist chooses to change bars on the trapeze, he must let go of one to grab the next. If he does not let go of the first bar, he will never make it to the other side. He will get stuck in the middle and fall. He must *choose* to make the change. This same phenomenon applies to changes in your life. You may have to let go of old patterns, old habits, and old ways of thinking to grow and be successful.

Businesses, like people, need to embrace change to be successful. Blockbuster is an example of a once-thriving company that failed to adapt when it should have done so. Blockbuster was founded in 1985 and provided home movies and video game rental. At its peaks in the 1990s, Blockbuster employed 84,000 people worldwide and had 9,000 outlets. When Netflix and on-demand streaming became popular, Blockbuster's business model needed to change, yet it refused to embrace the on-demand digital model. Blockbuster filed for bankruptcy in 2010.

See Susan's story about feeling loss during change.

Susan's story:

When Susan served on the Leadership Team building a "Hospital of the Future," the team worked for three long years toward the goal of opening the new Medical Center. The day finally came to move from the temporary headquarters into the new facility. Now, several years later, Susan can still recall her unexpected feelings of loss and sadness as she left her familiar office, parking place, and phone system.

She was perplexed by her feelings of resistance. Moving into the new facility had been the goal of all the hard work!

Even when the change is your idea, it can cause several behaviors and feelings that can impede your progress, if not understood. Often reaching new goals affects other aspects of your life. For example, if you decide to continue your education, this decision will probably involve extra expenses. It will also affect your relationships with family and friends because you will need to reallocate time to attend class and do homework. If your goal is to become healthier, your new food choices may affect your family members, some of whom may resent the switch from potato chips to apple slices. If you decide to focus time on your relationship with your significant other, your friends may not appreciate that you participate in fewer sporting events or girls' night out, for example.

Deborah's story:

Deborah recalls with dismay an encounter she had with a close friend who gave her an ultimatum about friendship. Stephanie told Deborah that she wanted more of her time, or she would drop Deborah as her best friend. At the time, Deborah was working full time, writing her Ph.D. dissertation, and in the beginning years of her marriage. The friendship with Stephanie did not survive.

Questions to Ask Yourself

Think about the following questions as you consider the changes you wish to make.

- *What do you anticipate are the positive and negative impacts of the changes you plan to make?*

- *How might you prepare for them?*

- *What do you need from people in your life to support you in your change?*

- *How can you learn to embrace the unknown?*

- *How many times have you passed up an opportunity because of your underlying belief or judgment about it? Be aware of the tortoise brain phenomenon that we describe below.* (This is shown as an exercise in *LifeQ* **PRACTICE #9.3** at the end of this chapter)

THE TORTOISE BRAIN

Just like a tortoise, this reptilian part of your brain may slow you down and keep you from emerging from your protective shell. Some scientists refer to this reptilian part as the *lizard brain*. We prefer referring to it as your *tortoise brain*. The tortoise brain (amygdala) is a physical part of your brain near the brainstem. It takes responsibility for your survival by causing fear, enabling you to attack, and pushing you to reproduce. Another name for this reptilian part of your brain is "Resistance." It wants to limit your exposure to anything new and risky, and this includes change, growth, and development. The Tortoise tells you why you should not take action to do something and gives you lots of excuses for why it will not work. It abhors change, achievement, and risk.

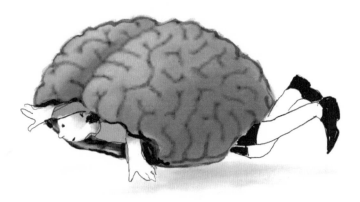

Tortoise Brain

Tortoises have survived on earth for more than 200 million years, while humans can be traced back to 2.5 million years. This brain part was useful in prehistoric times when humans faced life and death situations daily. The tortoise brain focuses on survival. It is that voice in your head that tells you to "be careful, back off, hide from danger, and play it safe." Today, as in the past, your tortoise brain's role is to keep you safe. As such, your tortoise brain wants to prevent you from changing. It may be controlling you and trying to prevent your success. Until you learn to recognize and tame this reptilian part of your brain, it will be challenging to achieve the goals you desire and to live the life that you want. The trick is to discern when the inner tortoise warrants your attention, and when you should ignore it. With your tortoise's focus on your safety, it can prevent you from taking risks, being bold, accomplishing goals, and living the life you envision with a high *LifeQ.*

Don't Let Your Tortoise Brain Sabotage You

How do you recognize when your tortoise brain is rearing its head and sabotaging your success? You must learn to acknowledge it and then tame it. You can acknowledge your tortoise's voice by the "What if?" questions resounding in your head. *"What if I don't succeed?" "What if I can't lose weight?" "What if I can't find a publisher?" "What if everyone laughs at me?" "What if I'm not smart enough?"* The language from your tortoise brain often contains the words "we" and "let's." *"We need to take a break." "Let's grab a cup of coffee." "Let's call grandma to check-in."* The voice becomes louder and louder the closer you get to success, whether it is shedding the last few pounds for a healthy body, finishing that MBA, completing the proposal, or writing your story.

In contrast to your reptilian tortoise is the *primate* part of your brain, which is considered the thinker. When your primate brain is more active, you are likely to reason, reflect, plan, and strategize. You can consciously tap into the large part of your *primate brain,* the neocortex, the modern, creative brain that can feel joy, gratitude and has become skillful in intellectual pursuits like science, creativity, and reaching goals.

TIPS for controlling your Tortoise Brain

Stay aware of the tortoise and how it wants to control your behavior. It wants to keep you in your metaphorical protective shell. Awareness is the first step. According to author Seth Godin, this reptile "is not merely a concept. It's real, and it's living on the top of your spine, fighting for your survival. But, of course, survival and success are not the same things." [8]

When your tortoise brain sends you warnings, flip your thoughts to something positive that you enjoy or someone you love.

- Suspend your instinct to be fearful and judgmental of others. Instead of fearing that people might laugh at you, envision them applauding your success.

- Shift the phrase "What if?" from a negative to a positive tone. "What if I win the award?" "What if my job interview goes well?" With positive thoughts, your brain releases endorphins that make you feel better, perform better, and attain success.

- Keep sticky notes with affirmations within eyesight and read them out loud daily.

- Surround yourself with people who support you and your goals.

- Wear a rubber band around your wrist and snap it when you are doubting yourself and playing negative tapes in your brain. It takes 21 days to cement a new habit into your way of life, so take control of your thinking, tame your Tortoise, and turn negative self-talk positive.

- Tell your tortoise brain, "Thank you for sharing, Tortoise, but I'm not interested. Come back when my life is truly in danger."

THE FOUR STAGES OF CHANGE

Every person who experiences a change goes through four predictable stages. By understanding this phenomenon, it is easier to deal with the totality of the change, whether you initiate the change, or it happens to you. These four stages are:

- Stage 1: Resistance

- Stage 2: Confusion

- Stage 3: Exploration

- Stage 4: Commitment

The key to moving progressively through the four stages is to continually focus on your goal, your vision for what you want. Solicit support from your family, friends, or coach and ask them to help you focus on your goals and vision.

Stage 1: Resistance

All change, even positive change, involves resistance. Change means a shift from the known to the unknown and the unfamiliar. Stage 1 usually means you will need to give up something, so you will need to adjust before you can become fully productive again. You may experience positive feelings like excitement, enthusiasm, determination, as well as negative feelings. Behaviors and emotions during Resistance Stage may include:

• **Excitement**	• **Resentment**
• **Enthusiasm**	• **Anger**
• **Determination**	• **Sarcasm**
• **Stubbornness**	• **Withdrawal**
• **Apathy**	• **Sadness**
• **Anxiety**	

As an example, you have as a goal to exercise five times per week because your vision for your overall health is to live a life filled with physical, mental, emotional, and spiritual health. You may get up the first two days 30 minutes earlier than you have been to exercise. The third day, your muscles are sore, you are tired from a tough couple of days at work, and it is raining. You want to sleep in that morning. Here is the test. Will you give in to the desire to sleep until 7:00? Fifty percent of people will. Will you? Now is the time to visualize your goal and see yourself achieving the goal. Put on your tennis shoes! You can do it!

Stage 2 Confusion

Confusion is the second stage of the change process. The resistance is over, but you realize that what was familiar and known is gone. You used to sleep until 7 a.m., and now you get up and get moving by 6:30. Behaviors and emotions during Confusion Stage may include:

• **Erratic performance**	• **Grumbling and complaining**
• **Doubting ability to reach goals**	• **Blaming others**
• **Frustration**	• **Sickness**
• **Poor listening**	• **Arguing**

The Confusion stage is the most critical in adjusting to change. You will need to make sure your priorities and expectations are clear because this is the stage when you are wondering whether the goals are worth the work. Your willpower and commitment will be challenged. The battle is mental, and conflicting messages are confusing. One of the messages you hear is, "The goal is worth the effort." The other message is disagreeing and saying that "This goal is just too difficult and not worth the effort at this time… maybe next year." It may be appropriate to include a reasonable adjustment of the goal. For example, it may be that setting the goal of exercising five days per week may be too much considering other commitments in your life. To continue your path to an abundant life with physical, mental, emotional, and spiritual health, you may decide to adjust the goal to three or four days during some weeks.

Stage 3 Exploration

The Exploration Stage brings positive energy and optimism. You have passed through the stages of Resistance and Confusion and start to see the finish line. You are focused on the future and confident that you can reach this goal. With success in your sight, you begin to focus on the possibility of attaining other goals, too. Behaviors and emotions during the Exploration Stage include:

• **Renewed energy**	• **Increased self-confidence**
• **Less anxiety**	• **High self-esteem**
• **Optimism**	• **More in control**
• **Excitement**	

Whether your goal is to become healthier with a higher **BodyQ**, earn that next degree **MindQ**, or raise your **LoveQ** by deepening your relationship with your partner, the Exploration Stage is positive. You will feel renewed energy, optimism, and more in control of the outcome. Just as the first 10% and last 10% of any project are the hardest, the same is valid for setting and reaching goals. Once you head toward the final 10%, you may think you can relax. No! Don't relax! Now is the time to stay focused. For example, a person may not lose that last five pounds or complete their final college course for their degree. The Exploration Stage can be tricky. It may look like you have made the change, but often individuals linger in Exploration for long periods without progress and growth. Continue to take daily action steps toward your goal.

Stage 4 Commitment

Stage 4 is the Commitment Stage. You have made it through the hard part and now are reaching your goal. You feel productive, successful, and confident. Your self-esteem with respect to your goal is high, and so is your energy. Now is the time to celebrate. When you praise and reward yourself for being successful, you build confidence and enable yourself to set goals and take risks in the future. Many people enjoy creating rewards along the pathway to reaching their goals. For example, if the goal is to exercise four times per week, they may reward themselves when they complete a month of exercise. Others may celebrate when they have uncluttered a room or cleaned out the garage. Some celebrate whenever they complete a course that leads toward their careers. Examples of rewards can be a trip to a spa, a new set of golf clubs, and a week to do nothing but watch TV reruns. Behaviors and Emotions during Commitment Stage include:

• **Belief in oneself**	• **Balance**
• **High energy**	• **High productivity**
• **Feel successful**	• **Able to set future goals**

SIMULTANEOUS CHANGES AND THE STAGES OF CHANGE

Reaching goals is not always a linear process. You will hit plateaus and encounter detours along the way. When you are working toward achieving several goals simultaneously, you will be in several stages of change at the same time, just as Robert is in the example following.

Robert's story:

*Robert has been working on several goals at once. His first goal is to improve his physical health and increase his **BodyQ** score. For the weight-loss part of his plan, he is currently in Stage 2 (Confusion) as he struggles to eat better and stay on track with his diet. At the same time, he is in Stage 3 (Exploration) in his goal to exercise three times per week. He is inspired because his endurance level has almost reached the goal he set. Simultaneously, he just added the goal to have more fun and recreation and increase his **FunQ**. Additionally, he committed to spend time with friends at least once a week and impact his **FriendsQ**. Robert's progress toward these new goals is in Stage 1 (Resistance) because he is struggling and juggling schedules and workload to begin the work of changing some priorities.*

What Stage(s) of Change Are You in Currently?

The speed you travel through the stages of change varies with each person. It also varies with the type of goal that you set. As part of your strategic planning to achieve your goals, consider what could happen to thwart your progress during each stage and create ways to overcome the obstacles and distractions as well as develop rewards for yourself along the pathway to success. Use the tool *LifeQ* PRACTICE #9.2 at the end of this chapter to gauge the stage you are currently for each of your goals.

Change Will Never Be Over

Change does not stop happening. If you are waiting to begin designing your life story until things "settle down," you will never be ready. The fact that change will continue is a concept that is crucial to understand. Life will always be filled with change, and the rate of change is accelerating.

When we ask clients to "Draw a picture of change," it can be fascinating to see their ideas about change put into illustrations. Many people draw a linear view of change that starts with one symbol and ends with one other character, as shown below. This picture implies that a change stops when it gets to the ideal state. However, change never stops. We have found that a healthier way to view change is to continue the evolution into many different shapes until eternity. See the picture below.

HOW CHANGE WORKS

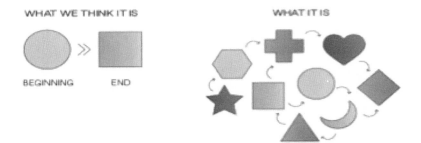

IT TAKES TIME TO CHANGE AND GROW

Humans are slow learners. Often, you must relearn a lesson 40 or 50 times to get it. How often have you reprimanded yourself and thought, "Not again! I've already learned that"? You need repeated exposure. You also probably have a lot to unlearn. It requires hard work to remove bad habits and replace them with good ones. The Bible calls this work "taking off the old self" and "putting on the new self." [9] Growth is often painful and scary. Every change involves a loss. Even if your old ways were self-defeating, they were at least comfortable and familiar, like a worn-out pair of shoes. Finally, good habits take time to develop. You cannot claim to be kind unless you are habitually kind. You must practice your habits, and that takes time!

WHAT'S NEXT?

The next step is to become aware of your underlying beliefs and patterns. Sometimes the most significant challenge you encounter in your quest to increase your **LifeQ** *score and implement your strategic plan is* **how you think***. It is crucial to recognize and, if possible, remove underlying beliefs and patterns that block your progress toward living your most abundant life. Sometimes we do not even realize they are there, like programs running in the background on our computers. Chapter 10 explores the importance of investigating your underlying beliefs & patterns.*

CHAPTER 9 *LifeQ* -TIPS AND CHAPTER RECAP

- **Keep the Serenity Prayer in Mind.** "God, grant me the serenity to accept the things I cannot change, the courage to change the things I can, and the wisdom to know the difference."

- **Label your change Type I, II, II. Focus your energy on Type I & Type II Change.**

  □ I "I can *control* this Change."

- II "I can *influence* this Change."

- III "I can *neither control nor influence* this Change."

- **Study the Stages of Change**

  - Resistance

  - Confusion

  - Exploration

  - Commitment

- **Design your Strategic Plan to offer solutions to help you** when you experience distractions and obstacles that could impede your progress.

- **People who have an optimistic outlook can thrive during change, whereas those who are pessimistic are more prone to have difficulty** when life throws them a curveball.

- **Remember that self-management is the most challenging chore during times of change.**

- **It is easy to become distracted, to run into obstacles and go off course.** Stay alert to time-robbers like Facebook and email, keep "Hoover people" from sucking your energy, and use positive affirmations to feel powerful.

- **Learn from creatures in nature that seem to embrace change and thrive.** The musical "The Lion King" is an excellent example of the "Circle of Life" where you can embrace natural changes as well as take charge of your success.

- **Establish Priorities and Goals – Visualize Your Success!** Planning for the impact of changing your life clears your vision and builds your confidence and strength.

- **Find your sense of humor** Laugh often. Children who are four years old laugh 400 times/day. Laughing increases your endorphins, which are 200 times more potent than morphine as well as boosts your immunity from diseases.

- **Embrace the Chinese symbol for change.** Danger is the top character. Opportunity is the bottom character.

Activities to Celebrate Successes

- Start a success journal. Reflect on the path you took. Document your successes.

- Share news with friends, family, and colleagues. Thank everyone.

- Accept and enjoy the compliments.

- Support someone else in reaching his or her goal

- Watch a favorite TV show or movie.

- Take a day off from work. Treat yourself to a day of relaxation.

LifeQ Practice #9.1 ASSESS YOUR OUTLOOK

Apply the following scoring indicators to the statements below.	Strongly Agree A	Agree B	Neutral C	Disagree D	Strongly Disagree E
1. It is important that I keep learning new things.					
2. In changing times, I usually expect the best.					
3. I get upset easily.					
4. If something can go wrong for me, it will.					
5. I have a good sense of humor.					
6. I'm optimistic about my future.					
7. I have goals for the future.					
8. I hardly ever expect things to go my way.					
9. I expect more good things to happen to me than bad, overall.					

Scoring for **ASSESS YOUR OUTLOOK**:

Subtotal your scores for items 1, 2, 5, 6, 7, and 9 as follows:

A = 4 points B = 3 points C = 2 points D = 1-point E = 0 points _____

Subtotal your scores for items 3, 4, and 8 as follows:

A = 0 points B = 1-point C = 2 points D = 3 points E = 4 points _____

What does your score mean? The higher your score, the more optimistic you are. The maximum score is 36 points. Those who have an optimistic outlook can thrive during change, whereas those who are pessimistic are more prone to have difficulty when life throws them a curveball. Optimists, far from protecting their fragile vision of the world, confront trouble head-on, whereas pessimists bury their heads in the sand of denial. Review your answers and choose two areas that you could impact now.

© 2016 Susan A. Murphy, MBA, Ph.D.[10]

LifeQ Practice # 9.2 STAGE(S) OF CHANGE

IN WHAT STAGE(S) OF CHANGE ARE YOU CURRENTLY?

Study the examples given. Then in the boxes for each of your goals, describe your Stage of Change and Actions Steps.

GOAL/PROMISE	STAGE	ACTIONS STEPS TO TAKE
Lose 10 lbs. by 10/31	# 2 Confusion	Do not purchase junk food for home starting now. Ask Janet to help me. I will email her every week with my progress.
Pass licensing exam by 12/31	#1 Resistance	1. Call agency regarding exam schedule Monday 2. Order practice exams 3. Schedule study time on calendar – now.

LifeQ PRACTICE # 9.3 **Think about several questions as you consider changes:**

- *What do you anticipate are positive & negative impacts of changes you plan to make?*

- *How might you prepare for them?*

- *What do you need from people in your life to support you in your change?*

- *How can you learn to embrace the unknown?*

- *How many times have you passed up opportunities because of your underlying belief or judgment about it? Be aware of the tortoise brain phenomenon.*

LifeQ PRACTICE #9.4 WHAT IS YOUR PERSONAL DISTRESS LEVEL?

Check all signs (physical, emotional, and mental) that you are currently experiencing.

PHYSICAL SIGNS	EMOTIONAL SIGNS	MENTAL SIGNS
___ Heart pounds or skips a beat	___ Irritable, easily annoyed, and angry	___ Low concentration
___ Tightness in chest	___ Indecisive	___ High degree of worrying
___ Breathing is rapid and shallow	___ Jealous	___ Low creativity
___ Dry throat, mouth, and lips	___ Overeating	___ No fantasies
___ Tight muscles/pain especially in neck, shoulders, lower back	___ Aggression	___ Living in past
___ Muscular tics or twitching	___ Crying	___ Feelings of worthlessness and depression
___ Frequent headaches	___ Isolation	___ Forgetfulness
___ Urinary frequency	___ Blame others	
___ Rash	___ Self-critical	
___ Hemorrhoids	___ Abuse alcohol or drugs	
___ Frequent indigestion, diarrhea, constipation	___ Nagging	
___ Insomnia	___ Unsure of yourself in routine situations	
___ Elevated blood pressure	___ Apathy	
___ Feel tired throughout the day		
___ Easily catch colds or develop flu		
___ Grind teeth when sleeping		
___ Herpes Simplex		
___ Loss of appetite		
___ Loss of sex drive		
___ Cold, clammy hand		

SCORING FOR PERSONAL DISTRESS QUOTIENT

Add up the checkmarks.

If you score:

More than 32: You are highly distressed.

20–32: You are moderately distressed.

Less than 10: You are calm and peaceful.

WHAT DOES YOUR PERSONAL DISTRESS LEVEL MEAN FOR YOUR LONG-TERM HEALTH? Too much stress can negatively affect you physically, mentally, emotionally, and spiritually. During times of change, it is especially important to be aware of the impact on your health. If you are highly distressed, it can lead to cardiac issues, strokes, breathing issues, and underlying health issues. By understanding the Four Stages of Change, learning how to cope with the impact of change, developing SMART goals, and remembering that change is inevitable, and growth is optional, you can lower your personal distress quotient.

© 2016 Susan A. Murphy, MBA, Ph.D. [11]

LifeQ PRACTICE #9. 5 NEXT WEEK'S ACTION PLAN

- What have you learned about yourself after reading this chapter?

- What actions will you take this next week to start to design the life that you want to live?

CHAPTER 10

PATTERNS OF BEHAVIOR AND LIMITING BELIEFS

Why are underlying limiting beliefs and patterns of behavior problems when you are trying to live an abundant life with a high *LifeQ*? The control your limiting beliefs and patterns have over you is immense and is one of the main reasons so many people never reach a fraction of their true potential. What makes uncovering your limiting beliefs and patterns so tricky is that most people do not realize that they have them. These beliefs become ingrained, invisible, and we rarely question them. Daniel's story illustrates consequences that can occur when your limiting beliefs bypass your conscious mind and stop you from attaining the success you want.

Daniel's story:

Daniel awakens to an empty house and realizes that once again, he is alone. Although he tells his friends that he wants to be married to a loving wife and have a home full of children, his dating patterns suggest otherwise. For the past seven years since college, Daniel keeps choosing love interests who treat him poorly and are unfaithful. That is what he discovered again last evening when he dropped by Stacy's house unexpectedly and found his wife-to-be in the arms of another man. Once more, Daniel finds himself alone and in pain with a broken heart. This episode is the third time this has happened to him, and he realizes this is no longer a coincidence. It is a pattern, and now he is determined to find out what is driving his bad choices.

Friends and family had been telling Daniel for years that he should examine his dating patterns. The more they told him, however, the more he resisted. Now he realizes that he may have been more influenced by his parent's divorce than he thought. He was eight years old at the time, and his conscious mind keeps telling him that after 20 years, he should be "over it." Now, as an adult, he may subconsciously believe that a long-lasting, trusting marriage is impossible. He also believes he is unlovable. Once he can discover the "why" behind his beliefs and behavior patterns, Daniel can begin to choose what he wants to do differently.

Why Is It Important to Identify Emotional Patterns of Behavior and Limiting Beliefs?

You will be unable to live your most fulfilling, abundant life unless you understand your patterns of behavior and your underlying beliefs. Your beliefs will continue to impact your behavior and impede your ability to achieve your goals. They are inextricably connected, but we are going to look at each separately. That's the only way to identify them and overcome them.

In 1949 Canadian behavioral psychologist Donald Hebb proposed that learning something new linked neurons in new ways. Hebb found that when two neurons fire at the same time repeatedly (or when one fires, causing the other to fire), chemical changes occur in both so that the two tend to connect more strongly. Hebb coined the phrase, *"Neurons that fire together, wire together."* [1]

Whenever you respond to a situation with a specific action, you are using a pattern. For example, the case could be the phone ringing, and the associated action could be reaching for the telephone receiver. You perform these types of activities without any conscious thought, which is why researchers generally think of these types of actions as arising from your subconscious mind.

The more often you perform an action or behave a certain way, the more it gets physically wired into your brain. Remember Dr. Hebb's saying, "neurons that fire together, wire together." Recognizing patterns is important because it helps us predict and anticipate events and situations that could arise, saving energy and forecasting dangerous situations. Sometimes these patterns can be obstacles to living our best life. But there is hope, and it is called neuroplasticity. *Neuroplasticity* is the ability of the brain to change its physical structure and function based on input from your experiences, behaviors, emotions, and even thoughts. That means that with awareness and action, we can change our patterns.

Your memory stores every situation that happens in your life and the actions you took to respond to these situations. Think of the power past experiences have on your life! Every time a crisis occurs, your brain checks to see if that situation is in your memory. If it is stored, and it has an action associated with it, the brain will use the action related to the situation stored in memory. The telephone rings, you reach for it. The traffic light turns red, and you push the car brake pedal. You feel hurt, you lash out with angry words. Let us continue using Daniel's story as an example. He has a situation where his parents fought incessantly, and there was infidelity on his mother's part.

Situation: *Stacy, who is Daniel's fiancée, answers her ringing cell phone. Almost immediately, Stacy starts to blush, turns away from Daniel, and then begins to whisper into her phone.*

Memory Data—Thoughts: *Daniel has the memory of his mother frequently whispering into the phone the same way Stacy does now. He recalls one night when his father yelled at his mother when she came home late. It was a terrible fight, including screaming and accusations about his mother's infidelity. After that fight, his father left the house for days. Daniel thinks that the same thing is happening in this situation. He believes that Stacy is being unfaithful.*

The feeling was triggered: *Little Daniel was feeling powerless and confused, and he recalls that nobody came to check on him. He felt alone and scared. This current situation of possible betrayal brings* *him right back to this memory. As he remembers it, he feels the same way he did as a child. He is anxious, worried, and fears the worst: being left alone and betrayed.*

Action: *When he was little, Daniel could not do anything about the situation. But now, as an adult, he can take action and deal with this situation head-on. Daniel demands Stacy show him her phone, and Daniel starts checking her emails and recent calls. He refuses to let Stacy go out with her friends. Daniel becomes very insecure and paranoid. They seem to fight always.*

The result—Repeated Pattern and Self-fulfilling Prophecy: *Stacy starts to pull away, feels suffocated, and has an affair.*

Identifying Emotional Patterns and Underlying Beliefs Can Be a Difficult Task.

Why are patterns so problematic when you are trying to live an abundant life with a high *LifeQ*? The problem with patterns is that your brain may link inadequate or even self-defeating responses with current situations. Your mind bypasses your consciousness, and you repeat the old answer. It is essential to look for your patterns.

Start looking for patterns in situations that did not turn out the way you wanted. Look at what you thought, said, and did. What did you do over and over again that did not work? If you do not think through these situations and analyze why they did not come out well, you are likely to repeat them. Do you remember the movie *Groundhog Day?* It is a comedy about a weatherman, Phil Connors, who is in a time warp on the very worst day of his life. The weatherman is broadcasting news about Groundhog Day in a small Pennsylvania town and keeps reliving his worst day over and over again. Instead of living for 50 years, some people seem to live one year 50 times! They make the same mistakes because they never stop and examine the lessons from their experiences.

We encourage clients to ask themselves annually, "What happened this last year? What worked and what did not? What patterns do I want to keep repeating, and what do I want to change so I can live a more fulfilling, successful life?

A typical example of a pattern that always fails, in the long run, is to test other people's love for you. This could be the case with Daniel and his unsuccessful relationships. Imagine that your parents were divorced during your childhood, destroying your ability to feel trusting and lovable. As an adult, when people try to get close to you, you sabotage relationships. You do not want to be hurt again, so you want to protect yourself. You never let your guard down. You might falsely accuse your partner of being unfaithful, or you might become unfaithful yourself. You test your partner to see if he or she will still love you or leave you. Often, when the first test does not confirm your suspicions, you try harder and escalate your testing behavior. When your partner does go, you justify your behavior and say to yourself, "See, my fears are legitimate, I am unlovable." Your self-fulfilling prophecy is confirmed.

EMPOWERING BELIEFS HELP YOU INCREASE YOUR *LifeQ*

The next chapter focuses in-depth on how to turn around limiting/negative beliefs, so in this chapter, we will only briefly introduce you to a simple, potent process. In *The Magic of Believing*, Claude Bristol wrote, "This subtle force of repeated suggestion overcomes our reason. It acts directly on our emotions and our feelings and finally penetrates to the very debts of our subconscious minds. It is repeated suggestions that make you believe." [2] You can overcome any limiting belief.

1. Identify a limiting belief that you want to change.

2. Determine how the belief limits you.

3. Decide how you want to be, act, or feel.

4. Create a turnaround statement that affirms or gives you permission to be, act, or feel this new way.

Following is an example of overcoming a limiting belief:

- My limiting/negative belief is that I must do everything myself. I have to be strong and independent. Asking for help is a sign of weakness.

- The way this belief limits me is that I do not ask for help, and I end up staying up too late and not getting enough sleep.

- The way I want to feel is connected and collaborative. I want to be vulnerable, and that does not make me weak. It takes courage to ask for help when I need it. I want to delegate some of the things I do not like doing, and that are not the best use of my time.

- It is ok to ask for help. I am worthy of receiving all the help I need. [3]

A SELF-FULFILLING PROPHECY AFFECTS BEHAVIOR

A *self-fulfilling prophecy* is any positive or negative expectation that affects another person's behavior in a manner that causes those expectations to happen. Examples of self-fulfilling prophecies include:

- A boss who expects employees to be disloyal, lazy, and quit will often treat employees in a way that elicits the same response that the boss expects.

- A boss who expects a high-performing employee to do well might spend extra time with the employee working on a project so that both the employee and project are successful.

- A student who believes she will fail a science course even if she studies might stop studying and then fails the course. The prophecy comes true. [4]

SELF-FULFILLING PROPHECY

Throughout your life, you will encounter significant events that can create your patterns of behavior. Just as Daniel was impacted by the divorce of his parents when he was eight years old, there are significant events in your life—positive and negative—that impact your patterns.

How can Daniel change his patterns? Does he have control over his responses? Yes! Daniel can learn new responses to a situation, although it may take time, effort, patience, therapy, and listening sessions with friends.

Adverse significant events include divorce, death of a loved one, loss of a job, diagnosis of a severe illness, abuse, and neglect by parents. Other adverse events may include more long-term issues that affect you, such as a physical deformity or mental impairment. For example, clients have told us how being dyslexic impacted their belief system throughout their lives because, for many, their diagnosis did not occur until adulthood. Many dyslexic children have been called "stupid" or "lazy," and those labels become self-limiting beliefs that significantly affect their patterns of behavior throughout their lives.

The events that have an impact on your self-limiting beliefs do not need to be huge in scope. It could be there may have been a single event when kids laughed at you when you answered a question incorrectly in class, or bullied you on the playground, or teased you about an ugly haircut or dreadful outfit. This one-time event may have influenced your subconscious belief system in a negative way that affects your confidence level throughout your life.

Below is a process that our clients use to turn around the negative impact of significant events in their lives. *LifeQ* **PRACTICE 10.4,** at the end of this chapter, is a template to describe your significant events, the negative effects of those events, and your new affirmations to change underlying beliefs and patterns of behavior.

Your Emotional Family Legacy: Changing Your Destructive Patterns

1. The first step in changing patterns is to *realize they exist.* You must search out the patterns. *What situations are triggering your self-defeating responses?*

2. *What events in your life created the patterns?* When you discover which events created your patterns, you have more information about your hot buttons.

3. *Dig deep.* You usually do not process all the information when events occur but run with the first few segments and draw conclusions. It only takes 5% similarity to an event in your past for your brain to identify it as equivalent. Although you do not control things that come to your mind, you do control what to do with them.

4. Then, ask yourself, *"Why did that situation make me react that way?"* Answering this question may take a great deal of inner searching to bring deeply rooted patterns out of the depths of your mind. Once you find the pattern, then you must try to remove it and replace it.

5. *Focus attention on meaningful, satisfying behavior patterns.* When you do, your body releases an enzyme, serotonin, which contributes to feelings of well-being and pleasure.

SAMPLE: SIGNIFICANT EVENT, IMPACTS OF EVENT, AND AFFIRMATIONS

The following exercise provides an opportunity to think through significant events in your life and what impact they may have had on you. Try to remember your specific events, especially those that caused anxieties and fears. For each event, try to remember how you felt, conclusions about life you may have drawn, and the costs to you in the long run.

1. First, look at the sample pattern chart.

    Think of events and times during your life (before you were ten years old) that might have shaped your viewpoint and your emotional patterns. Family legacies can be both positive and negative. For example, many families are fiercely loyal to their members, which can create a positive sense of security and family bond. However, that loyalty can also become harmful when traumatic events are not acknowledged, and the behavior is not changed. Below are some questions to assist you in taking stock of your emotional family legacy. *LifeQ* **PRACTICE # 10.2**

    Then fill in your own Pattern Chart *LifeQ* **PRACTICE # 10.4** at the end of this chapter. This exercise will increase your attention by encouraging you to become more aware of your behaviors. Then, try to imagine some new thinking that would improve or change your negative emotional patterns. Write about it in the box provided.

2. After that, think about what affirmations, what positive messages, you can begin to send yourself.

WHAT'S NEXT?

In the next chapter, you will dig deeper into your self-limiting beliefs and behavior patterns. You will discover the most common self-limiting beliefs, identify which ones are affecting your patterns, and learn four tips for changing those beliefs and patterns. You will determine which fears affect your behavior and discover how to stop worrying and live more in the present. By understanding more about your self-limiting beliefs and how they impact your behavior, you will be able to increase your **LifeQ** *and overall abundance.*

CHAPTER 10 *LifeQ*-TIPS AND CHAPTER RECAP

- The more often you perform an action or behave a certain way, the more it gets physically wired into your brain.

- The events that can have an impact on your self-limiting beliefs can be huge, like death or divorce of parents, or small like being laughed at during your speech in grammar school. These events may influence your subconscious belief system in a negative way that affects your confidence level throughout your life.

- You usually do not process all the information when events occur but run with the first few segments and draw conclusions. A current event only needs to be 5% like a past event for your brain to identify it as equivalent.

- Focus attention on meaningful, satisfying behavior patterns. When you do, your body releases an enzyme, serotonin, which contributes to feelings of well-being and pleasure.

- The Holmes and Rahe Stress Scale suggests a strong correlation between significant life events and illnesses. The word "disease" has two syllables: *dis* and *ease*. "Dis" in Latin means lack of and difficulty with, so when there is a lack of ease, there can be a disease. [5]

LifeQ **PRACTICE # 10.1 TAKE THE HOLMES AND RAHE STRESS SCALE INSTRUMENT TO BE MORE MINDFUL OF HOW SIGNIFICANT EVENTS CAN AFFECT YOUR HEALTH AND STRESS LEVEL.** Significant Events Cause Stress and Can Negatively Impact Your Health. Significant events continue to occur throughout our lives. As you explore the Significant Life Events in your life, the Holmes and Rahe Stress Scale suggests a strong correlation between life events and illnesses. This scale lists 43 life events based on a relative score. It was developed in 1967 by psychiatrists Thomas Holmes and Richard Rahe to determine whether stressful events might cause illnesses. [6, 7] Not only is it helpful to determine your score to be aware of stress levels, but it may also provide you insights into some significant life events that you have not yet considered important. As mentioned previously, these significant events can lead to developing underlying beliefs and patterns that can negatively impact the fulfilling, abundant life that you want to lead.

HOLMES / RAHE SOCIAL READJUSTMENT RATING SCALE. The sum of the life change units of the applicable events in the past year of an individual's life gives a rough estimate of how stress affects health. If you have two of the same life events, double the life change units.

Life event	Life change units
Death of a spouse	100
Divorce	73
Marital separation	65
Imprisonment	63
Death of a close family member	63
Personal injury or illness	53
Marriage	50
Dismissal from work	47
Marital reconciliation	45
Retirement	45
Change in health of family member	44
Pregnancy	40
Sexual difficulties	39
Gain a new family member	39
Business readjustment	39
Change in financial state	38

Death of a close friend	37
Change to a different line of work	36
Change in frequency of arguments	35
Major mortgage	32
Foreclosure of mortgage or loan	30
Change in responsibilities at work	29
Child leaving home	29
Trouble with in-laws	29
Outstanding personal achievement	28
Spouse starts or stops work	26
Beginning or end of school	26
Change in living conditions	25
Revision of personal habits	24
Trouble with boss	23
Change in working hours or conditions	20
Change in residence	20
Change in schools	20
Change in recreation	19
Change in church activities	19
Change in social activities	18
Minor mortgage or loan	17
Change in sleeping habits	16
Change in number of family reunions	15
Change in eating habits	15
Vacation	13
Major Holiday	12
Minor violation of law	11

Score of 300+: At risk of illness.

Score of 150-299: Risk of illness is moderate (reduced by 30% from the above risk).

Score <150: Only have a slight risk of illness.

The normal range is less than 150 points.

37% of respondents have health problems with 150-199 points.

50% of respondents were ill within the year, with 200-299 points

80% can experience illness within two weeks of hitting 300 points

90% of people already had a major change in health status with 350+ points.

LifeQ PRACTICE #10. 2 PARENTS' EMOTIONAL HISTORY

- *How did your parents suffer? Did they feel deprived? Individually? Together?*
- *What caused your parents' anxieties?*
- *How did your parents use their power? Or, did they feel powerless?*
- *Whom did your parents blame, if anyone? Whom did they criticize, if anyone? What were the consequences?*
- *What were your parent's ambitions? Did they have unaccomplished dreams? If so, what were they?*
- *Were they abusive physically, mentally, emotionally? To you? To each other?*
- *What about your childhood impressed others? When and for what did you receive praise? Were your parents proud of you?*

Often, children take on the legacy of their parents. They either imitate or rebel against their beliefs and actions. Think back over your responses to the questions above.

- *Do you feel or act the same way as your parents did?*
- *Are there any situations in which you are rebelling against the beliefs and actions of your parents?*

LifeQ PRACTICE # 10.3

Now that you were able to go back and refresh your memory, think of moments when you felt pain due to an event you experienced. What are your most significant events?

LifeQ PRACTICE #10.4

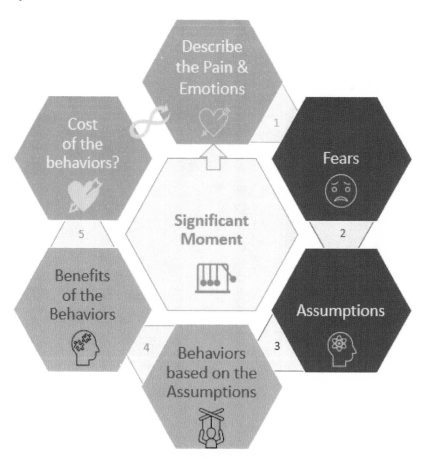

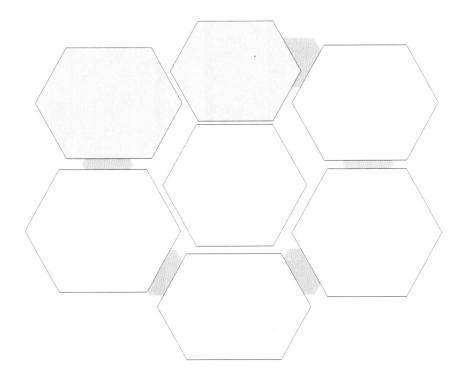

LifeQ PRACTICE # 10.5 NEXT WEEK'S ACTION PLAN

- What have you learned about yourself after reading this chapter?

- What actions will you take this next week to start to design the life that you want to live?

#### CHAPTER 11

DIGGING DEEPER INTO YOUR BELIEFS AND PATTERNS

It is easy to overlook the power of self-limiting beliefs and spend years wondering why you cannot seem to move forward and make lasting changes in your life. Though you might have grand dreams of living a more abundant life, limiting beliefs will keep prodding you to act in ways that are counterproductive to those dreams. Everything you do—and don't do—is based on an internal set of subconscious beliefs. In some situations, these beliefs can be helpful, but they can also cause huge problems by placing limitations where none exists. For example, if you hold a subconscious belief that you do not have what it takes to create a successful career, you will find yourself taking jobs that offer little opportunity for promotion, advancement, or even satisfaction. No matter how badly you want to experience more success in your career, you will continue to think and act in ways that make it impossible to do so.

"With all my baggage, I'll never get there!"

Self-limiting beliefs can be difficult to change because you often do not realize they exist. They reside in the subconscious mind and rarely make themselves known in obvious ways. You usually become aware of them when you decide to make changes in your life and keep bumping up against invisible walls. The subconscious mind is much more powerful than the conscious mind, and it is the subconscious that shapes how you live your life. The subconscious mind operates at 40 million bits of data per second, whereas the conscious mind processes at only 40 bits per second. [1]

In Niki's story, you will see how self-limiting beliefs can be passed from one generation to the next without awareness. Once you become aware of your beliefs, you can take positive steps to change your behavior for a more abundant life and higher *LifeQ*.

Niki's story:

Niki was perplexed as she left her boss's office. Niki's boss, Augustine, once again gave her a glowing annual performance review. Augustine praised Niki for doing work that exceeded expectations and for volunteering for extra assignments. One question that stunned Niki was when Augustine asked Niki if she was enjoying her job. Augustine said he was concerned about Niki's long hours at the office. She was usually the first person to arrive and last to leave. Niki had never thought about whether she enjoyed her job.

As Niki pondered the question, she realized that she had always worked very long hours. She had a fear of losing her job and running out of money. Frequently, she could imagine her mother's voice saying, "Money doesn't grow on trees and always save for a rainy day." Niki's grandmother had been a child during the Great Depression and told endless stories about breadlines and poverty. Granny still bought day-old bread and continuously talked about not having enough money. Niki realized she was living her life through the scarcity lens of her grandmother and mother. By examining the root cause of her beliefs and patterns, Niki realized she was not enjoying her job as much as she could. She decided to embrace an abundance mindset. Niki decided to work more efficiently and leave the office on time a few days per week. She even began tipping more generously for outstanding service. Within a month, Niki noticed she was enjoying her job as well as her time away from the office.

What do underlying patterns and self-limiting beliefs have in common?

Underlying patterns and self-limiting beliefs are intertwined and serve to reinforce each other. It is a matter of which came first, the chicken or the egg. The diagram on p.180 illustrates this sequence of developing patterns from your beliefs. It is a continuous cycle that can start at any point.

Niki's Beliefs, Emotions, Actions, and Results could be:

- **Beliefs:** Money is scarce, and poverty is real

- **Emotions:** Fear of failure, fear of losing her job, fear of going broke

- **Actions:** Worked very long hours, did extra work, exceeded expectations at work

- **Results:** Did not enjoy her job, had few extracurricular activities

An easy way to remember this vital sequence for developing patterns is by using the word "BEAR," which incorporates the first initial of each word: **B**eliefs, **E**motions, **A**ctions, and **R**esults.

It is crucial to figure out what kind of limiting beliefs you suspect you may have. Asking specific questions and writing down your answers can be an illuminating way to find out.

CREATING PATTERNS

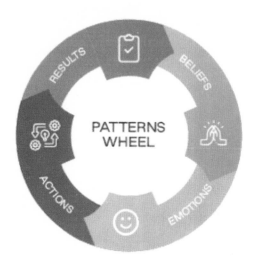

Below are some questions to help you begin understanding your self-limiting beliefs.

What are your self-limiting beliefs?

Self-limiting beliefs are often subconscious beliefs that can block you from making a career move, falling in love, and taking charge of your health. They limit your *LifeQ* Abundance Score. You may not consciously realize these beliefs are holding you hostage and preventing you from creating the life story that you want. What are your most potent self-limiting beliefs? Consider the common beliefs listed below and check the ones you see operating in your life.

- I am too old.

- I am not smart enough.

- I am not worthy or enough.

- Relationships take my freedom.

- Lovers always leave/cheat on me.

- I have already tried everything.

- I do not have enough education.
- It is selfish of me to want more.
- I do not feel that I deserve it.
- I am afraid of trying and failing.

- I do not have the willpower.
- All the good ones are taken.
- I am not lucky. I never win.
- I must have money to make money.

Do some of these self-limiting beliefs resonate more strongly with you than the others? By becoming aware of your most profound subconscious beliefs, you can begin the process of shining light on them and exposing how they affect your thoughts and behavior patterns. Once you have identified a limiting belief, write it down like these examples. Shine a light on it!

- *I don't feel that I deserve a healthy, loving relationship, so I will never have one.*

- *I am not smart enough, so I will never have a better career than I do now.*

- *I do not have the willpower, so I will never be able to lose weight.*

- *I am afraid of trying and failing, so I will never make more money than I do now.*

As you write down your answers, you will most likely notice some limiting beliefs popping up in your responses. For example, when you answered the question about why you are not yet making the amount of money you desire, your answer might have been, *"I'm earning as much as I can at my current job, and there are no other prospects for me to get a better job right now."* As much as that might appear to be accurate, it is a limiting belief. In other words, you *think* it is true, but it is merely your perception. The problem is that your perceptions and your actions make it real. Perhaps you are not happy with your weight and health. Your self-limiting belief is that *"I do not have time to exercise."* Again, when you *think* it is true, you are harboring a self-limiting belief, and it is governing your behavior.

Self-limiting beliefs often become mantras that you repeat in stressful situations.

We often learn self-limiting beliefs early in life. Before the age of 16, most adults have heard "No" or "You can't do that," more than 148,000 times. You may find that you frequently say, "I can't do that," or "it's too late," or "I should have done it sooner."

Think about your self-talk as you look for a parking spot when you are running late for a meeting: *"I'll never find a parking place,"* or *"I should have planned better,"* or *"This always happens to me,"* or *"I'll never get my act together."* [2] Think about how this affects your behavior. You may drive recklessly. You cannot concentrate during the meeting. You cannot stop thinking that others are judging your tardiness. As a result, you do not bring up that great idea you had on the way to the meeting.

HOW CAN YOU CHANGE YOUR SELF-LIMITING BELIEFS?

Four ways to change your self-limiting beliefs are:

- Change your self-talk

- Reverse the curve

- Say thanks, but no thanks

- Visualize and energize

Change Your Self-Talk— "Up Until Now…"

One way is to say to yourself, "Up until now…this may have been true, but not now. Now, this is true…" For example, "Up until now, I have been unable to control my weight. Now I can eat healthily and reach my ideal weight." Your subconscious learns that the past no longer is in power. You are free to choose a new life and a new future!

Reverse the Curve

Tell yourself that you no longer choose to believe that way and that from now on, you will look for evidence that shows that the contrary is true. You can begin believing in the opposite. For example, if you used to think, "I am unlucky, and nothing good ever happens to me," look for "facts" that are evidence that you *are* lucky and good things *do* happen to you. To change your beliefs, open your mind, and start searching for the facts that support the opposite beliefs—the ones that are not limiting.

"Thanks, but No Thanks"

Realize that self-limiting belief often take the forms of *I have, I can't,* and *I don't.* Examples are: *"I have so many problems." "I can't do that." "My upbringing won't let me." "I don't know how." "I'm not attractive enough."* Once you realize this, you can replace it with a positive declaration of what you want. Try mentally adding, "Thank you for sharing...." before stating your new belief. By thanking your mind for its input, you disarm your perception of danger, helping replace your self-limiting belief with a unique view that supports what you want.

Some examples of "Thanks, but No Thanks" include:

- "I have so many problems" becomes "Thank you for sharing, but what I ***really*** believe is that all the help I need to resolve my problems is finding its way to me now."

- "I can't do that" becomes "Thank you for sharing, but what I ***really*** believe is that I can do that when I'm ready, and I'm getting more prepared to do that every day."

- "My upbringing won't let me" becomes, "Thank you for sharing, but what I ***really*** believe is that even though I was taught not to do that, it makes sense to decide for myself whether I should do it or not.

- "I don't know how" becomes, "Thank you for sharing. I may not know how to do that, but I'm going to ask more questions and to learn."

- "I'm not attractive enough" becomes "Thank you for sharing. I take pride in my appearance and am going to do things to improve it."

Visualize and Energize

Another way to alter your self-limiting thoughts is to make a list of your self-limiting beliefs, perform a visualization exercise daily, and imagine the opposite is true. For example, visualize yourself accepting a great new job or discovering unexpected opportunities to boost your income.

Visualization can be a powerful tool for changing self-limiting beliefs because the visualization process speaks directly to the subconscious mind and plants empowering messages that can override the limiting beliefs. Before you begin the visualization process, it is a good idea to figure out what kind of limiting beliefs you suspect you may have. It will take time and consistent effort to change your belief into what is possible. However, the more you focus on consciously believing in the possibilities, the more you will begin to let go of your inner limitations and open to better circumstances. A significant part of this process is that you do not need to know "how" something is possible. You simply need to be willing to believe it is, and that is often enough to attract new opportunities.

BE MINDFUL! DON'T MAKE YOUR HISTORY YOUR DESTINY

Do not hang onto decisions, beliefs, or events that are negative. It is time to create new choices and beliefs.

What you think is what you get.

How you think is everything. Your thoughts drive your actions. Your minds, both your conscious and subconscious, are critical to success and a higher *LifeQ*. You become what you think about. Thoughts become real!

Throughout history, philosophers, historians, and even poets have written about the power of the mind. The Bible proclaims, "All things are possible to him that believes it." Even 2,500 years ago, Buddha said, "All that we are is the result of what we have thought." [3] Norman Vincent Peele said, "Change your thoughts, and you change your life. If you think in negative thoughts, you will get negative results; if you think in positive terms, you will achieve positive results. In three words 'believe and succeed.'" [4] William James, the first great modern philosopher of the subconscious, wrote, "The greatest discovery of my generation is that human beings can alter their lives by altering their attitudes of mind. If you wish to be rich, you will be rich. If you wish to be learned, you will be learned. If you wish to be good, you will be good. You must really wish these things and wish these exclusively." [5] Ralph Waldo Emerson stated, "A man is what he thinks about all day long" and "The ancestor of every action is thought." [6] Henry Ford, visionary leader, inventor said, "Whether you think you can or think you can't, you're right." [7]

Your thoughts determine your character, your career, your everyday life. If you do not have goals and your thoughts are confused and full of fear and doubts, your life becomes full of fear, anxiety, and doubts.

Use Your Conscious and Subconscious Mind

The Magic of Believing by Claude Bristol is an excellent resource for understanding the power of your mind. Bristol wrote about the importance of both your conscious and subconscious mind in reaching goals. Your conscious mind is the source of *thought*, and your subconscious is the source of *power*. Your subconscious works while you are awake and asleep. It can fast-forward and see you already being successful! Bristol said powers of the subconscious include intuition, emotion, inspiration, imagination, organization, memory, and dynamic energy. The subconscious mind assimilates all that is needed for you to reach success. You simply need to keep focused on the goal without "letting-up," no matter how long it takes. Patience and focus are essential.

It's No Joke!

An important point about our subconscious is that it does not have a sense of humor. It can't take a joke! Every time your conscious mind says, "I can't do that" or "That's too hard," our subconscious mind says, "You're right!" Every negative thought you have becomes a goal. If you say, "I'll never be promoted," or "I'll never finish college," or "I'll never find love," your subconscious says, "That's right." [8]

Managing Your Thoughts Is Key to Achieving Peace and Happiness

Unmanaged thoughts lead to tension, conflict, and stress. Managing your thoughts leads to confidence, strength, security, and serenity. Dr. Bruce Lipton, a research scientist, believes that if you positively interpret things, you start living a healthier and better-quality life, regardless of your genetic makeup. A new attitude, positive or negative, sends messages to the cells in your body and can reprogram cellular health and behavior. Positive thoughts can even change the cellular structure, turning diseased cells into healthy ones. [9]

Meditation, hypnotherapy, exercise, drug therapies, and prayer are becoming mainstream approaches to integrated health. Another useful strategy is examining your perception of stressful events. Have you noticed how people can experience the same stressful event and have different reactions to it? Two people can be stuck in the same traffic jam. One goes into road rage, and the other remains calm. The impact of stress can be how you *process* the stress you experience. Adele and Barbra Streisand experience stage fright before performing, while Bruce Springsteen considers the warm-up music before his concert his "get ready music!"

The 5.6 Positive Principle

Optimism is a critical part of a positive mental attitude. Negative thoughts can be compelling, getting in the way of progress toward meeting goals, and achieving success. Research performed by academics Emily Heaphy and Marcial Losada indicated that for every negative comment, it takes 5.6 positive ones to overcome its impact. That is, nearly **six positive** comments for every negative one! Negative thoughts and words can affect your success and lower your *LifeQ* score.[10] See *LifeQ* **PRACTICE #9.1** "Assess Your Outlook," illustrates your outlook about your life – optimistic or pessimistic.

Optimism is Advantageous!

Did you know optimists live on average two years longer than pessimists? Optimists see opportunities on the horizon, while pessimists often keep their heads and eyes focused downward. One way to turn from being pessimistic to optimistic is to change your self-talk. If you tend to be pessimistic, wear a rubber band around your wrist. When you start thinking or saying negative things, immediately say "Cancel!" and snap the rubber band. Optimism and enthusiasm can be contagious. Share with a friend!

FEARS AND WORRIES: DEVELOP AWARENESS AND GRATITUDE

A still mind can assess a situation more accurately than one that is anxious, and therefore is less likely to overlook a present danger or miss an opportunity. By understanding the power of your fears and worries, you can begin to limit their destructive hold on you as you strive for abundance and fulfillment.

THE POWER OF FEAR

Since the beginning of time, people have feared every imaginable thing. *Fear* is an unpleasant emotion caused by the belief that someone or something is dangerous, likely to cause pain or a threat. [11] It is natural to resist straying too far out of your comfort zone because of fear of the consequences of doing so. Fear underpins your beliefs and thoughts and interferes with your happiness. Anxiety may make you reluctant to act and make changes that carry risk. However, if you live your life this way, you are likely to miss out on many things that you would like to include in your life. Do not let fear hold you back.

Asking your boss for a raise or speaking up in a meeting or asking someone you admire on a date all involve risks of some kind. All can raise fears of rejection or embarrassment. All carry the possibility of great reward. Common fears include:

- *Fear of failure* keeps you from trying.

- *Fear of success* sabotages your every effort.

- *Fear of looking foolish* keeps you from speaking up.

- *Fear of speaking* keeps others from seeing your brilliance.

- *Fear of loneliness* pushes you into unhealthy relationships.

These fears can elicit negative feelings of disappointment, frustration, regret, and shame. Having fears can also cause you to become so preoccupied with what you don't want that you may attract the wrong results. You can become paralyzed by your fears, find yourself playing it safe to avoid achieving your feared result and settle for something much less than the life you are capable of having. Interestingly, you learn most of your fears. The only fears you were born with are fear of loud noises, fear of bright lights, and fear of falling. [12]

The antidote to fear is love, self-love, self-respect, and courage. Acting with courage in a fearful situation is a technique that boosts your regard for yourself to such a degree that your fears subside and lose their ability to affect your behavior, your decisions and undermine your happiness.

Everyone is afraid of something. It is normal to be concerned about your physical, financial, and emotional safety. It may give you the courage to ask yourself, "What have I got to lose? What is the worst thing that can happen? Will I lose money? Job? Relationships? Prestige?" Then think of everything that you could do to make sure that the very worst does not occur. A courageous person is not an unafraid person. As Mark Twain said, "Courage is resistance to fear, mastery of fear—not absence of fear." [13] Courage is being afraid and doing it anyway. Wayne Gretzky, the ice hockey star, said, "You miss 100% of the shots you don't take!"[14]

DALE CARNEGIE TECHNIQUE FOR CONQUERING FEAR-BASED THOUGHTS

Dale Carnegie was an American writer from the last century who lectured about self-improvement and interpersonal relationships. His ideas and books are timeless, especially *How To Win Friends And Influence People.* Carnegie recommended that when you have fear-based thoughts, try automatic writing. *Automatic writing* is a process of writing without conscious planning or thinking. You just let the words flow without censoring or editing yourself. This robust process enables you to bypass your conscious mind and connect with more potent, subconscious thoughts that could be triggering your fear. [15]

Although these consequences would not be fun to experience, you could undoubtedly handle them if they occur. Carnegie suggests that you accept the worst possible consequences you think could happen, and then decide to move forward anyway. This technique can be incredibly empowering because you reduce the size and magnitude of your fear by realizing that you can handle the things you would otherwise avoid. When you consider that the worst-case scenario is dying and you are alive, you will find a way to deal with life's challenges.

Worrying is a Pattern that Prohibits Mindfulness and Lowers Your *LifeQ.*

Worrying is like praying for what you do not want. Mindfulness is difficult to achieve when you are worrying. Worrying can negatively affect your *LifeQ* in all areas. Since mindfulness includes being fully aware of what is occurring in the present moment by acknowledging and accepting your feelings, thoughts, and body sensations, worrying about the future prohibits you from living in the present. "Worry does not empty tomorrow of its sorrow. It empties today of its strength," author Corrie Ten Boom wrote in *The Hiding Place.* [16]

In his book *The Little Book of Letting Go,* Hugh Prather calls worry "mental debris" or "a mental pollutant." Although Prather believes that worry is natural, he says so are tooth decay, accidents, and jealousy, but that does not mean worry is useful or beneficial. Worry "fragments the mind, shatters focus, distorts perspective, and destroys inner peace." As Prather explains, just because you tend to worry, does not mean you have to feed or nourish that tendency. [17]

The word *worry* comes from the Greek word for a divided mind. Worry of any kind is hazardous to your health. Among other effects, researchers believe that people who worry are, on average, 2.5 times more likely to develop Alzheimer's than more carefree folks. There is a saying: "Worry is like a rocking chair: it gives you something to do but never gets you anywhere." [18] There is wisdom in Winston Churchill's quote, "Let our advance worrying become advance thinking and planning."[19] See *LifeQ* **PRACTICE #11.3 Exercise To Stop Worrying**

WHAT'S NEXT?

The next step is to explore your Self-Esteem. In the upcoming chapter, you will discover your level of self-esteem and the benefits of healthy self-esteem. We will provide you with proven tips for enhancing your confidence and self-esteem. Healthy Self-Esteem is an essential element of being able to have a high LifeQ.

CHAPTER 11 *LifeQ*-TIPS AND CHAPTER RECAP

- Remember **BEAR** for Creating Patterns—**B**eliefs, **E**motions, **A**ctions, **R**esults.

- Practice living in abundance and gratitude. Make it a way of life.

- Your presence is a present. A gift you can give a person is to be fully present.

- Focus on your strengths and accomplishments. Your beliefs impact your behavior and how successful you are at achieving your goals. Beware of negative self-talk. Humans tend to dwell on their weaknesses and limitations. As a result, they often settle for far less than they can achieve.

- The first step in changing patterns is to *realize they exist.* Remember that your mind plays a huge role in creating your life story.

- For changing self-limiting thoughts, one way is to say to yourself, "Up until now...this may have been true, but not now. Now, this is true..."

- Visualization can be a powerful tool for changing limiting beliefs. The antidote to fear is love, self-love, self-respect, and acting with courage.

- Worrying is a pattern that inhibits mindfulness and lowers your *LifeQ*. Take steps today to decrease your worrying about the future.

LifeQ PRACTICE # 11.1

DO YOUR BELIEFS HARM YOUR LIFE STORY?

Age	Work	Success	Failure
Money	Stability	Risk	Relationships
Friends	Marriage	Children	Love/Self Love
Sex	Dreams	Spirituality	Happiness
Family	Fun	Body	Freedom
Education			

Choose 3 of the areas (above) that you believe have a negative effect on your life story.

Answer these questions:

- *My limiting/negative belief is* _____

- *Who or what influenced you? How did you form it (based on which experiences)?*

- *What is this belief costing you daily?*

- *What will holding on to this belief mean for you in the long term?*

- *If you could eliminate this belief, what could be the substantial benefits to you?*

- *Turn the negative belief into a positive statement, write it down. The turnaround statement that affirms or permits me to do this is:*

- *Write down three action steps you will take to change this belief.*

LifeQ **PRACTICE #11. 2 Write About A Fear You May Have.**

- *I feel afraid because . . ."*

- *What is the worst thing that could happen?* If you ask for a raise, your boss might say no.

- *And then what will you do and feel?* You might feel powerless and like a victim or this answer might propel you to take action: learn new skills, start a business, look for a new job.

LifeQ **PRACTICE # 11.3**

EXERCISE TO STOP WORRYING AND INCREASE YOUR AWARENESS

Bring Yourself into the Present Moment

Close your eyes, slowly breathe in and out 10 times, mentally counting each out-breath (breathe in, breathe out, and mentally count: "1, 2, 3, 4, and so on). Once you complete the count, open your eyes, and follow the steps below.

- Make a written list of your worries, fears, and doubts.

- Describe the worst-case scenario.

- Cross out the worries that are not likely to happen. Do not waste your energy on them!

- Then score items on your list (1 = not really problem, 10 = life-threatening issue).

- Decide that it is time to face a few of your worries, fears, or doubts. What has been the cost of these fears to you, and what are the benefits of facing them?

For any item higher than a five, write three possible solutions. **See example below:** What are your worries, fears, doubts?	Describe the worst-case scenario.	How likely is this to happen? 0 = not likely 10 = a real issue	What is the cost of this belief to you? How is this holding you back?	What benefits would you gain if you faced this fear?	How will you face the fear? Write 3 Action Steps
Critics will ridicule me once I finish my book	*I finish the book, and nobody wants to publish it, and if they do nobody wants to read it*	6	*Make excuses not to write every day. Cannot sleep, worry, resentment Smoke, over-eat, eat unhealthy food, drink too much*	*Honor my passion and purpose Be at Peace Make more money. Clarity Joy*	*I will write for ½ hour every day. I will increase to an hour after three months. Read a book on developing characters Join a book writing group*

LifeQ PRACTICE # 11.4

- **NOW ask yourself:** *Who or what triggers your worries?* Usually, it is our negative self-talk, but sometimes a relative, friend, or coworker cannot resist saying things that make us question our competence. "You always freak out when it comes to deadlines."

"You always freeze when giving presentations." "You are so disorganized." Minimize your time with them. If that is not practical, make a list of the people and their comments that make you question yourself. When one of these people makes a derogatory comment, give yourself a point for recognizing their patterns.

- Review the "Worry List" that you created in Step 1 above. Change the "Worry List" to a third-person voice. "He is worried about botching his presentation." This third-person gives you an emotional distance to see your worries more clearly. There is no self-judgment because it is as if you are thinking about someone else. By taking the "I" out of the sentence, it is much easier to come up with a solution.

- Put a checkmark by the worries that you cannot control. Try reciting the Serenity Prayer for help in accepting things you cannot change. *"God, grant me the serenity to accept the things I cannot change, Courage to change the things I can, And the wisdom to know the difference."*

- Choose a daily "worry time" of no more than 15 minutes. When worries creep up, say to yourself, "I will worry about that between 7:15-7:30 p.m." Deliberately turn your attention to something else until it is "worry time." Ensure you will not be interrupted and not close to bedtime.

- Don't complain about how worried you are. It reinforces the worry, and no one wants to hear about it.

- Look at your original and edited "Worry Lists" and see whether you tend to exaggerate negative issues and minimize positive ones. Do you tend to overreact and over-worry?

- Do not set yourself up for failure by expecting to be worry-free. Now you have a record of your worries, you can see the patterns, you can accept the worries you cannot control, and you can better manage those you can. As Mark Twain reminded us, *"I am an old man, and I have known a great many troubles, but most of them never happened."*

LifeQ PRACTICE #11.5 NEXT WEEK'S ACTION PLAN

- What have you learned about yourself after reading this chapter?

- What actions will you take this next week to start to design the life that you want to live?

CHAPTER 12

BOOST YOUR SELF-ESTEEM

Raising your self-awareness can positively affect your self-esteem. *Self-esteem* refers to how well you think of and value yourself, how much you are worth in your own eyes, and the power you allow yourself to have. It is your reputation with yourself. Your level of self-esteem affects your interactions with everyone in your life, most especially "you." Everything you think, say, and do influences your self-esteem in some way. Self-esteem closely intertwines with your patterns, underlying beliefs, and ability to live your most fulfilling life story with a high **LifeQ**. Aristotle defined true happiness as the "expression of the soul in considered actions." You must look at the actions and experiences that have formed and continue to create "you."

WHAT IS SELF-ESTEEM?

Matthew McKay, a psychologist, describes *self-esteem* as: "One of the main factors differentiating humans from other animals is the awareness of self; the ability to form an identity and then attach a value to it. In other words, you can define who you are and then decide if you like the identity or not." [1]

Self-esteem is a state of mind; it is the way you think and feel about yourself. People with high self-esteem possess feelings of confidence, worthiness, and positive self-regard. These individuals feel good about themselves, and they feel a sense of belonging and security. Aside from respecting themselves, they appreciate others as well. Success in life is often attributed to those with a strong sense of self because they feel confident taking on challenges and risking failure to achieve what they want. These individuals have more energy for positive pursuits because they do not expend their energy on negative emotions, feelings of inferiority, or working hard to take care of or to please others at the expense of their self-care.

As you read about Caroline's and Mike's encounters, think about whether you have had similar events that occur in your life.

> ### *Caroline and Mike's story:*
>
> *Caroline and Mike are sister and brother. Their father was a strict, critical man, and their mother seemed afraid of her shadow. Throughout their childhood, Caroline and Mike felt they rarely did anything "right." If they did not ace a school exam, their father insisted on knowing who the stand-out students were and which questions Caroline and Mike missed. There were rarely any rewards or positive responses when either of them did well in anything.*
>
> *Caroline and Mike are adults now. Caroline lives her life with her father's voice, always in her mind telling her that she is "not good enough," "not smart enough," and "will never amount to anything." Sometimes she hears her father's critical words coming out of her as she speaks to her children. Caroline's low self-esteem has prevented her from applying for promotions, setting many personal goals for herself, and taking risks to try new things.*
>
> *On the other hand, when Mike realized that he was sabotaging his success and happiness, he sought coaching with us. He discovered how his low self-esteem was negatively affecting his marriage, his child-rearing, and his career. Through hard work, Mike was able to uncover where that negative self-talk originated in his childhood. Once he discovered the source of his self-sabotage, Mike took steps to learn techniques that helped him work toward obtaining and maintaining a positive sense of self. Today, Mike is living joyfully with a high **LifeQ**. He is filled with gratitude for his excellent health and feels successful and fulfilled in his family life and his career.*

It is easy to see that people like Caroline might find it challenging to succeed in their endeavors because of the constant feelings of inferiority and worthlessness. Be cautious not to confuse self-esteem with arrogance. Self-esteem is an awareness of what you are worth and that you are deserving of good things; there are many contributing factors to your self-esteem, none of which is arrogance or conceit.

Self-Esteem Has Many Factors

The amount of self-esteem you have depends on many factors. Your parents' attitudes, your teachers' feedback, and your life experiences all play an integral part in your self-esteem. Race, religion, the media, culture, and your gender also may influence how you feel about yourself.

Caroline and Mike's constant and unsuccessful struggle to make their father proud played a significant role in forming their inner selves. Caroline's inability to take chances and Mike's poor relationship with his children are direct results of how their father drilled their inadequacy into their conscious and subconscious minds. Likewise, their mother's passivity just strengthened the idea that father knew best. Sometimes adults lose self-esteem and feel bad about themselves because of failures or disappointments in life or because of the way others in their lives have treated them.

It is essential to know that you can strengthen your self-esteem at any time in life. All you need to do is decide to do so. Ideally, healthy self-esteem is a result of positive childhood experiences. However, if your self-esteem needs bolstering, begin by examining where your negative feelings originated.

What Causes Low Self-Esteem?

When you experience negative emotional responses to experiences from your past, you can develop low self-esteem. Criticism, teasing, punishment and abuse, poverty, economic deprivation, and failure in school can impact your feelings of self-worth.

"I'm not sure I'm the right one to be living my life!"

The extent to which you value or believe in yourself begins early in life. Growing up hearing that you are not working hard enough, you are not talented enough, or that everything you do is subpar can create significant thought patterns that form habits of thinking—your beliefs. Before long, you begin to think in ways that limit your growth and self-development, and you begin to doubt yourself and feel dissatisfied. You can become afraid to accept challenges because you believe that you cannot accomplish anything meaningful. You start to think that you are unworthy; even when you do accomplish extraordinary things, you may brush the achievement aside and chalk it up to good luck. The deeper these thought patterns take root, the lower your self-esteem falls, until you cannot envision what it is like to feel good about yourself.

As you read about Marilyn's experiences, think about where you may see yourself in her story.

> ### Marilyn's story:
>
> *Marilyn is a talented, professional woman who works for a large bank in San Francisco. Susan met her at a conference and was immediately impressed by her intelligence, education, professionalism, and likeability. As Susan introduced herself, she told Marilyn that she enjoyed meeting women who are the "full package"—women with intelligence, personality, and who present themselves so well. Marilyn seemed surprised by the compliment and confessed that her body felt like Swiss cheese. "Whenever I receive a compliment like yours, it goes straight through the holes in my Swiss cheese and doesn't stick. I cannot accept it." Susan asked how her husband and kids felt when she does not accept their positive compliments and love. Marilyn said that "They don't like it and have almost stopped saying such things." Marilyn's honesty in revealing her feelings about not being able to accept compliments impressed Susan. She encouraged Marilyn to seek professional help to increase her self-esteem for the sake of Marilyn as well as her family and friends.*

So many people have been cautioned since childhood not to be egotistical or proud. Because of that upbringing, there is a tendency to negate a compliment when one comes their way. Marilyn could benefit from reflecting on where this attitude originated. In doing so, she might be able to locate the source of her "Swiss-cheese-ness" and realize that not accepting a compliment is a bit of an affront to the person who gives it. When someone is thoughtful enough to stop what he or she is doing and recognize something about you, you owe it to that person to appreciate and accept the praise. Remember that receiving a compliment does not mean that you are taking an ad out in the *New York Times* telling everyone how great you are. You are merely saying "thank you" and bumping up your self-esteem at the same time.

At the end of this chapter are several *LifeQ* **PRACTICES** to help you become more aware of your self-esteem level, including an instrument from *In the Company of Women*. Special thanks to Dr. Pat Heim, Susan's co-author from *In the Company of Women*, for granting permission to use the Self-Esteem tool. [2]

HOW DO YOU EVALUATE YOUR SELF-ESTEEM?

When you evaluate the level of your self-esteem, look at intrinsic qualities, such as whether you believe you are a useful person, how much you trust yourself, and how self-satisfied you feel. Are you pleased or unhappy about what you have accomplished in your life so far? How well do you relate to others? How comfortably do you accept responsibility for your actions? You cannot define who you are in a vacuum. You do so through a world of cues that give you feedback about how the world sees you. It is hard to hold a positive self-image if those around you send negative messages—even if they are wrong. Sometimes people will intentionally try to make you feel bad about yourself. Once you accept their opinion of you, your sense of self-esteem may take an accelerating downward spiral.

What Are the Benefits of Having a Healthy Self-Esteem?

There are many rewards for developing a healthy self-esteem level. These include:

- Being able to pursue your dreams and desires with energy and focus

- Not being held back by fears and insecurities

- Feeling empowered to take risks

- Feeling able to surround yourself with positive, supportive people and relationships

- Making good choices and reaching your goals.

Disguised Low Self-Esteem

Low self-esteem is sometimes hidden by other behaviors used to compensate for the deeper-rooted, more painful feelings you may wish to avoid. These behavior patterns may shield you from underlying feelings of sadness, inferiority, self-hatred, fear, or insecurity. They allow you to compensate for these unacceptable or painful feelings by giving you a false sense of being "okay" or "right" or "better" than those around you. Low self-esteem often masks itself through behaviors including:

- "Know-it-all" behavior, a false front of superiority
- Perfectionism
- Being a control fanatic
- Bullying
- Being too nice
- Boastful or attention-seeking behavior
- Jealousy
- Hyper-critical behavior
- Addictions to alcohol, drugs, food
- Anger

HOW TO INCREASE YOUR SELF-ESTEEM

There are several ways to increase your self-esteem. These include:

- Groom daily, exercise, de-clutter,
- Challenge yourself and increase competence.
- Avoid perfectionism.
- Stop your inner critic and improve your positive self-talk.
- Stay away from "Hoover" people.
- Use positive body language.
- "Let go."
- Find your sense of humor.

- Develop an attitude of gratitude.

- Reject the impostor phenomenon.

- Practice forgiveness.

Start with these obvious, but essential steps to increase your self-esteem:

◘ **Groom** even if working from home. You will feel successful, respectable, and ready to take on anything the day might bring.

◘ **Exercise regularly** to relieve stress, increase energy, improve memory, boost confidence, and stimulate the production of endorphins that are mood elevators.

◘ **Clear the clutter.** The Feng Shui definition for clutter is "postponed decisions and the inability to move forward." Clutter can keep you from making progress.

- **Challenge yourself and increase your competence.** *"The secret of getting ahead is getting started. The secret of getting started is breaking your complex overwhelming tasks into small manageable tasks, and then starting on the first one."– Mark Twain*

How do you do that? By exploring and practicing. You can start small, and once you succeed; you imprint a victory in your neural pathways as a new habit and belief about yourself. Small wins will make you feel good, and they add up to big achievements.

- **Avoid perfectionism.**

Perfectionism is destructive and impossible to achieve. A few steps to overcome it:

◘ **Make mistakes and learn from them.** *"A person who never made a mistake never tried anything new."- Albert Einstein* What is one thing I can learn from this? What is one opportunity I can find in this situation? What can I be grateful for now?

- ☐ **Treat yourself the way you would your child or pet.** Learn to be kind and compassionate with yourself. Put a statute of limitations on your mistakes.

- **Say "Stop!" to your inner critic and Increase your Positive Self-Talk**

"We become what we think about." – *Earl Nightingale* It is easy to find comfort in negative self-talk, and a surprising 77% of self-talk is negative. Dr. Shad Helmstedder's research suggests that by the time people reach 16 years of age, they have heard "no" and "you can't do that" 148,000 times. [3] We recommend wearing a rubber band around your wrist and snapping it when you say anything negative about yourself like, "You're always late. No wonder you can't find a parking space." or "You won't get this promotion, so don't even try." Self-esteem is fragile and is easily damaged. When you hear yourself using negative self-talk, consider saying, "Thanks for your input, but I'm not interested!"

- **Stay Away from "Hoover" People**

"Keep away from people who try to belittle your ambitions. Small people always do that, but the really great make you feel that you, too, can become great." – *Mark Twain*

Although we discussed "Hoover people" in earlier chapters, it bears repeating the discussion. No doubt, you have met some of these folks over the years. We named them "Hoover" in honor of the extraordinary, powerful, and best vacuum cleaner by that name. They are the ones who, regardless of how great things might be going, can always find the dark cloud. Imagine that you have just walked into work after a great weekend. You had a promising date, you went for a run and caught up with an old friend, and you saw that movie you'd been dying to see. You are beaming with positivity, ready to take on the workweek until Ms. Hoover comes along. When she hears about your weekend, she convinces you that your date was not nearly as interested as you initially thought. Next, she tells you that your new car is not very economical after all and questions how you could spend your hard-earned money on that ridiculous movie. Suddenly, your "I'm-ready-to-take-on-the-week" persona has devolved into feeling like the dirt and dust at the bottom of the vacuum cleaner bag.

You must not allow Hoover people to suck your positivity out of you. Often, they may be dealing with their self-esteem issues, or they just do not want to see anyone else happy if they are not. Remember that other people's happiness is not your responsibility. If they want to suck the excitement and joy out of life, let them do it alone.

- **Use Positive Body Language**

  Positive body language can change your thinking to positive, confident thoughts. It has become common knowledge that thoughts can change behavior, now we have found that the reverse is also true. Body language can change the way you think. Positive body language can change your self-talk, increase your testosterone level, and decrease your cortisol hormone level. For example, Toastmaster International recommends that speakers give direct eye contact to the audience plus stand straight with feet about 6 to 12 inches apart with balanced weight evenly on the balls of their feet. These actions help speakers feel anchored, balanced, and confident.

- **Let Go**

  "We cannot direct the wind, but we can adjust the sails," Dolly Parton. Letting go means acknowledging where your feelings and emotional reactions originate, accepting them, and then taking action to change yourself and your responses. Letting go of the past is not about burying it or trying to forget it. Many people

block out bad memories from the past, only to find them surfacing in later years in the form of fears, illnesses, and phobias.

- **Find your sense of humor**

  "A day without laughter is a day wasted," Charlie Chaplin. Laughing is like internal jogging, increasing your confidence and self-esteem. Some days you are the bug; other days you are the windshield. Some days you are the statue; others you are the pigeon. Laughing increases endorphins, which are 200 times more potent than morphine.

- **Develop your attitude of gratitude**

  When you acknowledge how much people have done for you or how much you have accomplished, you feel more confident. It is not happy people who are grateful; it is grateful people who are happy. Consciously focus on being grateful every day. For example, when you awaken and before falling asleep, think of several reasons to be thankful. Count your blessings.

- **Reject the Impostor Syndrome**

  The *Impostor Syndrome* (also known as impostor phenomenon or fraud syndrome) is a psychological pattern in which one doubts one's accomplishments and has a persistent internalized fear of being exposed as a "fraud." This term describes feelings of inadequacy. You believe that you lack competence, skill, or intelligence despite information that indicates that the opposite is true. Impostors have chronic self-doubt and feelings of intellectual fraudulence. It is the feeling that you are not successful, talented, and smart, and you are only pretending that you are. Some studies show that an estimated 70% of the population has felt the Impostor phenomenon at least once. [4] Even famous and very successful people experience it. Maya Angelou once said, *"I have written 11 books, but each time I think, 'Uh-oh, they're going to find out now. I've run a game on everybody, and they're going to find me out.'"*

The Impostor Syndrome occurs most frequently among high achievers, both men and women. One of its self-defeating attitudes is the fear of *"being "found out" or "unmasked" or "a fraud."* You may think, "I give the impression that I'm more competent than I am" and "I hope others won't discover there's a lot of knowledge I lack." As an "Impostor," you may believe that you do not deserve your success and the perks that come your way. You may have a persistent belief in your lack of competence, skill, or intelligence despite the strong evidence that you are competent, skillful, and intelligent.

Another self-defeating attitude is that you may think that your *"success was a fluke"* and you *"got lucky this time."* You fear that you will not be able to succeed the next. You may believe that your successes have not come from your efforts or internal abilities but rather from fate, luck, timing, charm, or having manipulated others. How do you cope with feeling like you are an Impostor? Fortunately, there are some steps you can take to deal with these impostor feelings and enable you to enjoy the highest *LifeQ* possible for you. Become aware of your thoughts. Awareness is the beginning stage of coping with Impostor Syndrome. Become mindful of your Impostor feelings as "just thoughts." Start to identify when the thoughts and feelings occur. Write your thoughts down and start to recognize they are not a reflection of your talents and skills.

If your Impostor feelings are acute, consider getting support from someone who can help you understand the difference between Impostor feelings and reality. Sharing your feelings with someone close to you can reduce your anxieties. You may begin to realize that many others feel like Impostors, too. Surround yourself with uplifting people who will support and encourage you. Make a list of uplifting people in your life and spend time with them. Recognize and celebrate your achievements. When you suffer from the Impostor Syndrome, you are usually quite critical of yourself and tend to brush off achievements. Write down your accomplishments and keep the list handy to remind you that you have achieved a lot.

Recognize when you are a minority. Impostor feelings are often prevalent in situations where there is a difference in age, education, gender, position, and resources. Pay special attention to your Impostor thoughts when you are going into such a situation, so you will not be caught off-guard. When your Impostor self begins thinking, "I'm not smart enough" or "The company made a big mistake hiring me," challenge these automatic Impostor thoughts and feelings and create more balanced ones. Counter with "This company put me through a thorough interviewing process, plus I've had years of business success."

- **Practice forgiveness**

  When someone has hurt you, it can eat away at your self-esteem, often reinforcing your feeling like an Impostor. You will probably have a lot of negative self-talk that distracts you from practicing mindfulness because you keep re-living the event that damaged you.

  When you forgive someone, you pardon the mistake or offense. Forgiveness is not a feeling; it is an act of the will. It is a decision to let go of negative emotions like anger, resentment, and thoughts of revenge. By embracing forgiveness, you allow love, peace, joy, and gratitude to enter your life and can move forward unencumbered.

  Everyone has been hurt by the words or actions of people in his or her inner circle. It could be that your unfaithful partner, your mother-in-law's criticism of your parenting skills, your best friend's spreading gossip about you, or your trusted colleague's double-crossing you in business have inflicted these wounds. When someone you care about hurts you, it is tempting to hold onto your resentment and seek revenge. However, if you do not embrace forgiveness, you may be the one who pays most dearly.

A Chinese proverb says, *"If you're going to pursue revenge, you'd better dig two graves."* In other words, your anger and resentment can destroy you.

Forgiving does not mean *forgetting* the transgression or condoning hurtful behavior. The saying "Fool me once, shame on you. Fool me twice, shame on me" applies here. Experience is the best teacher, and we do not recommend that you completely forget about being wronged. Clara Barton, the founder of the Red Cross, was reminded by a friend of a cruel thing that somebody did to her years before. Barton acted like she did not remember, and the friend asked, "Don't you remember?" Her famous reply was, "No, I distinctly remember forgetting it." [5]

What are the benefits of forgiveness? The act of forgiving can have a positive effect on your **LifeQ**. Forgiveness impacts your **SoulQ, EmotionQ, BodyQ,** and all aspects of your relationships. Forgiveness enhances your spiritual and psychological well-being and strengthens your immune system through lower levels of stress and hostility. Also, it can lead to healthier relationships and higher self-esteem. When you are holding onto grudges from past grievances, you are living in the past. You are not enjoying the present. As you will find in Yvette's story, holding onto anger and hurt prevents you from living your life with joy and abundance.

Yvette's story:

Yvette never recovered from the anger and bitterness she felt when her husband filed for divorce 40 years earlier. She lived a miserable, joyless, loveless life and died at 85 years still wearing her wedding band. She spent her days filled with hatred, jealousy, and self-pity because her husband had left her for another woman. While her ex-husband began a new life with his new bride, Yvette remained stuck in the past and never realized her life's potential.

Do you always need to confront the person who harmed you? No, sometimes it is more appropriate to forgive privately. For example, one client felt the cruelty of his parents had damaged him, and he harbored a considerable grudge that negatively impacted his life. Peter wrote a letter forgiving them for his mistreatment and flew to Scotland to their gravesites, where he read the letter out loud to them. Now, Peter has moved on and can live positively in the present. All religions preach the importance of forgiveness. The Lord's Prayer includes, *"Forgive us our trespasses as we forgive those who trespass against us."* Gandhi said, *"The weak can never forgive. Forgiveness is the attribute of the strong."*

Steps for forgiving include:

- Reflect on the situation and how you have reacted to it. How has this transgression affected your life, your health, your well-being? Make a list of the benefits of letting go of your resentment and anger. What is the value of forgiveness?

- Consider the situation from the other person's point of view. Why would he behave the way he did? Were his intentions really to harm you? Frequently, the other person did not intend to hurt you.

- Reflect on times that you have hurt others and on those who have forgiven you.

- Commit to forgive the person who has offended you.

- Choose to change your mindset from being a victim to one of having control over your situation and life. You might even find compassion for the person who has hurt you.

- If you are stuck, talk with a counselor or impartial loved one. Consider writing in a journal or meditating.

- Practice gratitude. It is difficult to be angry and grateful at the same time.

- Visualize the new life that you want. See yourself in the future as free of this suffering.

- Realize forgiveness is a process. You may need to forgive some hurts repeatedly.

- Search your heart for relationships that need forgiveness. Why not give yourself a precious gift and forgive those who have hurt you? Once you do, you will be able to focus all your energy on the present and future and create an abundant life that is your destiny.

How do you forgive yourself?

It may be yourself who needs to be forgiven by you. If so:

- Consider writing a letter to yourself and include the story of what happened. How were you and other person's feelings affected by the actions? What were your reasons for your behavior? Is there a benefit to continue to punish yourself?

- Take responsibility. "Okay, I did it. It was the best I was able to do at that time." Write about what you have learned from your experience. What are the ways to make amends? When it feels complete, read it out loud to yourself. Let yourself communicate your emotions. It is time to release this negativity to the Universe.

- The final element of forgiveness is learning what we can do differently in the future.

CONFIDENCE AND SELF-ESTEEM ARE KEYS TO SUCCESS

Leaders at NASA and Facebook realize that self-esteem and confidence are the keys to success. Even high performers like rocket scientists need a boost sometimes, so their leaders consciously instill confidence and encouragement into the corporate culture. The slogan at NASA's Jet Propulsion Lab is *"Dare Mighty Things."* Posters at Facebook headquarters read, *"What would you do if you weren't afraid?"* Good leaders know that when you feel good about yourself, you tend to be the very best person you can be. Eleanor Roosevelt said, *"No one can make you feel inferior without your permission."*

When it comes to working on your Personal Strategic Plan, it is crucial to do the planning and goal setting for the life that you want, and then to act. The Nike SWOOSH invites action with the slogan, *"Just Do It!"* It does not need to be perfect. Just Do It! When you take action, you achieve successes that build more confidence, which encourages you to achieve even more wins! Develop a mantra of *"Focus & Finish."* Do not let being perfect get in the way of being good.

WHAT'S NEXT?

*The next chapter will help you develop your strategic goals to drive your Personal Strategic Plan. We propose that by changing the word "goal" to the word "promise," you increase your chances for success in achieving what you want for your life. The adjective "SMART" stands for Specific, Measurable, Achievable, Relevant, and Timely and is critical in ensuring you accomplish your goals/promises. A template for your **LifeQ** SMART Goals is provided for you with step-by-step guidelines to design your Strategic Plan.*

CHAPTER 12: *LifeQ* -TIPS AND CHAPTER RECAP

- Your self-esteem is all in your mind. It is possible to increase your level of self-esteem at any age. The good news is that you have control over what you think and say and do.

- Your thoughts drive your behavior, and your behavior can change your thoughts.

- Ingredients of self-esteem include your sense of your value, your accomplishments, your relationship with others, your belief in your abilities, your sense of responsibility, and how others perceive you. By assessing the areas of your self-esteem, you can celebrate areas that are healthy and set goals to increase your scores in low areas.

- Behaviors like bullying may mask low self-esteem, being hyper-critical of others, controlling, and "know-it-all" behavior.

- The benefits of healthy self-esteem include being able to pursue your dreams, achieve goals that are important to you, and have a high *LifeQ* score.

- The act of forgiving has many pluses, including achieving greater spiritual and psychological well-being, more robust immune systems through lower levels of stress and hostility, healthier relationships, and higher self-esteem. When you hold onto grudges from past grievances, you are living in the past and not enjoying the present.

LifeQ PRACTICE # 12.1

Your Self-Esteem Profile from: *In the Company of Women* [6]

The following questionnaire will help you assess your self-esteem. Bear in mind that this is a snapshot of how you are feeling at this moment, not an overall assessment of who you are. Self-esteem can vary according to life events and the situations in which you find yourself. On the questionnaire below, place a checkmark in the blank that most corresponds to how accurate or inaccurate you feel each statement is at the moment.

	Not at all True				Very True
	1	2	3	4	5
1. I believe I have a number of good qualities.	___	___	___	___	___
2. When I set a goal, I reach it.	___	___	___	___	___
3. I find that I rarely can trust others.	___	___	___	___	___
4. I am very productive.	___	___	___	___	___

	Not at all True				Very True
	1	2	3	4	5
5. I have trouble saying "I'm sorry."	____	____	____	____	____
6. New people whom I meet respond positively to me.	____	____	____	____	____
7. I trust myself in a wide range of situations.	____	____	____	____	____
8. I do not feel very successful.	____	____	____	____	____
9. I am open to others, even if they are different from me.	____	____	____	____	____
10. I am able to do things as well as most people.	____	____	____	____	____
11. I accept responsibility for myself.	____	____	____	____	____
12. Others try to take advantage of me.	____	____	____	____	____
13. I wish I had more respect for myself.	____	____	____	____	____
14. My accomplishments are rarely recognized.	____	____	____	____	____
15. I like to deal with people, and they like me.	____	____	____	____	____
16. I can shape my own destiny.	____	____	____	____	____
17. My failures are generally my fault.	____	____	____	____	____
18. My co-workers treat me with respect.	____	____	____	____	____
19. I feel others are worth more than I am.	____	____	____	____	____
20. I continue to develop my capabilities.	____	____	____	____	____

	Not at all True 1	2	3	4	**Very True** 5
21. I get close to others and share.					
22. I act with self-control.					
23. I believe that the only kind of luck I have is bad luck.					
24. People at work do not have confidence in my abilities.					
25. I accept myself and my feelings.					
26. I know I can accomplish anything I choose.					
27. I'm suspicious when I get a compliment.					
28. I have difficulty making important decisions.					
29. When I make a mistake, I have trouble admitting it.					
30. My colleagues see me as a valuable member of our team.					
31. I believe I am a useful person.					
32. I wish I were able to reach more of my goals.					
33. I become defensive when others give me feedback on things I've done.					
34. I feel useless at times.					
35. I take an active role in resolving my own conflicts.					
36. Others speak negatively about me behind my back.					

	Not at all True				Very True
	1	2	3	4	5
37. My self-talk is often negative.	_____	_____	_____	_____	_____
38. I have much to be proud of.	_____	_____	_____	_____	_____
39. I am a good listener and friend.	_____	_____	_____	_____	_____
40. When I experience a setback, I find it hard to get back on track.	_____	_____	_____	_____	_____
41. I am competent to cope with and accept life's challenges.	_____	_____	_____	_____	_____
42. Others appreciate my talents, abilities, and my uniqueness.	_____	_____	_____	_____	_____

SELF - ESTEEM PROFILE SCORING

Self-esteem can be segmented into six categories: Values, Accomplishments, Relations with Others, Abilities, Responsibility/Accountability, and Others' Perception of you. To evaluate the level of your self-esteem in each of these categories, transfer your score for each statement to the blank below that corresponds to the number of the statement.

VALUES: This category is a measurement of how much you respect and trust yourself; how you see your unique qualities and your usefulness; how positively or negatively you talk to yourself. Record the numeric values you gave to the following questions in Columns A and B below. Then total each column. To get your final score, subtract your Column B total from your Column A Total.

To evaluate the level of your self-esteem in each of these categories, transfer your score for each statement to the blank below that corresponds to the number of the statement.

VALUE:	ACCOMPLISHMENTS:
This category is a measurement of how much you respect and trust yourself; how you see your unique qualities and your usefulness; how positively or negatively you talk to yourself. Record the numeric values you gave to the following questions in Columns A and B below. Then total each column. To get your final score, subtract your Column B total from Column A total.	This category measures how you feel about the goals you have achieved in your life, your level of success, and how strongly you believe that you can attain more. Add and then subtract your scores as above.

COLUMN A	COLUMN B	COLUMN A	COLUMN B
# 1 =	# 13 =	# 2 =	# 8 =
# 7 =	# 19 =	# 20 =	# 14 =
# 25 =	# 37 =	# 26 =	# 32 =
# 31 =		# 38 =	
COLUMN A TOTAL =	COLUMN B TOTAL =	COLUMN A TOTAL =	COLUMN B TOTAL =
COLUMN A – B =	VALUE TOTAL =	COLUMN A - B =	ACCOMPLISH-MENT TOTAL =

RELATIONS WITH OTHERS:		ABILITIES:	
This category measures how you feel about yourself in dealing with others and whether you can trust and open up to them, participate in authentic communication, and develop deep friendships.		This category measures how you feel about your capabilities to be productive, to shape your own destiny, and to bounce back after a setback.	
COLUMN A	COLUMN B	COLUMN A	COLUMN B
# 9 =	# 3 =	# 4 =	# 28 =
# 15 =	# 27 =	# 10 =	# 34 =
# 21 =	# 33 =	# 16 =	# 40 =
# 39 =		# 22 =	
COLUMN A TOTAL =	COLUMN B TOTAL =	COLUMN A TOTAL =	COLUMN B TOTAL =
COLUMN A – B =	RELATIONSHIP TOTAL =	COLUMN A - B =	ABILITIES TOTAL =

RESPONSIBILITY/ACCOUNTABILITY: This category measures how well you feel you accept life's challenges, how much control you believe you have over your circumstances, and your ability to take ownership of and apologize for your mistakes.		OTHERS' PERCEPTION OF YOU: This category measures how you believe others see you, your innate worth, and talents and abilities	
COLUMN A	COLUMN B	COLUMN A	COLUMN B
# 11 =	# 5 =	# 6 =	# 12 =
# 17 =	# 23 =	# 18 =	# 24 =
# 35 =	# 29 =	# 30 =	# 36 =
# 41 =		# 42 =	
COLUMN A TOTAL =	COLUMN B TOTAL =	COLUMN A TOTAL =	COLUMN B TOTAL =
COLUMN A – B =	RESPONSIBILITIES TOTAL =	COLUMN A - B =	OTHERS TOTAL =

INTERPRETING YOUR SCORES IN EACH OF THE SIX CATEGORIES

For each of the above six categories, notice where you have scored the highest and lowest. The possible range is –11 to + 17. Does it surprise you that you scored high in relationships and lower in accountability? Any score below +4 indicates a category that is important for you to focus on when improving your self-esteem. For example, if your VALUE score is low, you might consider becoming more positive in the way you talk to yourself. If your ACCOMPLISHMENTS score is low, consider making a list of and then celebrating all the important goals and successes you have already achieved in your life. Then note your current goals and develop a plan for attaining them.

OVERALL SELF-ESTEEM SCORING Add the Totals from:

VALUE	
ACCOMPLISHMENTS	
RELATIONSHIPS	
ABILITIES	
SENSE OF RESPONSIBILITY/ ACCOUNTABILITY	
OTHERS' PERCEPTION OF YOU	
GRAND TOTAL FOR SELF-ESTEEM	

INTERPRETING YOUR OVERALL SELF-ESTEEM SCORE

The possible range of overall scores of the self-esteem questionnaire ranges from 102 to -66. If your score is:

- *+60 and above:* Your self-esteem level is high, and you have a healthy, respectful view of your personal worth. You have already done a lot of work on yourself to be at this level. Congratulations!

- *+ 40 to + 59:* This score is impressive, showing that your self-esteem level is solid in most areas. You have clearly spent time and effort on developing your talents, uniqueness, and relations with others around you. To raise your self-esteem score even higher, focus on categories where your score showed a bit of room for improvement.

- *+20 to +39:* Your self-esteem level is fairly high compared to many others, although there are still some areas where you do not give yourself as much credit as you deserve. Focus on improvement in the categories where you are below +4, and your self-esteem level will increase to even healthier levels

- *+1 to + 19:* Your self-esteem could definitely use a lift. You have a tendency to underestimate yourself and how well others perceive you. You may find it difficult to increase your sense of power with the low level of self-esteem you currently have, and you may wish to work on building your self-esteem (we will suggest ways to do that throughout this book) in order to better your relationships with others.

- *Less than Zero:* You have scored low in many categories, and this indicates you may not feel very good about yourself or your unique talents and personality. Your low self-esteem may negatively impact your view of the world, and it can diminish your ability to have authentic, healthy relationships with yourself and with others.

LifeQ PRACTICE #12.2

SELF-ESTEEM JOURNAL	Week:						
ACTION STEP	MONDAY	TUESDAY	WEDNESDAY	THURSDAY	FRIDAY	SATURDAY	SUNDAY
Groom							
Smile							
Exercise							
Clear the Clutter							
Meditate/Pray							
No perfection needed							
Stay away from toxic people and situations							
CANCEL!!! I forgive myself!							
Increase competence:							
Repeat affirmations:							
Three things I am grateful for:							

LifeQ PRACTICE #12.3

- Create a "New You." The following exercise helps you to explore your inner strengths and provides a framework from which to build your new self-image. By starting to change the way you look at and feel about yourself, you will change your life and increase your *LifeQ.*

List your positive qualities, talents, and skills in the following categories:

- ◻ Work:

- ◻ Personal:

- ◻ Include your list of accomplishments (You developed this list in previous chapters).

- ◻ Now list some things you would like to change about yourself personally. (For example: "I would like to change the way I talk negatively about myself.")

- Ask others who know you well to tell you the positive things they see in you. Write down what they say. Read these lists frequently.

- Choose a few positive affirmations like "I am valuable and deserve to be loved." "I like and respect myself and feel better about myself every day."

LifeQ PRACTICE # 12.4 WHAT ROLES DO YOU PLAY IN YOUR LIFE STORY?

What Is Your Level of self-esteem in each role—Low, Medium, High?

Self	_____	Spouse	_____
Leader	_____	Parent	_____
Sibling	_____	Son / Daughter	_____
Friend	_____	Manager	_____
Employee	_____	Colleague	_____
Board member	_____	PTA member	_____

Next Step: Compare the two highest scoring roles to your two lowest scoring roles. Is there a difference in how valuable and accomplished you feel in these roles? How strong is your relationship is to others? How does each position make you think about your abilities, and how accountable do you feel? How do you believe others think about you in that role? What can you do to strengthen your level of self-esteem in the positions with the two lowest scores?

LifeQ PRACTICE #12.5 THIS WEEK'S ACTION PLAN

- What have you learned about yourself after reading this chapter?

- What actions will you take this next week to start to design the life that you want to live?

PART 2

DEVELOP YOUR WINNING STRATEGY

CHAPTER 13

SETTING YOUR SMART GOALS AND MAKING PROMISES

*W*hy should you spend time learning how to set goals? Goal setting does three essential things. Goals set a direction for you; goals make you conscious of where you are going; and setting goals gives you a destination, so you know when you have reached it.

Keeping your mind focused on your goals is crucial to attaining them. Just like an airplane flies off-course 99% of the time due to turbulence and wind, you can frequently go off-course when pursuing your goals. Planes and people need to readjust their strategies as they head toward their goals continually. In the story of Marcel and his daughter Maria, you will be able to contrast Marcel's *dream* of going to Poland with Kristin's *goal* of going to Poland.

Marcel's and Maria's story:

Marcel's life-long dream was to travel from his home in Indianapolis to visit the birthplace of his parents in Poland. He had imagined this trip ever since he learned about geography in school and found Poland on his Dad's large model globe. Throughout his life, he would tell others of his dream and that "Someday I will visit the land of my forefathers and see if I have other relatives still living in Poland." Marcel never took that trip although he lived to be 85 years old. He just never got around to it. And his "Someday I'll travel to Poland" became a different destination of "Someday Isle."

Marcel's daughter, Maria, frequently heard about her father's dream of traveling to Poland. Maria committed herself that she would visit her ancestors' land by age 35. Not only was Maria enthusiastic about the trip, but she also wrote down her goal of traveling to Poland by her 35th birthday and promised herself she would make the trip happen. She researched the travel cost, the best time of year for travel, and took Polish language courses. Maria celebrated her 35th birthday in the Polish town where her grandparents married.

WHY IS GOAL SETTING IMPORTANT?

Goal setting is key to becoming successful. Have you ever noticed that people who become successful continue to be successful? Those who are not successful continue to be unsuccessful. The secret is GOALS.

Why don't people set goals? What gets in the way of goal setting? Three things that can hamper goal setting are fear of failure, low self-esteem, and the perception that there is just not enough time to set goals.

KEY TO SUCCESS AND KEY TO FAILURE

As we discussed earlier, you become what you think about. Throughout history, this is one point where most historians and philosophers agree. Your thoughts and beliefs drive everything you do. If you are not thinking about the direction you want to go, you may end up somewhere else. It is critical to become aware of what you are thinking. If you think about a concrete goal, you become that goal. Every negative thought you hold in your mind becomes a goal. If you say, "I can never remember people's names!" Your subconscious mind says, "That's right, Dummy!" If you do not have goals, and your thoughts are goal-less, confused, fraught with fears and doubts, then your life becomes one of confusion, fear, anxiety, and doubt.

GOALS VS. PROMISES

Most people are great at setting goals and lousy at achieving them. More than 100 million Americans make New Year's Resolutions every year, yet fewer than 10% keep them. Most of them abandon these goals after one week. In fact, because of the failure rate in reaching goals year after year, only 11% believe they will achieve these New Year's goals.

When clients say, "I'll try" when committing to a goal, there is an excellent chance that they will not succeed. Language is a powerful tool, and now we have clients talk about "promises." By saying, "I promise to you and myself, I will do it next week," the level of commitment increases. It even feels different. It affects you both mentally and emotionally.

People who make promises to themselves tend to keep the promise. A promise is your word. It is a proclamation. So, what is the difference between a goal and a promise? A *promise* is a declaration that something will or will not be done, a commitment. A *goal* is the result or achievement toward which effort is directed. [1]

Once we started recommending that our clients replace the word "goals" with the word "promises," they achieved a higher success rate. Promises trigger your values and beliefs on a subconscious level. It seems the person making the promise may have more at stake personally and emotionally than the person setting a goal. If you make a promise, you are more likely to develop promises that are achievable, realistic, and deserve your commitment. For example, compare the level of commitment in this example of a marriage proposal by a man to the woman he loves. "My goal is to be faithful to you for the rest of my life." And, "I promise to be faithful to you for the rest of my life." Which proposal seems more committed?

While goals usually come from an external source like your company, your boss, family, religion, or society, a promise is deeply internal. You typically think long and hard before making a promise. Imagine that you set a goal to be punctual. It is probably not going to happen. But when you promise your loved ones that you are going to be punctual, you will most likely keep your promise. If you break your promise and start being late for gatherings or deadlines, you will feel embarrassed and ashamed to admit that you failed.

When you make a "promise" to do something, it often becomes more than a "goal." When you set promises, you get your mind ready for success, and your brain records these successes in its neurons as a positive emotional reaction. Keeping promises makes you "feel good."

BEWARE OF MAKING TOO MANY PROMISES AT ONCE

We caution you from making all your goals into promises because that would feel overwhelming to make 12+ promises at one time. Once you start breaking promises that you make to yourself, then your word becomes less valuable to you. Be selective when making promises. Don't overload yourself with too many commitments, especially at the beginning of this goal-setting process. *You can create SMART Goals with staggered start dates, and then you can determine if you want to make a few of the SMART goals into SMART Promises.* Choose wisely.

"SMART" GOALS PROPEL YOUR MIND TO BE SUCCESSFUL

In Chapter 10, when we discussed the impact of your underlying beliefs and patterns, we emphasized that both your conscious and subconscious mind are critical to your success. Throughout history, philosophers, historians, and even poets have written about the power of the mind. Zig Ziglar gets it right when he says, "It is your attitude, not your aptitude, that determines your altitude." The conscious mind is the source of thought, and the subconscious is the source of power. Your subconscious is always working, whether you are awake or asleep. It can fast-forward and see you already being successful. The subconscious mind assimilates all that is needed for you to reach success—you just need to stay focused on the goal without "letting-up" no matter how long it takes. You need to learn to be patient and tenacious. [2]

YOUR CHANCES FOR SUCCESS ARE EXCELLENT

Many people who set goals wish they could achieve something without any strategic planning. That is not how most success occurs. We recommend that you set goals after strategically discovering your *LifeQ* and your values, purpose, patterns, and beliefs.

The dictionary defines the word *success* as "turning out as was hoped for," "a favorable result." To be successful, we believe you must set your goals for your life, and these goals may be different for each person. You are successful and have a "favorable result" when you attain the goals that you had "hoped for," and that gives meaning to your life. [3]

Zig Ziglar defines success is: "You should stand on the goal line of life and look into the end zone. What you want to see there sets the parameters for your definition of success." [4] In other words, it is crucial first to figure out what kind of person you want to become and what you want to achieve. Then spend the days of your life behaving in ways that will help you meet these goals. As Rev. Billy Graham once said, "I've never seen a hearse with a U-Haul behind it!" [5]

BENEFIT OF WRITING DOWN YOUR GOALS AND PROMISES

Several studies have shown that writing down goals increases your chances of success. A study of Harvard MBA alumni 10 years after their graduation looked at the correlation between written goals and success. Group A, comprising 84% of the class, had no goals at graduation and was making "X" dollars. Group B, including 13% of the class, had goals but had never actually written down those goals, and was making 2X the income of Group A. Group C, 3% of the class, had written down those goals, and was making, on average, 10X the income of the other 97% put together. The only differences among the groups were the clarity of the goals of the graduates, plus the act of writing down the goals. [6]

Have you noticed that when you take the time to write down your shopping list, you remember most of your items without glancing at it? Or when you scribble a terrific idea in your notebook that you think about it throughout the day? The human brain has as many as 60,000 thoughts per day, so writing down your thoughts prioritizes them and brings clarity and focus. The act of writing things down serves to lodge them into your long-term memory.

S.M.A.R.T. GOALS ARE "SMART"

What kinds of goals for success do you usually set? Are they broad goals, or do you use categories for personal and professional goals?

We set SMART goals for ourselves and teach clients to set SMART goals. The SMART stands for Specific, Measurable, Attainable, Relevant, and Time-bound. We use yellow stickies that say, "A dream without a deadline is merely a wish." With SMART goals, it is easy to tell when you have successfully reached a goal. If it is too broad, like "I want to make a lot of money," "I want to be successful," or "I want to improve my education," it is hard to tell when you have reached the goal. You can make those goals into SMART goals by declaring, "I see myself making at least $100,000 a year within two years." "I see myself owning my own home within five years." "I see myself receiving my college diploma in four years." Action steps for SMART goals are:

- **Specific:** Goals must detail what you want to achieve. A generalization like "I want to be rich" is not quantifiable. In other words, state the exact amount of money you wish to acquire. "My goal is to have one million dollars in assets within five years." "My goal is to publish my e-book by May 15th."

- **Measurable:** If goals are not measurable and quantifiable, they are just dreams. The progress and success of fulfilling a SMART goal can be measured.

- **Attainable:** Goals should have a little stretch. If too far out, however, your subconscious sees it as impossible. Goals must be realistic, achievable in a specific amount of time, and reasonable. You must also set a goal that you can achieve, or that you believe you can achieve. If you have never made more than $30,000 a year, a million dollars may be too far a reach, and you should start with a smaller goal.

- **Relevant:** Your goal must align with other pertinent goals that are reasonable, realistic, and resourced, and happening at the right time. The goal must be relevant to you, who you are, and how you want to be perceived. For example, if your goal of having a million dollars is, in fact, the plan your spouse made for you and is not a priority for you, then you will surely fall short of accomplishing that goal. If your spouse wants you to excel at golf and golf does not interest you, you will probably not excel at golf. It must be a result that you want and are determined to achieve. Include action verbs: "develop," "increase," "complete," "improve," and include the expected result.

- **Time-bound:** Setting the specific dates for achieving your goal is critical for SMART goals. If you do not set a date as to when you want to reach this goal, then it is just floating out in space to be accomplished someday in the future. Someday never comes. "Someday I'll achieve the goal" becomes the destination of "Someday Isle." Add a date to achieve the goal, for example, 12/31 of this year.

- Once the SMART goal is defined, you need to develop your strategy, including analyzing the benefits of achieving the goal, obstacles and solutions, steps and timelines, and the resources you need to complete each step. See *LifeQ* **PRACTICE #13. 3**

In the example below, Claire committed to a SMART promise that her home would be clutter-free by year-end. She knew that it would be a challenge for her to change her life-long cluttering behavior and that she would need to conquer the first stage of any change – Resistance to decluttering. Claire carefully identified strategic steps to ensure she reached the outcome that she wanted.

Claire's SMART Promise to be clutter-free.

Claire's story:

Claire had become a "stuff-aholic." She even paid for a storage unit for her extra stuff. Now she realizes that her cluttering habit has been cutting into her joy and draining her energy. She even stopped having friends over because she was embarrassed by her messy home. As she walked through her house during December last year, Claire was overwhelmed and frustrated as she looked at the piles of papers, magazines, clothes, gadgets, and knickknacks. Some of her clutter included important documents, assorted magazines with articles she wanted to save, and souvenirs from her travels. Her closet overflowed with 15 years of clothes and shoes, some of which she had not worn in more than 10 years, and others that still had the sales tags attached.

*Claire decided that the next year would be the start of her clutter-free life. The thought of that even felt good. She made a promise to herself that she would start decluttering on January 1. As the New Year approached, Claire began to feel resistance. She knew this would be a big project and would require her to change, and change has always been difficult for Claire. She laughed at herself as she started her self-talk about maybe she didn't need to do this. Every change begins with resistance, so she knew that her resistance would be an obstacle. She called two friends, told each of them about her promise, and begged them to hold her accountable. They agreed. Claire made a SMART Promise to **"Have the house clutter-free by next December 31."**. Claire set an additional SMART promise to **"Declutter one room every two months."***

Claire's Strategic Plan had the following steps:

- **Select four boxes** for items and apply labels: "Keep," "Maybe Keep," "Trash," and "Charity" or "Consignment."

- **Start small.** Tackle one drawer or shelf at a time. Do not empty all drawers simultaneously, but one at a time. Do not progress to another area until finished with the first small area.

- **Declutter one room at a time.** Claire chose the laundry room to start because she thought it would be the easiest, and she could build momentum.

- **Set a timer for 15 minutes when decluttering.** Claire read that by starting with 15 minutes of uninterrupted, focused time; she could make a lot of progress. Then, if she had time, she would set it for another 15 minutes. Do not declutter for more than 1 hour the first day to save energy and enthusiasm for the next day.

- **Keep learning about decluttering tips to help with decluttering projects.** Claire learned to avoid putting paper in horizontal piles. It is more peaceful to see open space on desks and surfaces. Take photos to remember items. One man took pictures of his 1,000 beanie babies before donating them. Stick to the rule: "When in doubt, throw it out."

- **Enjoy the process and stay on the lookout for hidden treasures in the clutter.**

- **Celebrate with a reward after each room becomes clutter-free.**

HAVING SMART GOALS AND PROMISES WILL HELP YOU BE SUCCESSFUL

We have used SMART goals and promises throughout our lives. In our stories below, you will see that by committing to SMART promises, we achieved significant successes. Jasenka made a SMART promise to become fluent in speaking Spanish. Susan set a SMART promise to earn a Ph.D. Our stories demonstrate how we achieved our goals and fulfilled the promises that we made to ourselves.

Jasenka's SMART Promise

For many years, Jasenka has wanted to live on every continent and learn other languages while there. She was already fluent in four languages and decided she wanted to learn Spanish next. On vacation to Argentina, she mused, "What could be a better way to learn Spanish than to spend time in a country that speaks Spanish?" **Jasenka made a SMART promise to move to Buenos Aires for five years, learn to speak and write Spanish fluently, and establish a successful coaching business.** *Her family and friends had questions: "How can you leave your life in America? How will you find clients? Where will you live?" While many people saw obstacles and reasons to discourage her from the move, Jasenka saw opportunity, growth, and a way to fulfill her desire to become fluent in Spanish. Her SMART promise was specific, measurable, attainable, relevant, plus time bound. She felt confident about her commitment since she had already learned German and English by immersing herself in Germany and the United States. Jasenka moved to Argentina and established a flourishing coaching business with clients whom she coaches in Spanish.*

Susan's SMART Promise

Achieving a Ph.D. takes hard work, tenacity, and focus. There are thousands of doctoral students who never finish their dissertations. Some drop out of their doctoral programs after a few months, while other students finally quit after 10 years or more. Susan created a **SMART promise to complete her Ph.D. by 2000.** *She knew that she needed to keep this goal visible to remind her to stay focused and get it done. Her good friend, Dr. Pat Heim, joked with her frequently, saying that the "D" in Ph.D. stood for "Done." To stay focused, Susan displayed yellow stickies around her office, on her computer frame, and even her bathroom mirror that said "Ph.D." Her business cards had "Ph" after her name that reminded her that she needed to add the "D." A colleague gave her an empty diploma frame that Susan mounted on her office wall. Writing* *a SMART promise, keeping it visible every day, plus having a positive support team of cheerleaders helped Susan be successful and earn her Ph.D. by her deadline.*

"WHY" IS MORE IMPORTANT THAN "HOW" YOU WANT TO ACHIEVE A GOAL

The "5 Whys" process is used in business to understand the root cause of any problem. It was first used in Toyota Motor Corporation by Taiichi Ohno. We like to apply it to goal setting to show the reasons why reaching a goal is worth the effort. Knowing the "WHY" your effort is worth it can be very motivating. Although the "5 Whys" is most widely used in quality improvement processes, we find it useful in many situations where our clients are searching for a better understanding of challenges, problems, and motivation to achieve goals.

In the example below, Brenda wants to break her habit of being late. She decides to get to the root cause of her motivation to achieve the goal. Brenda drills down and asks herself honestly: "Why do I want to be punctual?"

BRENDA'S GOAL: "I WANT TO BE PUNCTUAL"

- *WHY do I want to do this?* My punctuality will show my respect for my husband, who becomes angry at my tardiness and embarrassed when we arrive late for events.

- *WHY do I want to do this?* When it is my turn to drive the carpool, my children are embarrassed every time I am late because they disrupt their school classes and teachers scold them in front of their classmates.

- *WHY do I want to do this?* My children will stop receiving demerits for arriving late.

- *WHY do I want to do this?* By arriving at meetings on time and completing business reports on time, I will show my boss that

I am a serious professional who is disciplined and manages my time well. Being punctual would improve my chances of promotion and more pay that would be good for my family.

- *WHY do I want to do this?* Supporting my family is my most important value.

Achieving goals and keeping promises requires discipline and focus. It is incredibly easy to find yourself off-course during your pursuit. Therefore, you must list sound reasons for investing your time and energy. If you do not know deep down in your gut the "WHY" behind your effort, you can easily thwart your chances for success. Following is Brenda's story of how she broke her habit of being late.

Brenda's story:

Brenda was always running late. She knew this habit was affecting her ability to advance at work. She wanted more responsibility, but her lateness indicated sloppiness and unreliability to her boss, who had spoken to her about this several times. Also, Brenda's habitual lateness caused stress in her personal relationships. Her children were angry at always being dropped off late to school and events. Her husband and friends felt annoyed and disrespected each time they had to wait for her. Brenda's habitual lateness negatively impacted her **LifeQ,** *including* **CareerQ, FamilyQ, LoveQ,** *and* **FriendsQ.** *Brenda realized that one of her main goals had to be that she be punctual.*

Brenda made a SMART promise that she would begin immediately to be punctual for meetings, meet due dates for projects, and be on time for her family. She knew it would be a challenge because being late had become a habit for Brenda. Although she had some setbacks and was not always on time during the next few weeks, she was determined to do this. There was too much at stake in her personal and professional life. She set her watch ahead by 10 minutes, reminded herself daily of what was at stake, and gave herself positive self-talk every morning and evening. After a few weeks, Brenda's boss noticed the change and gave her positive feedback about her transformation to being punctual. A few months later, he gave Brenda a coveted assignment and told her he would not have done that before when he felt he could not depend on her. Also, her relationship with her family and friends improved because they no longer thought she valued her time more than theirs.

Following is how Susan's family sets SMART goals.

Susan's story:

At the beginning of each year, the Murphy family writes goals for the next year ahead. About 25 years ago, Susan's husband witnessed her writing her goals and said, "What about having team goals and goals for me, too?" Susan said, "Great idea!" So ever since then, at the beginning of every New Year, the Murphys write three sets of goals— for Team Murphy, for Jim, and for Susan. As Susan describes their annual goal-setting process, "We post these goals in several places around our home, so they are always visible. At the same time, we document all the accomplishments we had from the previous year. We have all our successes from the past 25 years saved on our computers. It is fun to look back and see all that we have accomplished together. Having goals has helped us live a life full of adventure and new experiences every year. One of the Murphy promises is to take an international trip yearly, so every January instead of saying, "'Should we or shouldn't we take an international trip next year?' we say, 'Where shall we go?'"

THE TEMPTATION TO LOWER YOUR GOALS

"Structural Tension" occurs when your goals seem difficult to reach because they are too far away from your current reality—your current state. The farther your vision of what you want to accomplish is from your current reality, the higher the tension level and the greater the discomfort. To decrease this "structural tension," you can either move your current reality (your current state) toward your vision or lower your vision (your goals) to be closer to your current reality. You often will be tempted to decrease your goals because that is easier than stretching to achieve the goal.

When Jasenka decided that she wanted to speak fluent Spanish by moving to a Spanish speaking country, she could have easily succumbed to the structural tension and downgraded her vision and goal. She could have taken the easier path and stayed in California while continuing to study Spanish in classes and online courses. The structural tension was almost unbearable as she packed her belongings to move to Argentina and said "Goodbye" to her family and friends in California. Jasenka was tempted to avoid the structural tension and stay in California. However, she pursued her goal and moved to Buenos Aires where she met and married Antonio, whose first language is Spanish.

An example of this from Susan's life is that Susan had a vision of writing a well-researched, successful book about challenges and opportunities that women experience when working with other women. She wanted to explore why workplace relationships among women are often either extraordinarily productive or quite destructive, while men's relationships at work do not become as personal. Susan's first step was to write down the goal of writing a bestseller within two years about women working with women. As Dr. Pat Heim and Susan were doing research, there were many times that they found the "structural tension" between the "vision" of a completed book and their "current reality" of being amid mounds of research to be stressful and uncomfortable. During those times, it would have been much more comfortable to downgrade the vision of "write a bestselling book within two years" and change the vision to "publish articles and present our research to audiences." Because they kept the lofty vision alive, not only did Pat and Susan publish the successful book, *In the Company of Women* is now available in several languages.

As we write this book, we are launching our newest company, SynerQ. We have been working toward this goal for several years and have been tempted on numerous occasions to succumb to the structural tension of achieving our enormous goal. SynerQ is a software platform that measures and improves employee engagement through entertaining surveys, virtual reality, and gamification. Whenever one of us has gotten discouraged, the other has encouraged us to keep focused on our lofty goal, our vision, and our values. As Thomas Edison said, *"Our greatest weakness lies in giving up. The most certain way to succeed is always to try just one more time."* Now, **www.SynerQ.co** is a reality!

DETERMINE IF A SMART GOAL IS WORTH EFFORT AND COST TO ACHIEVE

Sometimes in the business world, tough decisions must be made, and ambitious goals lowered. When creating a Personal Strategic Plan for your life, you may need to adjust a particular SMART goal when you realize it is not worth the effort and cost to achieve it. We recommend you assess each goal and promise at least every three months to ensure it is still consistent with your vision, purpose, and values and worth your focus, time, and energy.

SPREAD OUT YOUR GOALS

There is no need to start the pursuit of every goal at the same time. Consider staggering your goals, so you start working on one in January, then calendar the start date for the next one, for example. June 15. If you are developing a new habit or behavior, be gentle with yourself. It takes at least 21 days to form a habit.

VISUALIZE YOURSELF ACHIEVING YOUR GOAL

As we discussed in Chapter 8, the Law of Attraction says that like attracts like and when you focus on something, it will manifest. Have you ever noticed that if you are thinking about buying a red sports car that you see lots of them?

IDENTIFY SOMEONE TO HOLD YOU ACCOUNTABLE

In Chapter 14, you will discover how to create your own Personal Board of Directors who can hold you accountable, help you deal with obstacles, and celebrate success. You will be more likely to be successful when someone collaborates with you on your progress regularly.

FIND YOUR SENSE OF HUMOR!

Be willing to laugh at yourself and forgive yourself so you will get back on track when you find yourself off-course.

PLAN FOR OBSTACLES

Strategically think about what could go wrong and move you off-track toward your goal. Have a plan, a backup plan, and a backup plan for the backup plan. USA Swimmer Michael Phelps used his backup plan during the 2008 Beijing Olympics. In his quest for his eighth gold medal, his goggles filled with water when he dove into the pool to start the race. Virtually blind, Phelps activated his backup plan and started counting his strokes. He knew exactly how many strokes he needed to get to the other end of the pool. He remained calm, focused, and won the gold medal. Planning for obstacles while simultaneously visualizing success increases your chances of achieving your goals.

Plan for Obstacles!

DETERMINE REWARDS FOR SUCCESS

What kinds of rewards and recognition inspire you? How do you like to celebrate success? Perhaps you enjoy going to movies, buying new clothes or shoes, getting a massage, buying a new golf putter, going to a concert, or taking a weekend getaway trip. At the time you set your SMART goal, you can encourage and motivate yourself by deciding how you will reward yourself when you achieve it.

INGREDIENTS OF YOUR PERSONAL STRATEGIC PLANNING TOOL

For each of your SMART goals, we recommend a one-sheet planning tool that encapsulates essential ingredients for your plan. Consider the following elements:

- SMART Goal or SMART Promise: Written in the form of a statement

- Start Date, Target Date, and Actual Completion Date

- Benefits from achieving this goal (What positive results will you enjoy?)

- Potential Obstacles and Fears with Solutions and Opportunities

- Specific Action Steps, the target date for each step, resources needed for that step, and completion date

- Is this goal in alignment with my values? Yes or No

- Is achieving this goal worth the time and effort involved? Yes or No

- Messages for My Subconscious and Positive Affirmations to Myself

BELOW ARE EXAMPLES OF *LifeQ* GOALS, OBSTACLES, ACTION STEPS

BodyQ

SMART GOAL: I do not need cholesterol medication by 12/31.

BENEFITS FROM ACHIEVING THIS GOAL: I will be healthier, feel better, and live longer. I will spend less money on prescription drugs.

OBSTACLES AND FEARS: Eating unhealthy food has become a habit, and I am fearful that I will not be able to stop eating high-fat food. My schedule is hectic, and I am concerned that I have no extra time to focus on this goal.

POSSIBLE SOLUTIONS: I can visualize having a healthy cholesterol level and could incorporate the Law of Attraction to manifest healthy cholesterol. I could find someone to coach me on this life change, and who can hold me accountable.

ACTION STEPS: I will consult a nutritionist about developing a dietary plan to include foods that will decrease my intake of cholesterol-rich food within the next week. I will create an exercise plan and implement it into my daily routine by tomorrow evening. I will identify a coach to hold me accountable within two weeks.

MESSAGE TO MY SUBCONSCIOUS AND POSITIVE AFFIRMATIONS: My health is essential to me, and my cholesterol is at a healthy level. I am in control of my body and diet. I am powerful and make sound decisions about my food and exercise.

FunQ

SMART GOAL: I will learn to dance the salsa by June 21.

BENEFITS FROM ACHIEVING THIS GOAL: Dancing salsa will be a fun activity for me as well as serve to release my stress. I will meet new people in my classes and on the dance floor.

OBSTACLES AND FEARS: I do not have extra money for salsa lessons, and I have limited time available to invest in this new activity.

POSSIBLE SOLUTIONS: I could find organizations that offer free salsa classes or salsa dance DVDs so I could teach myself.

ACTION STEPS: Search and find organizations that offer free lessons. I will look on-line, in newsletters, at recreation centers, and community colleges for classes. Look for DVDs that show the salsa dance steps to begin learning the movements and music.

MESSAGE TO MY SUBCONSCIOUS AND POSITIVE AFFIRMATIONS: I deserve to have fun and learn to dance the salsa. I am a good dancer with a good sense of rhythm. I am confident I can learn salsa. I can achieve whatever I set as a goal.

EnvironmentQ

SMART GOAL: I own a house of my own within two years.

BENEFITS FROM ACHIEVING THIS GOAL: Owning my own home will provide housing stability as well as freedom from the whims of a landlord who could raise my rent or convert to a condominium for sale. It will be the first step in putting down roots in the community and building a nest egg for my future financial security.

OBSTACLES AND FEARS: A massive barrier is that I won't have money for the down payment.

POSSIBLE SOLUTIONS: I could borrow money from relatives to use for the down payment. I may be able to rent a home with a contract that allows for an option to buy it in the future when I have saved more money. I could take a part-time job or work extra hours to supplement my income.

ACTION STEPS: Figure out the location where I would like to live in my first home. Consider what kind of house I would like to own. Once I have explored what type of home I can afford and in which part of the city, consider options for obtaining the down payment. Interview realtors and attend open houses in the neighborhoods of interest. Visualize my new home and use the Law of Attraction to help manifest my dream.

MESSAGE TO MY SUBCONSCIOUS AND POSITIVE AFFIRMATIONS: I deserve to own my home and am confident and disciplined in saving money. I am powerful and invincible. When I make a decision, I follow through, remain focused, and stay on track. My life brims with prosperity and abundance.

FamilyQ

SMART GOAL: I will have a close connection with my family for the rest of my life starting 12/31.

BENEFITS FROM ACHIEVING THIS GOAL: Close family relationships will honor one of my top five values and will add to my fulfillment and happiness. A supportive family will add to my sense of security and strengthen my confidence.

OBSTACLES AND FEARS: My schedule is very busy with limited time available for this new promise. I do not know where to start this quest since most people in my family are not proficient in building relationships, and some members are estranged. I am not confident that my family members are open to building a relationship with me.

POSSIBLE SOLUTIONS: I could learn the skills needed for conflict management and forgiveness. Start with the family members who seem to be ready to build relationships. Imagine what it would look like to have a good relationship with family members. Practice openness and show vulnerability with family members where relationships have the most potential.

ACTION STEPS: Identify one family member who would be a first step in building a closer relationship. Imagine how a good relationship with that relative looks and feels. Describe in writing the "why" you choose that relative and why it is important to you. Explore books and articles about conflict management and building relationships. Initiate a call or coffee date with your relative. Find out your relative's interests and discover areas of commonality.

MESSAGE TO MY SUBCONSCIOUS AND POSITIVE AFFIRMATIONS: I deserve to have a positive relationship with my family. I acknowledge my self-worth and confidence. I serve as a good family member who is supportive and caring. I can love and be trusted. I forgive those who have hurt me.

LoveQ

SMART GOAL: I am in a loving, supportive relationship with someone respectful, kind, caring, self-supporting, and emotionally healthy by the end of next year.

BENEFITS FROM ACHIEVING THIS GOAL: I could find happiness, intimacy, and a life partner to develop a long-term mutually supportive relationship.

OBSTACLES AND FEARS: I may not be able to find my love partner. I may be rejected and hurt by someone with whom I fall in love.

POSSIBLE SOLUTIONS: I could think about my interests and meet like-minded people, for example in book clubs, museums, educational seminars and classes, online dating sites. I could also explore my self-limiting beliefs about love relationships.

ACTION STEPS: Create a list of the characteristics that I want in a life partner. Determine which factors and values are non-negotiable. Focus on these characteristics and do not accept a second date with someone who does not embody the attributes and values that are important to me. Assess my interests and then explore classes and groups that attract others with similar interests. Tell friends about my desire to meet others who have my interests and values. Search online dating services and apply to ones that seem appropriate to attract my partner: follow-up and take calculated chances. Assess how I am doing every three months.

MESSAGE TO MY SUBCONSCIOUS AND POSITIVE AFFIRMATIONS: I am capable of loving and being loved and respected by a partner. I am compassionate and lovable. Happiness is a choice, and I choose to be happy. Having a healthy, loving relationship is a normal part of my life.

MoneyQ

SMART GOAL: I will save $25,000 every year starting now.

BENEFITS FROM ACHIEVING THIS GOAL: Saving $25,000 per year, I will be able to start building financial security.

OBSTACLES AND FEARS: I realize that I have scarcity fears around money. I believe I will never have enough. I am afraid I will lose my job at some point and will be unable to make or save money.

POSSIBLE SOLUTIONS: I could explore events in my life that contribute to my scarcity fears and start developing an abundance mindset. I can build my strategic business plan to increase my income. I can set aside a specific amount of money every month to save.

ACTION STEPS: Create a budget for my income and expenses. Document exactly where I am spending money and identify any high costs. Review insurance policies for specific areas that are over-insured (automobile, household, medical, etc.) Pay myself first and put money in my designated account for savings. Identify a financial coach to keep me accountable.

MESSAGE TO MY SUBCONSCIOUS AND POSITIVE AFFIRMATIONS: My life is abundant, and I am grateful. I choose financial freedom. I am powerful and have plenty of money and blessings, and. I make the right decisions and invest wisely. My ability to conquer my challenges is limitless.

CareerQ

SMART GOAL: I have a job within two years that I am passionate about and that commands at least $100,000.

BENEFITS FROM ACHIEVING THIS GOAL: By having a career that fulfills me, I will feel happier, less stressed, and more fulfilled.

OBSTACLES AND FEARS: I am not sure what careers would make me feel passionate. I cannot leave my current job to search for a new one because of my financial obligations.

POSSIBLE SOLUTIONS: Research what I would like to do professionally, evaluate my skills and talents, passions, and consider taking courses to increase my skills and marketability.

ACTION STEPS: Decide that it is time to take control of my career path. Step back and do an honest assessment of my situation: what type of work aligns with my purpose and values. Conduct a career SWOT analysis of my strengths, weaknesses, opportunities, and threats. Write down my talents and passions. Write down types of careers that would deplete my energy. Discover and assess my gaps in knowledge, skill, and behaviors. Interview people who are currently in fields that interest me to find more information. Remember that I am always networking. Keep my sense of humor and maintain my self-esteem during this process. Hire a Coach.

MESSAGE TO MY SUBCONSCIOUS AND POSITIVE AFFIRMATIONS: My potential to succeed is infinite. I deserve to have a career that I am passionate about, and that provides joy and financial rewards. I am the producer and director of my life story, and I choose to be happy in my career. My life is abundant and prosperous.

WHAT'S NEXT?

You have determined what you want as your goals, have identified your underlying beliefs and patterns, understand the stages of change, and are using the Law of Attraction to draw it to you. The next step is to develop your Personal Board of Directors. In the business world, a strong Board is a vital asset to a successful business. A talented, supportive Board is a crucial tool in your Strategic Planning Toolkit. The next chapter will introduce you to the JOHARI WINDOW that is a model for designing effective relationships with your Board Members as well as with every significant person in your life.

CHAPTER 13: *LifeQ*-TIPS AND CHAPTER RECAP

- **Make sure it is YOUR goal.** Too many people set out to achieve goals and promises for others and not themselves. The single best thing you can ever do to achieve a goal is to make sure it is yours. Your heart and desire must be in it.

- **Consider calling it a PROMISE when you are firmly committed to achieving it.** Subconsciously, you are more likely to keep a promise than accomplish a goal. A promise usually means a more profound commitment because it is your word.

- **Identify your goal.** If you do not know WHERE you want to be, then it does not matter which direction you go.

- **Use the resources around you.** Resources mean people, money, time, materials, and so forth. You can use the people in your life as positive motivators who will cheer you on and lift you.

- **Create a Plan.** No business is successful without a business plan, so why not create one to make your life more fulfilling and abundant while increasing your **LifeQ**? The steps to create a plan are:

    □ Identify a specific goal.

    □ Envision it.

    □ Write down WHY you want this.

    □ Define a time frame for it. Write down when you will accomplish it.

    □ Write down WHO will help you accomplish this.

    □ Do not worry about the HOW. You just need to know the WHAT and the WHY.

- **Review your plan every day.** Two things happen when you do this: you are consciously thinking about it, and you are subconsciously thinking about it.

- **Tell yourself you will succeed.** The most important voice we ever need to listen to is our own. *"Whether you think you can, or you think you can't, you're right."* Henry Ford

- **Tell supporters about your goal.** Some people will step up to offer to help you, while others may become naysayers. Choose to spend time with your supporters and stay away from those who distract you by their negativity.

- **Envision the results.** Sports legends Jack Nicholas and Michael Jordan used visualizing techniques to make successful shots. During tournaments and on the golf practice range, Nicholas always envisioned the destination for his golf ball before striking the ball. Michael Jordan did the same with his basketball free-throws. He was able to make free-throws with his eyes closed.

- **Start!** Do not let the fear of the unknown paralyze you and block your success. In business, this is called "analysis paralysis." You do not have to know all the answers. Just start. And you will be on your way to keeping your promises and living an abundant life.

LifeQ PRACTICE # 13.1

- **CHOOSE** 12 SMART Goals from the Components in your *WHEEL OF LifeQ* that describe what you want to achieve in the future. Your mind will start working on those Goals NOW even though you are planning to start performing the work on them later!

- As you write your Action Steps, consider what you are going to START, STOP, and CONTINUE doing for each goal. Also include messages and affirmations as well as who will keep you accountable.

- What messages do you tell your subconscious?

- What positive affirmations will you say to yourself so that you will achieve your goals?

- For each think of "5 Whys".

LifeQ PRACTICE # 13.2   Fill out the Goal Sheet for each Q

SMART GOAL

S.M.A.R.T: SPECIFIC, MEASURABLE, ATTAINABLE, RELEVANT, TIMEBOUND

_____

BENEFITS FROM ACHIEVING THIS GOAL

_____

REWARD

_____

OBSTACLES / FEARS	POSSIBLE SOLUTIONS
_____	_____
_____	_____
_____	_____
_____	_____

ACTION STEPS BY WHEN	RESOURCES NEEDED
1. _____	_____
2. _____	_____
3. _____	_____
4. _____	_____
5. _____	_____
6. _____	_____

WHO IS HOLDING ME ACCOUNTABLE? _____

AFFIRMATIONS & MANTRA _____

_____

LifeQ PRACTICE # 13.2 NEXT WEEK'S ACTION PLAN

- What have you learned about yourself after reading this chapter?

- What actions will you take this next week to start to design the life that you want to live?

CHAPTER 14

CREATING YOUR PERSONAL BOARD OF DIRECTORS

"*Y*ou are the average of the five people you spend the most time with," says business expert Jim Rohn.[1] The people around you matter. As in the case of Lori's story below, if you associate with people who do not like their jobs, you will become like them. If you hang around with people who do not care about growing in the company, you will not succeed in the company. In contrast to Lori, you will see with Manuel's story how his colleagues had the opposite effect on him. Manuel's success and *LifeQ* climbed because he spent time with people who were trustworthy, hardworking, positive, and contributing.

Lori's story:

At Lori's workplace, she mingles with a group of actively disengaged coworkers. Every day she goes to lunch with the same cynical crowd that talks endlessly about how bad things are. These people do not like their jobs, their boss, or the company. Their negativity is beginning to permeate Lori's outlook about work and life. Unfortunately, Lori is becoming like these naysayers. She is actively disengaged at work and is losing her zest for life.

Manuel's story:

Years ago, Manuel heard the saying, "birds of a feather flock together." He has found this to be true. As a result, Manuel is selective and spends his time and energy with people who can be positive influences on his life. His close friends are people who have similar values of integrity, contribution, and respect. At work, he spends his break

time with colleagues who are trustworthy, hardworking, and opti-
mistic. Manuel realizes that the people with whom he associates can
impact the quality of his life.

You need people around you who will challenge you and raise your **LifeQ** level. Even if it is uncomfortable at times, you want to surround yourself with people who are exponentially better in a variety of ways. If you are always the most talented and knowledgeable person in your sphere, you are not going to be growing. Although this may sound judgmental and even heartless, it is essential to understand the influence your inner circle has on your performance and state of abundance.

When you were a kid, your parents probably told you not to hang out with the wrong crowd. As adults, it is easy to forget these words of advice; however, it remains true. Whoever resides in your inner circle has a strong effect on whether you achieve your goals. To paraphrase author Jim Collins, *"Keep the right people on your bus, in the right seats of your bus, and ask the people who are not supporting you to disembark from your bus as soon as possible."* [2]

As you are creating your Personal Strategic Plan, it is time to develop your Personal Board of Directors. Businesses calculate who should serve as advisors, and so should you. A fulfilled and abundant life depends on this. Now is the time to remove toxic saboteurs from your inner circle. Consider your closest relationships and decide who should stay, whom you should reclassify, and whom else you can recruit to support you. Keep only supportive, positive people on your Personal Board of Directors. If someone is bringing you down, you must reduce his or her involvement in your life. Not doing so may hinder your energy, vision, ultimate success, and your **LifeQ.**

As an exercise, write down the five people with whom you spend most of your time and energy. Assign a numerical value that represents their positive influence on you to each person from 1 to 5, and then calculate your average (with 5 being the most positive influence possible). How does each person affect your average? They do not need to be Warren Buffet, the Dalai Lama, or the Pope, but all of them should make you better. They should elevate both your thinking and performance. (See *LifeQ* **PRACTICE #14. 1 IDENTIFY YOUR FUTURE PERSONAL BOARD OF DIRECTORS**) If one or more of them do not improve your life, consider letting them go.

Be open to changing your Board Members throughout your life. As you enter new stages, your Board of Directors may evolve. For instance, your five people in high school were probably very different from your five now. And it is not as though the high school friends needed to discarded, but their roles may have diminished. True friendship always endures, and now you are merely focusing your valuable time most appropriately. Conversely, if there are people who will help you improve, make a concerted effort to spend more time with them.

Put yourself under the microscope. Most great relationships are symbiotic, a relationship in which people bring out the best in one another. How can you do a better job of living a purposeful life, and what else can you bring to other people's lives to help them? Be mindful of whom you are helping, inspiring, and holding to a higher standard.

SHOW ME YOUR FRIENDS AND I'LL TELL YOU WHO YOU ARE

Choose your company wisely. Be relentless in surrounding yourself with individuals who bring out the best in you. One of the most important decisions we make in life is who will be in our innermost circle. It is crucial to choose strategically and cautiously those who surround you because their influence will have both short-term and long-term impact on your personal and professional life.

You may be talented and intelligent, but if you always surround yourself with negative and fear-based people, you are limiting your progression in life. Why would you want to spend time and energy with people who are holding you back instead of with those who can support and elevate you?

RELATIONSHIPS AFFECT GOAL ACHIEVEMENT

Your relationships affect your thoughts and actions. If you want to lose 20 pounds, it is essential to stay focused on your goal to be slimmer so you can make clear-cut diet decisions. However, if you are always surrounding yourself with people who overeat and stuff themselves with unhealthy foods, you make it harder to restrict yourself. You will be tempting your willpower. It will be a much easier task if you associate with like-minded people who have similar visions and, better yet, with people who have already been there before.

Of course, this does not mean you should sever relationships or cut away every single person who does not contribute to your goals. It just means you should reduce the amount of contact you have with people who do not enable you to become a better person. If you are entrenching yourself in relationships that are not elevating you or propelling you forward toward the life story that you want to live, you are not helping yourself—or anybody else. If you are not the best you can be, in the end, you are not the best you can be for others in your life.

"NATURE ABHORS A VACUUM"

Aristotle believed that every space in nature must be filled with something, even if it is just air. He concluded that *"Nature abhors a vacuum."* When you start to remove the naysayers from your life, the law of nature dictates that space will fill with something else.

Strategically choose to fill this vacuum with people who bring out the best version of you, and who will support you and challenge you to live your best life. Ensure their values are like yours. An excellent Personal Board of Directors will have the courage to tell you when you are straying from your path. They care about you enough to initiate difficult conversations with you because they believe in you and want you to be successful.

STRATEGICALLY CHOOSE YOUR BOARD MEMBERS

On business Boards of Directors, the composite usually consists of a variety of people who offer different areas of expertise. There are typically legal and financial experts, strategy gurus, and people with a background in the type of business they are serving. For example, a pharmaceutical company will have physicians on the board, and computer companies will have IT experts on the board. Successful Boards of Directors ensure that members have similar values as the business and will buy into the Mission and Vision Statements. There cannot be a conflict of interest that would influence their input to the business's direction; in fact, they abstain from voting on potentially self-serving topics.

JOHARI WINDOW

The Johari Window model can be important when designing your personal strategic plan and for working authentically with your Personal Board of Directors. As you are becoming more mindful and self-aware, understanding the concepts underlying the Johari Window and strategically applying them can accelerate your growth and development.

The original publication of the Johari Window was in 1955 by American psychologists Joseph Luft and Harry Ingham while researching group dynamics at the University of California Los Angeles. Now, many decades later, the Johari Window is especially relevant because of the importance today of being aware of your behavior and impact on others. These "soft skills" are needed to develop relationships at home and work. The name "Johari" is a combination of the psychologists' first names, Joe and Harry. [3]

The Johari Window is composed of four quadrants. Each quadrant represents the information known about a person. Examples of the types of personal data necessary in this model are behaviors, feelings, attitudes, knowledge, experience, skills, viewpoints, and emotions. The theory behind the model is that these quadrants illustrate how well you know yourself, how well others know you, and areas where you have blind spots.

JOHARI WINDOW

	Known to Self	Unknown to Self
Known to Others	Open Area	Blind Area
Unknown to Others	Hidden Area	Unknown Area

THE FOUR QUADRANTS

The four Johari quadrants are The Open Area, The Blind Area, The Hidden Area, and The Unknown Area.

Quadrant #1: The Open Area

Quadrant #1 contains information that both the person (in this case, YOU) and the others know. This information includes your behaviors, feelings, attitudes, knowledge, experience, skills, viewpoints, and emotions that are known by you as well as members of your Personal Board of Directors. The aim of any relationship should be to develop and expand this "Open Area" for every person. When your relationships have a very large windowpane in the Open Area, you and others (your Board Members) are the most authentic and productive. You can then build trust within your relationship, and you increase the chance for good communication, cooperation, and fewer misunderstandings, conflicts, and distractions with your Board members.

Quadrant #2: The Blind Area

Quadrant #2 is information unknown by the person (YOU) but known by the other Board members. By seeking feedback and encouraging disclosure from your Board members, you can reduce your blind spots and increase your self-awareness and mindfulness. One goal of your working relationship with your Board of Directors is to decrease the size of your Quadrant #2. By reducing Quadrant #2, you improve areas of your personality, attitudes, or behaviors that could be serving as obstacles to leading your most abundant life with a high *LifeQ*. Be sure to give your Personal Board of Directors permission to provide you with constructive feedback and make sure you are open to listening to them. Although it may not be easy to hear about some of your unproductive behaviors, thank your Board of Directors for being willing to share their opinions for you to grow.

Quadrant #3: The Hidden Area

Quadrant #3 represents the information that the person (YOU) knows about yourself but that you have kept hidden from your Board of Directors. This Quadrant could include secrets, fears, hidden agendas, or personal information that you have not revealed. It is natural to fear judgment and want to hold back some information about yourself. Through self-disclosure, you may choose to tell your Board members additional information about yourself to enhance trust, understanding, and communication.

Quadrant #4: The Unknown Area

Quadrant #4 is the information that neither the person (YOU) nor others in your group know about you. The types of data that may be unknown include an undiscovered ability or talent, a fear that you do not see that you have, an unknown illness, subconscious feelings, or underlying beliefs from your childhood. Sometimes, this hidden area remains uncovered during a lifetime. At other times, through self-disclosure or feedback, this information will surface. Your Board of Directors may encourage you to try new things to discover unknown talents and thus reduce the unknown area of Quadrant #4.

JOHARI WINDOW

By understanding this Johari Window Model, you and your Personal Board of Directors can make a conscious effort to increase your Open

Area in Quadrant #1. By using Self-Disclosure and Soliciting Feedback, you can more strategically live your most abundant, purposeful life with a high *LifeQ*.

The ideal Johari Window reflects when people are open, both in giving and receiving information. If they can act with honesty and integrity, it will lead to effective communications and few misunderstandings. These people have the largest 'open' area.

See *LifeQ* **PRACTICE #14.5** for Johari window questions to expand Quadrant #1 "Open" Questions for you and your Personal Board Members to consider

TIPS FOR CREATING YOUR BOARD

An excellent Personal Board of Directors will empower, motivate, and guide you. They will be able to give you a nudge in the right direction to help you meet your goals and achieve the success that you want. Your Board members will be willing to provide you with feedback and tell you the truth, even when you do not want to hear it. They will help you think outside of the box, give you authentic feedback, and a kick in the pants when you need one. Consider these suggestions when choosing your Board:

- *Create a diverse board.* Just as in business today, diversity leads to a variety of thoughts. Examples of Board diversity include having both men and women as well as members of different generations. Members can be in your industry as well as other fields. The perspectives may be different from yours, and that is what will add depth to your decision-making.

- *Include a virtual board member.* You may want to include a historical figure, someone you admire but have never met, or an impressive relative who is no longer around. Whenever you face a tough decision, imagine what this member would say about your circumstances and what advice he or she would give you. Some people choose Benjamin Franklin, John Adams, Mark

Twain, Jesus Christ, Eleanor Roosevelt, or Buddha—all whose biographies and teachings are readily available. If you want to be an entrepreneur, you may choose Richard Branson. If you desire to be a creative genius, you can call on Steve Jobs. If one of your career aspirations is to be a chef, you can list Iron Chef. List someone who has already achieved your goal.

- *Include experts in the LifeQ areas you want to increase.* Reflect on your *LifeQ* scores and ensure you have experts available who can provide support in places you want to improve. For example, if you plan to focus on *SoulQ,* find a spiritual Board Member to help you with your spiritual growth. If you want to improve your *BodyQ*, include an expert in health. If you are going to enhance your *MoneyQ,* find an expert in finance and financial planning to help you stay on track with your money goals.

- *Include a sympathetic board member.* This individual can provide a shoulder to cry on when you have disappointments. This position is in a tricky spot because you cannot host a continuous pity party. This board member must know when enough is enough, and when it is time for you to "get back in the saddle" and carry on designing your purpose-driven life.

- *Include a humorous board member.* This individual can serve to make you laugh at circumstances as well as yourself. Comic relief is essential, and laughter releases endorphins. A cheerful board member can help your life stay enjoyable and increase your *FunQ* and *MindQ.*

- *Always be looking for new board members.* Develop criteria for accepting someone new on your Board. Ensure your Board includes supporters with similar values and those who want to see you be successful. As mentioned earlier, find ways that you can contribute to the success of your Board members, too.

BOTTOM LINE: SURROUND YOURSELF WITH GREAT PEOPLE

As you create your Personal Strategic Plan, choose your Personal Board of Directors carefully. If you strive to be joyful, fulfilled, authentic, confident, and conscientious, surround yourself with people who embody these characteristics. Just as the people close to you influence you, you also affect the people who are close to you and love you. If you allow an opposing force into your life, you hurt yourself and ultimately affect everyone around you. Deliberately including happy, fulfilled, talented people on your Board of Directors will impact your behavior, and you will manifest the results and the life that you want.

CHAPTER 14: *LifeQ* -TIPS AND CHAPTER RECAP

The people around you matter. *"You are the average of the five people you spend the most time with,"* says business expert Jim Rohn. [4]

- Consider your closest relationships and decide who should stay, whom you should reclassify, and whom you can ask to support you. Keep only supportive, positive people on your Personal Board of Directors.

- Most great relationships are symbiotic, where people bring out the best in one another.

- "Nature abhors a vacuum." When you start to remove the naysayers from your life, fill that space with other Board Members. Strategically choose to fill this vacuum with people who bring out the best version of you and will support you and challenge you to live your best life.

- The Johari Window Model is useful for working with your Personal Board of Directors. The theory behind the model is that the four quadrants illustrate how well you know yourself, how well others know you, and areas where you have blind spots. Through feedback and self-disclosure, you can continue to increase your self-awareness and mindfulness and make the changes necessary.

- Create a diverse Board. Include a virtual board member; a board member who is an expert in *LifeQ* area(s) you want to increase; a sympathetic board member who can serve as a shoulder to cry on; and a humorous board member who can make you laugh. Finally, always be on the lookout for potential members for your Personal Board of Directors.

- The ideal Johari Window reflects when people are open, both in giving and receiving information. If they can act with honesty and integrity, it will lead to effective communications and few misunderstandings.

WHAT'S NEXT?

In the next chapter, you begin Part 3 of your strategic planning process for your LifeQ. After assessing your current reality and developing a winning strategy, it is time to act. Of course, we know you have already been taking action along the way. You have lived many years of your life until this point in time. As you strengthen your ability to think and plan strategically, you will continue to assess, plan, act, have setbacks, and repeat throughout your life. You will frequently land off-course due to unforeseen circumstances. In this next section, Part 3, you will need to think strategically once again as you reassess your plan.

LifeQ PRACTICE #14. 1 IDENTIFY YOUR PERSONAL BOARD OF DIRECTORS

- **What kind of person do you want to be?**

  ◦ What is the ideal self that you wish to become?

  ◦ What are the qualities you want to possess?

- **Who are the five people you spend the most time with currently?**

  - How did they get into your life?

  - What are the top three qualities each of them stands for?

  - How successful have they been?

  - How happy, optimistic, enthusiastic, and goal-focused are they?

  - Will they help you increase your *LifeQ* by pushing you when needed?

  - Are they willing to tell you when your ideas will not work?

- **Do they match whom you want to become in the future?**

  - Do their talents and qualities match whom you want to become?

  - Do they elevate you or bring you down? Do they align with your values?

- **Figure out if members of your Board of Directors are working against you.**

  - Do you have members on your Board who make negative judgments that haunt you? You may be giving them way too much power over your thoughts, emotions, and actions.

  - Are they sincerely happy for you when your life is going well, or are they sarcastic and take away your joy? You don't need or want naysayers and jealous Board Members who undermine your dreams. To avoid attacks from these naysayers, you may find that you obsess about living up to their standards. It is time to give them a pink slip and let them join someone else's Board!

LifeQ PRACTICE #14. 2

WHO ARE THE PEOPLE WHO EMBODY THE QUALITIES YOU DESIRE?

- Think of people and qualities whom you respect or aspire to emulate. They can be people who have already achieved the goals that you want. Perhaps they include Benjamin Franklin or Albert Einstein. If you plan to be an entrepreneur, you can mention Richard Branson. if you aspire to be a chef, you can list Julia Child. If you do not like every aspect of the person, list qualities that you admire.

  Sample: PEOPLE AND THEIR QUALITIES WE ADMIRE

  - ▫ *Richard Branson: Vision, Passion, Resilience*
  - ▫ *George Washington: Leadership, Humility, Faith*
  - ▫ *Mark Twain: Humor, Common Sense*

- **PEOPLE AND THEIR QUALITIES I ADMIRE:**

  - ▫
  - ▫
  - ▫
  - ▫

LifeQ PRACTICE # 14.3 DEVELOP PLAN TO BE IN CONTACT WITH YOUR BOARD

You could make direct contact via face-to-face, telephone, or social media. You can reach them through their books, podcasts, or videos. Perhaps you can use visualization like Napoleon Hill, author of *Think and Grow Rich.* [5] Every night before he went to sleep, he would have an imaginary Council meeting with his "invisible counselors." Hill's Council began with a group of nine and eventually expanded over time to 50 members. His Council members included people like Aristotle, Darwin, Einstein, Confucius, and Socrates. Through these nightly council meetings, he received immense inspiration, knowledge, and ideas, which he credited for his success in life.

JOHARI WINDOW ADJECTIVES

LifeQ PRACTICE #14.4 JOHARI WINDOW EXERCISE [6]

There are 56 Johari Window adjectives listed below that are possible descriptions for people using the Johari Window analysis. In this exercise, you choose several adjectives that you feel describe your personality. Each member of your Personal Board of Directors uses this same list of adjectives, and each member chooses an equal number of adjectives that describe you. Insert these adjectives into your Johari Window of four quadrants.

Quadrant #1 is the Open Quadrant, where the adjectives that you and others see in your personality. *Quadrant #2* is the Blind Quadrant, where the adjectives that your Board Members see in you that you do not see in your personality. *Quadrant #3* is the Hidden or Private Quadrant, where you place the descriptive adjectives that you hide from others. *Quadrant #4* is the Unknown Quadrant that neither you nor your Board Members see, either because they do not apply or because of collective ignorance of these traits.

LifeQ PRACTICE #14.4

Able	Accepting	Adaptable	Bold	Brave	Calm	Caring
Cheerful	Clever	Complex	Confident	Dependable	Dignified	Energetic
Extroverted	Friendly	Giving	Happy	Helpful	Idealistic	Independent
Ingenious	Intelligent	Introverted	Kind	Knowledge-able	Logical	Loving
Mature	Modest	Nervous	Observant	Organized	Patient	Powerful
Proud	Quiet	Reflective	Relaxed	Religious	Responsive	Searching
Self-assertive	Self-conscious	Sensible	Sentimental	Shy	Silly	Smart
Spontaneous	Sympathetic	Tense	Trustworthy	Warm	Wise	Witty

LifeQ PRACTICE # 14.5 ASK YOUR BOARD MEMBERS: "WHAT ARE FOUR WORDS THAT DESCRIBE ME?"

The answer to this question will give you some insight into your Brand (your reputation) and how people think of you. Reflect on whether the words they use to describe you match the view that you have of yourself personally and professionally. This process will provide insight for you into areas where things are going well and areas where there are gaps that could use some attention.

LifeQ PRACTICE # 14. 6 THIS WEEK'S ACTION PLAN

- What have you learned about yourself after reading this chapter?

- What actions will you take this next week to start to design the life that you want to live?

PART 3

TAKE ACTION AND TURN YOUR SETBACKS INTO COMEBACKS

CHAPTER 15

TAKE ACTION AND TURN SETBACKS INTO COMEBACKS

Whatcanbemorechallengingthanworkingonyourself?Congratulations on all your hard work! You have addressed the first two vital elements of your *LifeQ* Strategic plan: 1.) Become aware of your current reality and your position on your GPS and 2.) Develop Your Winning Strategy. *LifeQ* Part 3 is Take Action and Turn Your Setbacks into Comebacks.

YOUR PLAN

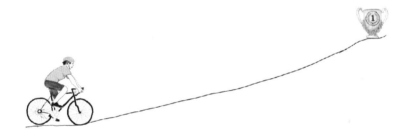

REALITY

We realize that your life journey started long before you learned about your *LifeQ* score and that you have already been "taking action" throughout your life. Plus, we know you have been moving toward your goals and taking action with every *LifeQ* chapter. Some of the goals and promises that you wrote about during the **WHEEL OF LifeQ** Chapters 3 and 4 may be goals that you have been contemplating for years. You may have even tried and failed to achieve some of them previously. We all know people who have lost and gained those same 20 pounds several times.

In business and life, it is easy to procrastinate and delay your launch date as well as to launch but then have setbacks that can be discouraging. So this part of the *LifeQ* Plan is crucial. The "T" in SMART goals and promises is essential. It is helpful to set a start date as well as a finish date. We jokingly tell our clients, "It is time to paint or get off the ladder!"

Why is it so tempting to procrastinate and so easy to quit when you encounter your first obstacle? That initial obstacle can trigger your fear of failure, lack of self-confidence, self-limiting beliefs, lack of willpower, or lack of discipline. Suddenly something else becomes your priority, and you talk yourself into the need to abort your plan.

TAKING ACTION

Nothing happens if you do not act. Dreams without action are illusions, and a goal without a deadline is merely a wish. Many readers of the Law of Attraction books fail to achieve their dreams. Nothing happens if you do not put in the work needed. Opportunities will come and go. When they arrive, you must answer the call with action. Otherwise, it is impossible to create the fulfilling and abundant life that you want.

YOU'VE GOT TO LAUNCH!

Successful people launch! There is a term in business called *analysis paralysis*. Analysis paralysis occurs when someone continuously studies and analyzes all the data and information but does not take action to move toward those opportunities.

A 12-year study of entrepreneurs at Babson College in 1980 by Robert Ronstadt concluded that all success happens because of the "Corridor Principle." Ronstadt observed that every person is proceeding down a corridor in life. Each person stands at the entrance to this corridor, looking down the dark hall that disappears into the distance. There is no guarantee about what will occur when proceeding down that dark corridor. The main difference between those people who succeed and those who fail is in their ability to "launch." The successful people were willing to launch themselves down the corridor of opportunity without any guarantee of what would occur. They were willing to risk uncertainty and overcome normal fears and doubts that many unsuccessful people find immobilizing. Once they launched down the corridor, they were able to see other opportunities that were not available at the beginning—opportunities to build new relationships, new skills, new career opportunities, or new investments. [1] "This means that great accomplishments begin with your willingness to face the inevitable uncertainty of any new enterprise and step out boldly in the direction of your goal." As the Tao Te Ching says, *"A journey of a thousand miles begins with a single step."* [2]

Jessica's story illustrates how to take those first steps and what to do when you hit inevitable obstacles and experience setbacks.

Jessica's story:

For as long as Jessica can remember, she wanted to be a doctor. She had excelled in college while focusing on the pre-med curriculum. During her senior year, Jessica had to leave college to return to her parents' home to care for her sick father. Jessica completed her degree online.

During Jessica's twenties, she became an office manager for a medical group, married her hometown sweetheart, and had three children.

Jessica's **LifeQ** scores were good in all areas except **CareerQ**. At 34, Jessica's desire to be a doctor had never waned. She thought about it every day. Jessica knew that she could no longer procrastinate. She had to take action, or the medical school opportunity would no longer be an option. Jessica and her family decided that Jessica should follow her dream and see if she could get into medical school.

Within two years, Jessica took her Medical College Admission Test and applied to 15 medical schools. She was ecstatic to be accepted by the same Medical School her physician father had attended 45 years earlier. Although she knew her life was about to change dramatically, Jessica was thrilled. Attending medical school required a lot of focus—course work, exams, pressure from professors, and the competitive environment. Most of the other students did not have the family responsibilities that she did. Also, naysayers, who had been Jessica's friends, did not understand why she wanted to go to medical school and often voiced their negative opinions.

Jessica knew that it was now or never to complete her studies and created systems to help her stay on track and stay resilient. She made a Vision Board with pictures of herself as a doctor and a medical license for "Dr. Jessica." She placed affirmations for encouragement on her mirrors, refrigerator door, and computer screensaver. Jessica identified several people to serve on her Personal Board of Directors, including an experienced physician, performance coach, and an encouraging friend. She set up a reward system so that at the end of every semester, Jessica would have a spa day, a family day, and a date night with her husband. With her family's blessing, Jessica established a daily schedule for studying hours that would keep Jessica on-track.

Seven years later, at the age of 42, Jessica celebrated the grand opening of her medical practice with her excited family and proud Board of Directors cheering joyfully.

Your progress so far!

You have made great strides to get to Part 3. You have done impressive internal work to pack your bags with your self-reflection, equipment, nourishment, and recruited your companions. Then you plotted your course and designed your plan. During the first part of developing your plan, you became aware of your current reality. You calculated your *LifeQ* score, celebrated your strengths, and discovered areas that you want to improve. You have clarified your purpose and values, figured out your patterns, and addressed many of your self-limiting underlying beliefs. You discovered that taking action is a crucial factor of making the Law of Attraction work for you. You learned about the Four Stages of Change and steps to take at each stage to move toward improving your *LifeQ*. You learned how resistance is a natural part of any change and to expect it. Next, you designed your plan by setting your SMART goals and promises. Finally, you selected your Personal Board of Directors. You have been taking many small action steps throughout this book and moving forward. Now it is time to take action and officially launch.

HOW TO TAKE ACTION AND OVERCOME PROCRASTINATION

Taking action is a crucial step in effectuating life changes. The first 10% and last 10% of any project are the toughest and taking that first step can be very difficult. As you are garnering inspiration to act, remember that every race ever won has a beginning.

What gets in your way when you are trying to move forward toward a higher *LifeQ*? Our clients struggle to increase their willpower and overcome procrastination. Both are needed to take action. Distractions can seem much more interesting than taking a step toward positive change.

For example, social media can eat up lots of time. There is a humorous saying, "One way to waste two hours, is to go online for five minutes!" Other impediments to moving forward could be your self-limiting beliefs, patterns, and low self-esteem. Each of these is invisible and can cause your powerful subconscious mind to block your success. A great example of the power of your subconscious occurred in 1954 when Roger Bannister broke the four-minute mile record. The record had stood since 1886, and there was a belief universally that no human could run faster than four minutes. Historians claim, "It had become as much a psychological barrier as a physical one." Once Bannister broke the record, another runner broke it again 46 days later, and a year later, three runners broke the four-minute barrier *in a single race*. Bannister singlehandedly shattered the self-limiting belief. [3]

To help you act toward achieving your goals and increasing your *LifeQ*, consider the following questions. They will help jumpstart your action steps, fortify your willpower, and overcome your procrastination. You cannot make changes to your *LifeQ* without using self-control, which is the willpower that allows you to do something difficult.

- *What is your main reason for accomplishing this goal?* Clarifying the "why" you want to achieve a goal is essential to keep you focused and motivated to act. "Why" is more important than "How."

- *How will you feel when you have finally accomplished the goal?* Imagine that you have achieved your goal and let yourself experience feelings that will accompany your success.

- *How will it improve your life?* Be specific and describe the positive impact this change will make in your life. Visualize your life after having achieved your goal.

- *What usually holds you back from starting to take action?* Consider your personal history. When have you been reluctant to begin acting after you have plotted a new path? It could have been fear of success, disbelief that you will achieve your goal, poor time management, or lack of self-discipline. Now once you have identified what can distract you in progressing toward your desired goal, willfully and methodically focus your thoughts and energy on your plan.

- *Have you committed to a daily action plan* that includes setting morning intentions and priorities, followed by evening reflections that analyze your daily progress?

- *How will you reward yourself during the journey to accomplish this goal?* It is not necessary to wait until you have achieved the entire goal. You can reward yourself every week or every month that you stay persistent, focused on the result, and making progress.

- *Can the steps you are planning be "chunked down" so that you can quickly begin your pursuit and have some successes early on?* In the business world, this is "picking the low-hanging fruit." Achieving initial successes has a magical effect of building momentum and can boost your willpower to achieve more success. As mentioned in Chapter 1, "A body in motion stays in motion!"

- *How often do you practice gratitude, compassion, and love?* From our experience, practicing gratitude, compassion, and love every day leads to behaviors and attitudes that strengthen your will-power and resilience.

HARNESS THE POWER OF RESILIENCE

Taking action toward the life that you want will rarely be without many twists and turns, stops, and restarts. Did you know that an airplane traveling from one destination to another is off-course 99% of the time? Because of external and internal factors, such as wind turbulence, air traffic controllers' directions, or a faulty compass reading, the airplane must continually adjust its flight path to reach its destination. Just like these factors that influence the flight path, you will experience interference as you journey through your life.

Comedians joke that "Life" can be defined as "something that gets in the way of your other plans." You can design a beautiful plan, and then "life" can get in the way. You may have an unexpected setback to your financial plan. A natural disaster like a hurricane, flood, or earthquake can damage your home. Another corporation may purchase your company and put your job suddenly in jeopardy. A truck may rear-end your car at a stoplight, causing damage to your vehicle and whiplash to your body. Your life partner may become seriously ill and require additional care from you.

Resilience is one of the essential qualities you need to include in your toolkit. It is "the capacity to recover quickly from difficulties; toughness."[4] The quality of being "unstoppable" is essential to guarantee your success. Learning to deal with difficulty improves your chance of being a success time and time again. Everyone falls, but not everyone stays down.

"Resilience is a personal act of defiance and affects everything, including problem-solving skills, physical, mental and emotional well-being, and innovation. Resilience is like super-competency, influencing many other related skills and abilities that you need to deploy to work, manage, and lead well." [5]

An extraordinary example of resilience is Hari Budha Magar, a mountain climber who is the first bilateral above-the-knee amputee to summit a peak higher than 19,000 feet and plans to climb Mount Everest. Magar lost his legs in a bomb explosion in Afghanistan while in the Nepalese army. "After the explosion, I didn't know what to do, how to live, or what would come next. Half of my body was gone, and at that point I didn't care if the other half went too." Magar claims that his "capability is in my mind, not my legs. I still have a brain to think, hands that move, a mouth to speak, eyes to see and ears to hear. I haven't lost much. Limitations are created and destroyed in the mind. Sure, I need bigger doors and bathrooms and have to rely on a wheelchair and handrails, but life is about adaptation." Displaying his resilience, Magar goes on, "When something doesn't work in the way we expect it to, we find different ways of doing things."[6] Confucius said, "Our greatest glory is not in never falling, but in rising every time we fall."

Resilience While Learning to Ride Your Bike

Learning to bounce back from adversity is essential for success. Do you remember learning to ride a bike? You reached deep inside yourself and put everything you could muster into riding your bike down the street. You fell anyway. You skinned your knees and elbows. Through your determination and focus (and probably with the encouragement of a parent, friend, or coach), you got right back up, brushed yourself off, and you tried it again and again. Eventually, success was yours. You were riding like you had been doing it forever.

What kept you going during those failed bike riding attempts? Resilience. The ability to pick yourself up and keep moving forward to accomplish your goals and achieve your dreams.

This same quality is essential to living the life that you want. The same principles of resilience that applied to your belief in your ability to ride your bike when you were a kid apply to your determination to live the life that you want now and fulfill your dreams. It is essential to realize that no one else is going to give your dreams the priority that they deserve. It is up to YOU. You are responsible for the fulfillment of your dreams.

Steps to Create Resilience

Fortunately, resilience is a developed skill that enables you to bounce back from inevitable problems, obstacles, or adversity.

1. Believe that you *can* achieve your dreams. You manifest what you believe, not only what you want. Remember, how you think is everything!

2. Accept complete responsibility for your situation. You are not a victim. The next time you find yourself thinking or speaking negatively or laying blame elsewhere, repeat the phrase, "I am

responsible" until you are no longer thinking negatively or projecting negativity. Your success in life is up to you.

3. Decide in advance that you will respond constructively and positively to every obstacle and adversity. Use the Law of Attraction to your advantage to combat the barriers and adversity. Ensure you are in a state projecting positive energy of gratitude, forgiveness, positivity, and love. By focusing on being happy and resilient, you will attract happiness and resilience into your life.

4. Do not be overly concerned about what other people think about you, your goals, and your level of success. What others think of you is none of your business! Most people are self-centered and are thinking about themselves instead of you.

Remember: it is not how far you fall; it is how high you bounce! Do not let temporary setbacks keep you from getting what you want. As you read the story below, think about how you react to tough challenges and adversity.

Oolong Tea and Embracing Resilience

A young woman went to her mother to complain that her life was too hard for her. She did not know how she was going to make it, and she wanted to give up. She was tired of fighting and struggling. It seemed when one problem was solved, a new one arose.

Her mother took her to the kitchen. She filled three pots with water and placed each on the stove over a high fire. Soon the pots came to boil. In the first pot, her mother put carrots, in the second she placed eggs, and in the last, she placed Oolong tea. She let them sit and boil; without saying a word.

After 20 minutes, she turned off the burners. Her mother fished the carrots out and placed them in a bowl. She pulled the eggs out and put them in a bowl. Then she ladled the Oolong out and placed it in a bowl. Turning to her daughter, she asked, "Tell me what you see."

"Carrots, eggs, and Oolong tea," the daughter replied.

Her mother brought her closer and asked her to feel the carrots. She did and noted that they were soft. The mother then asked the daughter to take an egg and break it. After pulling off the shell, she observed the hardboiled egg. Finally, the mother asked the daughter to sip the Oolong tea. The daughter smiled as she tasted its rich aroma. The daughter then asked, "What does it mean, mother?"

Her mother explained that each of these objects had faced the same adversity: boiling water. Each reacted differently. The carrot went in strong, hard, and unrelenting. However, after being subjected to the boiling water, it softened and became weak. The egg had been fragile. Its thin outer shell had protected its liquid interior, but after sitting through the boiling water, its inside became hardened. The Oolong tea was unique. After being in the boiling water, the tea leaves had changed the water's color and taste.

"Which are you?" she asked her daughter. "When adversity knocks on your door, how do you respond? Are you a carrot, an egg, or Oolong tea? Are you the carrot that seems strong, but with pain and adversity, do you wilt and become soft and lose your strength? Are you the egg that starts with a malleable heart, but changes with the heat? Did you have a fluid spirit, but after a death, a breakup, a financial hardship, or some other trial, have you become hardened and stiff? Does your shell look the same, but on the inside, are you bitter and tough with a stiff spirit and hardened heart? Or are you like Oolong tea? The tea changes the hot water, the very circumstance that brings the pain. When the water gets hot, it releases the fragrance and flavor. If you are like tea, when things are at their worst, you get better and change the situation around you. When the hour is the darkest and trials are their greatest, do you elevate yourself to another level?"

- Author unknown

How do you handle adversity? Are you a carrot, an egg, or Oolong tea?" May we all be powerful and resilient like Oolong tea! The happiest of people do not necessarily have the best of everything; they make the most of everything that comes along their way. They make lemonade from lemons. They embrace resilience. They proactively produce and direct the life that they want to live according to their values and purpose.

Turn Your Setbacks into Comebacks—How to Boost Your *LifeQ*

Success can come from failure; it always has. You can learn from your successes as well as your setbacks. Failure is a part of almost everyone's journey through life, and yet success frequently comes when you build on a previous reversal. Inventors, billionaire entrepreneurs, and Olympic athletes experience failures followed by victories.

By analyzing your feelings, actions, and decisions, you can use your setbacks and successes as springboards to more success. Winners do not let the failures define them. Winners dare to keep going forward. Dr. Warren Bennis, a leadership guru, found that successful leaders think of "failure" as a springboard of hope. The leaders whom Bennis interviewed for his book about Leaders "simply don't think about failure, don't even use the word, relying on such synonyms as 'mistake,' 'glitch,' 'bungle,' or countless others such as 'false start,' 'mess,' 'hash,' 'setback,' and 'error.'" [7]

You have already had many successes and many setbacks in your life, and you have moved forward from both. Success takes many forms. It could be earning your college or graduate degree, buying your first car, winning an award you coveted, completing the project you have been working on, starting your own company, and marrying your right partner. Your setbacks could be losing your job due to a layoff, falling off the wagon after six months of being in Alcoholics Anonymous, getting the flu when you were so serious about your exercise program, making a bad investment in stock, or getting a divorce. You had high hopes for success – and it just did not work out that way.

FAILED PRODUCTS THAT SURVIVED THROUGH RESILIENCE

Many successful products exist because of failure and the determination of resilient people. We mention three of our favorites here.

- WD-40, the household lubricant, was the 40th attempt by the aerospace industry in 1958 to create a degreaser solvent and rust protector.

- Bubble wrap began as a failed attempt to create insulated, textured wallpaper. It was a colossal failure in 1957 and did not sell well. That did not deter the two inventor engineers, Al Fielding and Marc Chavannes. They wanted to find another use for their product. A marketer at Sealed Air, which makes Bubble Wrap, finally came up with the perfect service for their product. In 1959, IBM started using Bubble Wrap as a packaging material to protect computers while being shipped. Annually, Bubble Wrap sales exceed $400 million. [8]

- Legend has it that 302 financial institutions declined Walt Disney's request for financing to create Disneyland. Disney was so passionate about creating the "Happiest Place on Earth" that he borrowed money against his life insurance policy to obtain funding.

HOW TO OVERCOME YOUR FEAR OF FAILURE

Failure is nothing to fear. It can be a direct path to success. Here are some ways to prevent setbacks from blocking your success in life:

- *Do not waste time feeling like a failure. Try to get over it as soon as you can. Snap out of it.* Do not waste time feeling bad about yourself. Failure is part of business and life.

- *Replace the word "failure" with another term like "setback" or "misstep."* Use a term that implies a temporary state.

- *Pick yourself up.* When you fail, get right back up and get back to work. Do not be discouraged by failure, and never let it stop you from pursuing your dreams.

- *Look for the good that comes because of failing.* Take advantage of unexpected opportunities that may present themselves.

"WHAT WOULD YOU DO IF YOU WEREN'T AFRAID?"

As mentioned in Chapter 12, several posters at Facebook headquarters ask, "What would you do if you weren't afraid?" The slogan at NASA's Jet Propulsion Lab is "Dare Mighty Things!" Fear of failure is pervasive and can prevent you from achieving the success that you want.

CHANGE REQUIRES MAKING CHOICES

You can do this! It is not enough to simply dream of changing or hoping that you will change. To change, you will need to choose to change. It must be intentional. It will not happen accidentally. It is about deciding to be different in three months or six months or a year or a decade from now. Are you going to be healthier, debt-free, more spiritual, or more loving? Make the choice today to improve your *LifeQ.* Your life is your most important business, and we want you to feel more fulfilled, joyful, abundant, and purpose-driven every day. Remember that what you do every day is valuable because you are exchanging a day of your life for it. Choose wisely.

REBOOT YOUR LIFE WITH PASSION, COMPASSION, HUMOR, AND GRATITUDE

Remember, life is 5% what happens to you and 95% what you do with it!Although life does not come with a re-set button, you can give your life a fresh start anytime you choose. If you are not happy with the life you are living, commit today to assess what is going well and the areas where you do not feel fulfilled, and decide what you want instead. Then, promise to act. As the Producer, Director, and Actor in your life story, you can choose to live a life story that honors your values and purpose. You have free will and can reboot your life whenever you choose.

LifeQ planning is not for the faint of heart. It takes time, effort, passion, persistence, and humor. *LifeQ* Planning is a necessary, dynamic process that continues until you take your last breath. As Ben Franklin said, *"If you fail to plan, you plan to fail."*

PLANNING ISN'T A ONE-AND-DONE PROCESS

Planning is not a one-time process. You will now be able to make changes in your *LifeQ* Plan whenever you want. These changes will honor your values, your life's purpose, and priorities. Your *LifeQ* score will change throughout your lifetime as you experience significant events. We recommend you take the *LifeQ QUIZ quarterly* to check on your progress. Determine what is going well and what could be improved. Create SMART goals to transform your life and achieve the success that you want. Maya Angelou said, *"The question is not how to survive, but how to thrive with passion, compassion, humor, and style."* Success is a lifestyle, make it yours!

> **"WHAT IS SUCCESS?** by Ralph Waldo Emerson
>
> To laugh often and much
>
> To win the respect of intelligent people and affectionate children
>
> To earn appreciation of honest critics
>
> To endure the betrayal of false friends
>
> To appreciate beauty

To find the best in others To leave the world a bit better whether by a healthy child, a garden patch, or a redeemed social condition

To know even one life has breathed easier because you have lived.

This is to have succeeded. [9]

As your coaches, we encourage you to *"Go Forth and manifest your dreams. This is not the End. This is your Beginning of living the life that you want!"*

CHAPTER 15 *LifeQ*-TIPS AND CHAPTER RE-CAP

- The first 10% and last 10% of any project are usually the toughest. Taking that first step is often very difficult.

- You cannot make changes to your *LifeQ* without self-control. It is the willpower that allows you to do something difficult.

- "A body in motion stays in motion! A body at rest stays at rest!"

- To take action toward achieving your goals and increasing your *LifeQ*, consider:

  - What is your main reason for accomplishing this goal?

  - How will you feel when you have accomplished the goal?

  - How will it improve your life?

  - What usually holds you back from starting to take action?

  - Have you committed to a daily action plan to set morning intentions and priorities followed by evening reflections that analyze your daily progress?

  - How will you reward yourself during the journey to accomplish this goal?

- ◻ Can the steps you are planning be "chunked down" so that you can quickly begin your pursuit and have some early wins?

- How often do you practice gratitude, compassion, and love? Resilience is an essential value for your toolkit because you will have adversity along your journey. Some steps to increase your strength include:

  - ◻ Believe that you *can* achieve your dreams.

  - ◻ Accept complete responsibility for your situation – you are not a victim.

  - ◻ Decide in advance that you will respond constructively and positively to every obstacle and adversity.

  - ◻ Do not be overly concerned with what other people think about you.

  - ◻ Celebrate your successes! Reward yourself when you attain them.

LifeQ PRACTICE #15.1 QUESTIONS TO PONDER FOR YOUR TRANSFORMATION

In Chapter 1, you responded to these six questions. Please complete the questionnaire once again.

DIRECTIONS: Answer YES / NO

Do you have a clear idea of your most fundamental principles, values, interests, and gifts?

YES: _____ NO: _____

Do you have a sense of purpose in your life?

YES: _____ NO: _____

Do you almost always have a positive attitude about life and wake up each day excited about life?

YES: _____ NO: _____

If your life ended tomorrow, would you be satisfied with who you were, how you spent your time, your relationships, your service to others, and what you accomplished?

YES: _____ NO: _____

Will you leave a legacy that impacts others in your circle in a positive way?

YES: _____ NO: _____

Will your life story be a legend passed on by future generations?

YES: _____ NO: _____

SCORING: There are six questions. The more questions you can answer "YES," the more you are living your life with purpose as you begin the journey with us. Each YES represents a lot of work and self-reflection. Our goal is that when you have completed the work in this *LifeQ* journey, you will score YES on all six questions.

LifeQ PRACTICE #15. 2 PUTTING IT ALL TOGETHER

One year from today, I will achieve my goal. Complete these statements as if it is one year from today.

Today is: _____

I am so grateful that my goal of _____ has been achieved.

This makes me **feel**_____

This allows me to fulfill my **life purpose,**
which is_____

This allows me to actualize my **life values.** The ones that are most important to me that are reflected by my goal are: _____

The **successful people** (mentors, friends, advisors, colleagues) who have helped me achieve my goal include: _____

The specific and measurable **results** I
achieved were_____

The **actions I took mentally and physically** to achieve my
goals include_____

To do this, I **gave up this limiting belief(s)** about myself:

_____

Now I counter that belief with this **positive mantra**
about myself_____

When obstacles and adversity blocked the pathway, I took these actions
to overcome them and become resilient: _____

I rewarded myself with _____ **when I reached**
my milestones along the way to this goal. Now I can reward myself for
achieving my huge goal with: _____

LifeQ PRACTICE #15. 3 THIS WEEK'S ACTION PLAN

- What have you learned about yourself after reading this chapter?

- What actions will you take this next week to start to design the life that you want to live?

#### CHAPTER 16

READY, SET, GROW!

Y ou have made a significant investment of time and effort in your future by finishing this book. You have embarked on a new way of thinking. It does not matter whether you read every word and completed every exercise, or merely skimmed through the chapters and glanced at the practices. Most likely, you picked up some of the most important concepts. This book will help you think more strategically about your life journey, and if you incorporate the principles into your life, abundance can be yours. Now, you are reassured that it starts with YOU. You have the power within you to create the life you want and the life of your dreams. The choice is yours. It is your birthright to manifest your destiny, but you must claim it.

Celebrate You!

Most successful businesses use a similar planning process, and each part of their plan is an essential building block that impacts the overall success of the company. You can choose to start your *LifeQ* plan at any point in any chapter as you develop your strategy. When you have setbacks, you can quickly assess which elements of the process you need to focus your attention.

We encourage you to retake the *LifeQ QUIZ* often to benchmark your progress and to make the needed changes for improving your *LifeQ* Personal Plan. Some clients take the *LifeQ QUIZ* every quarter as well as do an annual review of their plan. Many clients like to keep track of Components that are the target of their focus and assess their progress every month. From a quantitative perspective, you will be able to determine which areas are going well and the definitive steps necessary to improve your *LifeQ* Score. Refer to Chapter 5 when you need motivation so you can review stories of clients who strategically created more abundance while changing careers, adding fun and adventure, searching for love, surviving an empty nest, and embracing retirement.

At the center of your *LifeQ* are your values and purpose. These elements are fundamental to living a fulfilling, abundant life. As Thomas Merton said, *"People may spend their whole lives climbing the ladder of success only to find, once they reach the top, that the ladder is leaning against the wrong wall."* All your goals and promises must align with your values and purpose. Otherwise, you will find your ladder leaning against the wrong wall, and you will neither fulfill your potential nor manifest your destiny.

Keep in mind that life is not linear. Rarely do you set a critical SMART promise and reach it without twists and turns along the way. Just like airplanes traveling from one destination to another and impacted by wind resistance or outside influences, you are off course much of the time. We recommend you set the alarm so that every month you, a member of your Personal Board of Directors or your coach, hold you accountable for your goals.

When you realize you have gotten off-course, revisit the three parts of your *LifeQ* Strategic Plan to assess where to intervene. First, is there something in your current reality that has affected your trajectory? Is it time to perform another SWOT analysis? Are you clear about your values and purpose? Could it be that your self-limiting beliefs, patterns, or self-esteem are interfering with your success? Second, could it be because of flaws in your strategy? Are your goals and promises not SMART? Perhaps they are not measurable or time-bound? Do you need someone else on your Board of Directors to help with your strategy? Third, do you need to reboot and return to your launching pad for a restart? Is it time to recharge your battery? In business and life, progress does not move in straight lines. And just like your laptop computer and cell phone, sometimes your life journey needs a reboot.

LifeQ-TIPS FOR A FULFILLING, SUCCESSFUL LIFE

- Perform *LifeQ* Planning for your life. Start by Defining Your Values and Clarifying your Life Purpose.

- Complete the *LifeQ QUIZ* quarterly. Celebrate your Qs going well. Set *LifeQ* Promises for areas where you would like to increase your level of satisfaction and fulfillment.

- Write two SMART promises for each of the 12 sections for your *WHEEL OF LifeQ*.

- Examine your self-limiting beliefs and patterns of behavior. What situations contributed to your underlying beliefs? Are they blocking you? Should they be changed? Assess Your Outlook. Are you more optimistic or pessimistic? You are in charge of your thoughts, so train your mind to think optimistically. Continue to focus on the positive every day.

- Practice an attitude of gratitude every day. Choose five things in your life for which you are grateful and start and end each day by focusing on them. It is not happy people who are grateful; it is grateful people who are happy!

- Perform a SWOT analysis on yourself. Capture your Strengths, Weaknesses, Opportunities, and Threats on paper just as successful organizations perform a self-assessment. Which areas can you celebrate? Are there gaps in knowledge or any habits that need to change so you can increase your *LifeQ*?

- Keep only supportive, positive people on your Personal Board of Directors. Now is the time to remove toxic people from your inner circle. Consider your closest relationships and decide who should stay, whom you should reclassify to an outer ring of influence, and whom else you can recruit to support you.

- Keep yourself accountable and stay on course with your *LifeQ* Plan. Just like organizations manage their strategic business plans, you need to review your due dates and goal milestones.

WE ARE GRATEFUL AND WANT TO HEAR FROM OUR READERS

We are grateful that you invited us to serve as your coaches at this point in your life journey so we could introduce you to our *LifeQ* Strategic Planning process. We welcome you to send us your success stories so we can pass them onto others so that they can be motivated by and benefit from them.

You can find us online at www.LifeQBook.com, We welcome you to browse additional *LifeQ* resources and exercises. Contact us at **Info@LifeQBook.com**

And always remember, your life is your most important business.

APPENDIX

We created this appendix to provide you tools to help you as you work through the *LifeQ* process to create your best life. These tools can help you manage your progress and mark your challenges and successes.

APPENDIX *LifeQ* PRACTICE # 1

Mistakes: The Best Way to Learn

Scientists learn from making mistakes. The more mistakes they make, the more likely they are to achieve their goal. Think of three events in your life when you made a mistake and learned from it. You can use childhood mistakes or something more recent.

Mistake **How I felt when it happened** **What I learned from it**

APPENDIX *LifeQ* PRACTICE # 2

Successes. Learn from your successes. Celebrate what went well and repeat for more success.

Think of three events in your life, when you have been successful.

- What did I do to be successful?

- Why did it work?

- How did I feel?

APPENDIX *LifeQ* PRACTICE # 3

POWERFUL QUESTIONS WHEN YOU ARE STUCK

What do you want?

What is holding you back?

What is it costing you to continue to hold back?

How do you want to change your thoughts on this topic?

What new habits will you put in place to fortify your mindset?

What is the most meaningful action you can take right now?

What new skills or support will ensure your success?

WORKSHEETS: MORNING, EVENING, WEEKLY, AND MONTHLY PLANNING

Many people find that keeping track of their progress daily, weekly, and monthly helps them to be successful in attaining their SMART goals and SMART promises. Following are four sample worksheets.

APPENDIX *LifeQ* PRACTICE # 4

DAILY *LifeQ* PLANNER

- My intentions and priorities for today are:

- Three things I'm grateful for today:

- Act of gratitude, compassion, or love I plan to do today:

- What are the challenges that I am facing today…!

- My affirmations and tools to help me with challenges are:

- The Qs that I am working on today are:

EVENING ASSESSMENT FOR EVENING REFLECTION:

- How was my day?

- What went well?

- What did not?

- What did I learn?

- My Accomplishments:

- What did I intend to accomplish, but I did not:

- What patterns, blockages, or habits prevented me from achieving my goals?

- Three things I'm grateful for:

APPENDIX *LifeQ* PRACTICE #5

WEEKLY *LifeQ* PLANNER

- Three things that I'm grateful for:

- Acts of gratitude, compassion, or love I plan to do this week:

- Last week, I accomplished:

- What did I intend to accomplish but I did not?

- The 3 Qs that I am working on this week are:

- Update SMART Goal Worksheets

- Patterns, blockages, habits, and beliefs that might prevent me from achieving my goals?

- Affirmations to keep me on track and defeat negative self-talk:

APPENDIX *LifeQ* PRACTICE # 6

MONTHLY *LifeQ* PLANNER

- Three things I am grateful for:

- Significant Accomplishments last month:

- Setbacks last month:

- How I plan to recover:

- Update SMART Goals Worksheets:

- The 3 Qs that I am working on this week are

- Patterns, blockages, habits, and beliefs that might prevent me from achieving my goals?

- Affirmations to keep me on track and defeat negative self-talk:

ENDNOTES

Chapter 2 How to Build a Personal Strategic Plan

1. Bronnie Ware, *The Top Five Regrets of the Dying* (Carlsbad, CA: Hay House Inc., 2012).

PART 1 BECOME AWARE OF YOUR CURRENT REALITY

Chapter 3 WHEEL of *LifeQ* Introduction and *MINI LifeQ* QUIZ

1. "Intelligence." Merriam-Webster, 2011. https://www.merriam-webster.com/dictionary/intelligence.

2. Daniel Goleman, *Emotional Intelligence: Why It Can Matter More than IQ* (New York: Bantam, 1995).

Chapter 4 *WHEEL OF LifeQ* QUIZ

1. Jason Linder, "How Mindfulness Can Reshape Negative Thought Patterns," *Psychology Today* 18 April 2019. https://www.psy-chologytoday.com/us/blog/mindfulness-insights/201904/how-mindfulness-can-reshape-negative-thought-patterns.

Chapter 5 Putting *LifeQ* into Your Personal Strategic Plan

1. World Health Organization (WHO), 1948.

Chapter 6 The Value of Values

1. Aaron Tippin, *"You've Got To Stand For Something"* Lyrics were written by Aaron Tippin and Buddy Brock, 1990, https://en.wikipedia.org/wiki/You%27ve_Got_to_Stand_for_Something_(song).

2. Benjamin Franklin, *Memoir,* (CA: University of California Libraries, 1834).

Chapter 7 Finding Your Purpose

1. Loren Eiseley, *The Unexpected Universe* (Eugene, OR: Harvest House, 1969).

Chapter 9 Embrace Change

1. Bible, Book of Proverbs 17:22 American Standard Version - New & Old Testaments: E-Reader Formatted ASV w/ Easy Navigation (Kindle Locations 2-3). Kindle Edition. First published 1901.

2. J. Steward Black, *Harvard Business Review*, "Laughter Will Keep Your Team Connected – Even While You're Apart," May 27, 2020, https://hbr.org/2020/05/laughter-will-keep-your-team-connected-even-while-youre-apart.

3. Debra Swedberg and Brown, Constintine, "Laughter Yoga, Adults Living With Parkinson's Disease, and Caregivers: A Pilot Study," May–June 2016, https://www.sciencedirect.com/science/article/abs/pii/S1550830716000355.

4. Min Youn Cha et al. An Effect of Optimism, "Self-esteem and Depression on Laughter Therapy of Menopausal Women," *Korean J Women Health Nurs* 18, no. 4 (Dec 2012): 248–256, https://synapse.koreamed.org/DOIx.php?id=10.4069/kjwhn.2012.18.4.248&vmode=PUBREADER.

5. Mohsen Yazdani et al. "The Effect of Laughter Yoga on General Health Among Nursing Students," *Iran J Nurs Midwifery Res,* 19 no 1(Jan-Feb 2014): 36–40. https://www.ncbi.nlm.nih.gov/pmc/articles/PMC3917183/.

6. William B. Strean. Can Fam Physician. 2009 Oct:55(10):965-967. PMCID:PMC2762283.

7. Shad Helmstetter, *What To Say When You Talk To Yourself* (New York: Simon & Schuster, 1982).

8. Seth Godin, Seth's Blog (blog), *Quieting the Lizard Brain,* January 28, 2010, https://seths.blog/2010/01/quieting-the-lizard-brain/.

9. Bible. Romans 13:12; Ephesians 4:22-24; Colossians 3:7–10, 14. American Standard Version - New & Old Testaments: E-Reader Formatted ASV w/ Easy Navigation (Kindle Locations 2-3). Kindle Edition. First published 1901.

10. Susan Murphy. *Maximizing Performance Management, Assess Your Outlook.* (Englewood, CO: MGMA, 2016), 262.

11. Susan Murphy, *Maximizing Performance Management, Personal Distress* (Englewood, CO: MGMA, 2016), 270.

Chapter 10 Patterns of Behavior and Limiting Beliefs

1. Norman Doidge, *The Brain that Changes Itself: Stories of Personal Triumph from the Frontiers of Brain Science* (New York: Penguin Publishing Group, 2007).

2. Claude M. Bristol, *The Magic of Believing* (Upper Saddle River, NJ: Prentice-Hall, 1964).

3. Jack Canfield, *The Success Principles,* (New York: Harper Collins, 2005), 245.

4. Carolyn Kaufman, "Using Self-Fulfilling Prophecies to Your Advantage," *Psychology Today,* October 11, 2012, https://www.psychologytoday.com/blog/psychology-writers/201210/using-self-fulfilling-prophecies-your-advantage.

5. #5. American Heritage Stedman's Medical Dictionary. (New York: Houghton Mifflin Company, 1995.)

6. Thomas H. Holmes and Richard H. Rahe, "The Social Readjustment Rating Scale." *J Psychosom Res* 11 no. 2 (1967): 213–8. DOI:10.1016/0022-3999(67)90010-4. PMID 6059863.

7. Richard H. Rahe and Ransom J. Arthur, "Life change and Illness studies: Past History and Future Directions," *J Human Stress* 4 no. 1 (1978): 13–15. DOI:10.1080/0097840X.1978.9934972. PMID 346993.

Chapter 11 Digging Deeper Into Your Beliefs and Patterns

1. Bruce Lipton, *The Biology of Belief – Unleashing the Power of Consciousness, Matter & Miracles,* (Carlsbad, CA: Hay House Inc, 2008).

2. Shad Helmstetter, *What to Say When You Talk to Yourself* (New York: Simon & Schuster, 1986).

3. Max Muller and Max Fausboll, *Sacred Books of the East, Vol. 10: The Dhamma-pada and Sutta Nipata* (1881), accessed Nov.16, 2015, www.sacred-exts.com/bud/sbe10/sbe1003.htm.

4. "Norman Vincent Peele quotes," Good Reads, accessed Nov. 16, 2015, www.goodreads.com/author/quote/8435.Norman_Vincent_Peale.

5. www.goodreads.com/author/quotes/15865.William_James.

6. www.goodreads.com/quotes/541463-a-man-is-what-he-thinks-about-all-day-long.

7. www.goodreads.com/quotes/978-whether-you-think-you-can-or-you-think-you-can-t--you-re

8. Claude M. Bristol, *The Magic of Believing.* (Upper Saddle River, NJ: Prentice-Hall, 1964).

9. Bruce H. Lipton, *The Biology of Belief. Unleashing the Power of Consciousness, Matter and Miracles,* (CA: Hay House, 2005).

10. Jack Zenger and Joseph Folkman, *Harvard Business Review,* The Ideal Praise-to-Criticism Ratio, March 15, 2013, https://hbr.org/2013/03/the-ideal-praise-to-criticism.

11. Merriam-Webster.com. Merriam-Webster, 2011. https://www.merriam-webster.com/dictionary/fear.

12. Ronald Rood Quotes," Think Exist.com, http//thinkexist.com/quotes/Ronald_rood/.

13. https://www.goodreads.com/quotes/10131-courage-is-resistance-to-fear-mastery-of-fear---not

14. Paul A. Brown, Forbes, January 12, 2014, www.forbes. com/sites/actiontrumpseverything/2014/01/12/ you-miss-100-of-the-shots-you-dont-take-so-start-shooting-at-your-goal.

15. Dale Carnegie, *How To Win Friends And Influence People* (New York: Simon & Schuster, 1964.)

16. Corrie Ten Boom, *The Hiding Place* (Royal Oak, MI: Chosen Books, 1971).

17. Hugh Prather, *The Little Book of Letting Go* (New York: MJF Publishers, 2001).

18. Van Wilder, *Rocking Chair* (New York: National Lampoon, 2006), 85.

19. www.goodreads.com/quotes/340855-let-our-advance-worrying-become-advance-thinking-and-planning.

Chapter 12: Raising Your Self-Awareness Positively Affects Your Self-Esteem

1. Matthew McKay, *Self-Esteem* (Oakland, CA: New Harbinger Publications, 1996).

2. Pat Heim, Susan Murphy, with Susan Golant, *In The Company of Women: Indirect Aggression Among Women: Why We Hurt Each Other and How to Stop* (New York: Tarcher/Putnam, 2003).

3. Shad Helmstetter, *What to Say When You Talk to Yourself* (New York: Simon & Schuster, 1986).

4. J. Gravois, "You're not fooling anyone." *The Chronicle of Higher Education* 54, no. 11(2007): A1. Retrieved November 5, 2008, from Http://chronicle.com.

5. William Eleazar Barton, *The Life of Clara Barton: Founder of the American Red Cross, Volume 2* (Boston: Houghton Mifflin, 1922).

6. Heim et al, *In The Company of Women: Indirect Aggression Among Women: Why We Hurt Each Other and How to Stop.*

PART 2 DEVELOP YOUR WINNING STRATEGY

Chapter 13 Setting Your Smart Goals and Making Promises

1. 1. Webster New World Dictionary, Simon & Schuster, Inc. 1990, NY, NY (Victoria Neufeldt, editor-in-chief) p 589.

2. Claude M. Bristol, *The Magic of Believing* (Upper Saddle River, NJ: Prentice-Hall, 1964).

3. Webster New World Dictionary, Simon & Schuster, Inc. 1990, NY, NY (Victoria Neufeldt, editor-in-chief) p 589.

4.   Staci Stallings, *What is Success?*. https://www.streetdirectory.com/travel_
     guide/8284/self_improvement_and_motivation/what_is_success.html

5.   https://quotefancy.com/quote/776025/
     Billy-Graham-I-never-saw-a-U-Haul-behind-a-hearse.

6.   https://sidsavara.com/why-3-of-harvard-mbas-make-ten-times-as-much-as-the-
     other-97-combined/

7.   Bill Bartmann, youtube=http://www.youtube.com/watch?v=SSDu6LaMILE&hl=en_
     US&fs=1&. Accessed August, 2019.

Chapter 14 Creating Your Personal Board of Directors

1.   https://www.goodreads.com/
     quotes/1798-you-are-the-average-of-the-five-people-you-spend.

2.   Jim Collins, *Good to Great: Why Some Companies Make the Leap and Others Don't*
     (New York: Harper Collins Publishers, Inc., 2001).

3.   Original publication of the Johari Window was in 1955 by American psychologists
     Joseph Luft and Harry Ingham while researching group dynamics at the University
     of California Los Angeles.

4.   Jim Rohn. https://www.businessinsider.com/jim-rohn-youre-the-average-of-the-
     five-people-you-spend-the-most-time-with-2012-7

5.   Napoleon Hill, *Think and Grow Rich*, (VA: Napoleon Hill Foundation, 1937).

6.   Johari Window, Wikipedia: The Free Encyclopedia. Wikipedia Foundation, Inc.
     April 30, 2020, https://en.wikipedia.org/wiki/Johari_window.

PART 3 TAKE ACTION AND TURN YOUR SETBACKS INTO COMEBACKS

Chapter 15 Take Action and Turn Your Setbacks Into Comebacks

1.   Robert Ronstadt, "The Corridor Principle," *Journal of Business Venturing* 3 (1989):
     31–40. 10.1016/0883-9026(88)90028-6.

2.   *Tao Te Ching*, 4th century BC, silk manuscript, https://en.wikipedia.org/
     wiki/A_journey_of_a_thousand_miles_begins_with_a_single_step.

3.   https://hbr.org/2018/03/what-breaking-the-4-minute-mile-taught-us-about-the-
     limits-of-conventional-thinking

4.   Jesse Sostrin, Director at PwC's U.S. Leadership Coaching Center of Excellence,
     author of *The Manager's Dilemma: Balancing the Inverse Equation of Increasing
     Demands* (New York: Palgrave Macmillan, 2015).

5. Jesse Sostrin, Director at PwC's U.S. Leadership Coaching Center of Excellence, author of *The Manager's Dilemma: Balancing the Inverse Equation of Increasing Demands* (New York: Palgrave Macmillan, 2015).

6. Confucius said: *"Our greatest glory is not in never falling, but in rising every time we fall."*

7. Julia Hirsch, "This Buddhist Life: Hari Budha Magar," *Tricycle Magazine*, Summer 2018.

8. Warren Bennis and Burt Nanus, *Leaders: Strategies for Taking Charge* (New York: Harper & Row, 1985), 69

9. David Kindy, "The Accidental Invention of Bubble Wrap," SmithsonianMagazine.com, January 23, 2019, https://www.smithsonianmag.com/innovation/accidental-invention-bubble-wrap.

10. What is Success? Adapted from Bessie Anderson Stanley's poem "Success" (1904)